# Critical Muslim 36

## Destinations

*Critical Muslim* is published quarterly by C. Hurst & Co. (Publishers) Ltd. on behalf of and in conjunction with Critical Muslim Ltd. and the Muslim Institute, London.

All editorial correspondence to Muslim Institute, CAN Mezzanine, 49–51 East Road, London N1 6AH, United Kingdom.
E-mail: editorial@criticalmuslim.com

**The editors do not necessarily agree with the opinions expressed by the contributors. We reserve the right to make such editorial changes as may be necessary to make submissions to *Critical Muslim* suitable for publication.**



C. Hurst & Co (Publishers) Ltd., 41 Great Russell Street, London WC1B 3PL

ISBN: 978-1-78738-406-4 ISSN: 2048-8475

To subscribe or place an order by credit/debit card or cheque (pounds sterling only) please contact Kathleen May at the Hurst address above or e-mail kathleen@hurstpub.co.uk

Tel: 020 7255 2201

A one-year subscription, inclusive of postage (four issues), costs £50 (UK), £65 (Europe) and £75 (rest of the world), this includes full access to the *Critical Muslim* series and archive online. Digital only subscription is £3.30 per month.



A Cataloguing-in-Publication data record for this book is available from the British Library

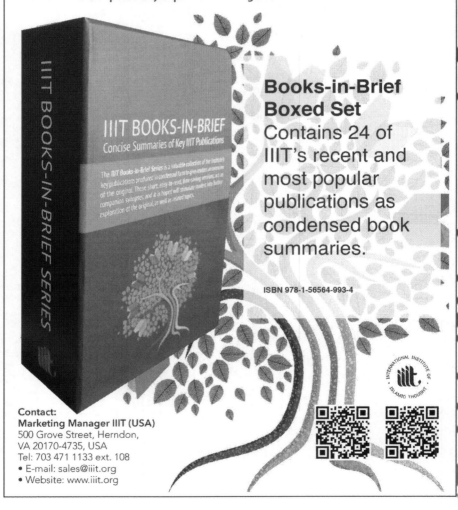

CM36

AUTUMN 2020

# CONTENTS

## DESTINATIONS

# DESTINATIONS

# INTRODUCTION: TO HELL AND BACK

*Samia Rahman*

Do any of us know where we're heading? It seems futile to contemplate destinations, physical or existential, when the world is on stuttered pause. Carefully cultivated plans, life's expected milestones and hard-earned goals are suddenly and indefinitely out of reach. Little if anything makes sense, yet we're told to push ahead with our pre-existing trajectories as if pandemia hasn't descended like a thick mist. 'Destinations might sound rational, but one has to wonder whether it is as elusive as destiny,' Ebrahim Moosa writes later in these pages. 'Why? Because the once solid pathways to ends and purposes have ceased to be pathways. They are as elusive as traces drawn on desert sands.' Veering off course via tangents and random meanders has become less of an option. Instead our worlds seem really quite small, the promise of any alternative destination stalled. As the African-American novelist and anthropologist, Zora Neale Hurston, suggests in *Their Eyes Were Watching God,* 'there are years that ask questions and years that answer'. I think we all know where we are with the year 2020. All that is left is to content ourselves with the here and now, one day at a time, and wait patiently for the year that will provide the answers.

Although, of course, alternatives still do exist. Instead of traversing the world, virtual and internal realities allow access to destinations from which we are physically barred, offering an escape from what we may, with some hyperbole, describe as this hell on earth. Some of these are infernal realities, the existential anguish of the realms of the darkest recesses of our imagination. The Qur'an describes hell in terms of *mathwā*, explains Moosa, ominously 'meaning an abode or destination with permanence' while the word *maṣīr* 'derived from the verb ṣayr, to journey, does not signify a comfortable journey; rather it means a journey involving effort'.

Perhaps hell is a state of mind rather than an endpoint. Ever since fear-inducing motifs peppered seventh century mystic Hasan al-Basri's '*zuhd*' or renunciation poetry, hell has been depicted as a destination we must do everything in our power to avoid. The influential scholar, who is celebrated as a founder of Sufism, regarded death, and the 'fork-in-the-road' options some believe it offers, as the ultimate destination. Is what comes before – life – therefore a toil that must be endured, driven by pious observance in order to divert from a destiny of damnation? The great Al-Ghazali seems to think so, apparently informed by al-Basri's unequivocal warnings. He tells us in his multi-volume tome *The Revival of the Religious Sciences*: 'your coming unto it [hell] is certain, while your salvation therefrom is no more than conjecture… fill up your heart, therefore, with the dread of that destination.'

Whether hell occupies a literal or metaphysical space, it involves a journey of *maṣīr*; and as it is such an undesirable destination, only with a great deal of effort can one avoid such a calamity and be granted a place in its antithesis - heaven. Quite, but not quite, the type of effort that C Scott Jordan details in his evocative exploration of Kuala Lumpur in this issue. 'Pinching myself to prove I am awake I proceed past an escalator entrance that seems as though it just materialised from below the ground, it was one of the ways into or out of the subterranean Kampung Baru LRT (Light Rail Train) Station, towards a massive cement square pillar. Within the pillar rises and falls a lift, around the tower's circumference wraps a tiered stairway, presumably to heaven. Electing exercise, I climb the steeper-than-they-look stairs, and began to sweat. It starts to rain; or rather, in KL it always pours, in spontaneous and overly dramatic fashion. As I reach the top of the pillar, I cannot tell rain from sweat but I'm not bothered because even the few prepared umbrella wielders were no match for this torrent of water.' Qur'anic references to paradise make frequent mention of water as a purifying life-giving source so Jordan could consider his heavenly climb in the pouring rain quite the spiritual cleanse.

Muhammad Iqbal, poet, philosopher and 'spiritual father' of Pakistan, believed heaven and hell to exist as states of mind, rather than actual locations to which humans would be sent after the quantifying of their deeds upon their demise. Never meant to be taken literally, the basis upon which a person is to be consigned to the mental anguish of hell or the euphoria of paradise would depend on their inner psychic and intellectual development. We often speak of struggle resembling spiritual experience, even if it is as banal as a gruelling climb up the stairs of a bridge in Kuala Lumpur. Similarly, Hafeez Burhan Khan writes of his wanderlust as a catharsis, with every step of any journey and each discovery of a new destination an emotional release and a moment of personal expansion. Momentarily freed from the mundanity of existence, he talks of his love of drifting through unloved landscapes, places in transition, marginalised urbanity and soaking in the memory of all that went before amidst buildings that echo with memories.

Choosing to remain rooted in the same place one's entire life, although not without its merits, seems to inspire a parochialism that fuels the small-minded populism we are witnessing in the world today. This is not a modern-day phenomenon however. As Robert Irwin writes in his essay on the Mamluks, 'the fifteenth-century Flemish merchant Anselm Adorno prefaced the account of his pilgrimage with an attack on those who were foolish enough to think there was no country except their own and that everybody else lived in dark shadows as savages. Those who had read widely or travelled out east knew better. From such sources one may get a sense for the texture of life and the conflicting faiths and passions of those times, and one may dream of how it was to have lived in the Mamluk Sultanate.'

The texture of lives lived elsewhere is a compelling reason to visit the treasure chest of destinations available to us, and hopefully will be available to us after Covid times. Whether it is to feast on great food, as Boyd Tonkin exquisitely recounts in 'Invisible Thessaloniki', or to discover hitherto unknown destinations, as Natalya Seitakhmetova, Zhanara Turganbayeva and Marhabbat Nurov lay bare in their treatise on the strands of Kazakh Cultures, there is forever something to discover and be immersed in. We lower our Western-centric gaze and allow voices intimately entwined in the history and contemporaneity of the Central Asian Republic to be heard, while patting ourselves on the back for elevating the other. 'Heaven is a Place on Earth', Belinda Carlisle sings. Well, surely hell is in the narratives imposed upon those unable to tell their own stories. After all, only some of us are privileged in our freedom to roam from one destination to another with ease. That it is purely down to the accident of nationality enabling this few to cross borders with ease is a shameful travesty.

Those without appropriate documentation, for whom legal passage across countries is all but denied, are condemned to risk their lives when the only channels open to them are illegal and unsafe ones. Displaced peoples seeking sanctuary from poverty, war, persecution or in search of opportunities are dehumanised and left to fester in inhumane conditions. The refugee camps scattered across the globe are a blight on our humanity. These places are hell on earth for people whose only crime is to dream of a better future. As countries closed their borders one by one in the extraordinary global shutdown of Spring 2020, in an attempt to keep out the deadly virus, some of us used to the freedom to travel, were experiencing an impingement on our ability to roam for the very first time. Tamanna Rahman had an inkling that her trip to Cuba, just before lockdowns were being imposed, was perhaps not totally wise, but so unprecedented and rapid was the suspension of travel that she could never have foreseen the precarious scramble she eventually had to undertake to return to the UK.

Ziauddin Sardar's recounting of his 1986 trip to Assisi, where he explained to Prince Philip, Duke of Edinburgh, that Muslims regard their role on the planet as vice-regents, or trustees entrusted by God with the earth's safe-keeping, illustrates how little has been achieved to stave off the climate crisis despite awareness of its imminence decades ago. Climate change and an increase in the frequency of pandemics looms on the horizon and instability will increasingly creep into the existence of those of us who take our comfortable lives for granted. To anyone seeking to jealously guard their little piece of paradise, keen to keep out those who find themselves in undocumented limbo hell, may they be warned that one day, sooner than they may think, it could so easily be them on the wrong side of border control. Any one of us could find ourselves in search of paradise, just like the much-loved Sudanese poet Abdel Wahab Yousif who died in August 2020. Known to his fans as Latinos, the talented young man drowned off the coast of Libya in a tragic attempt to cross the Mediterranean adrift in a flimsy and overloaded dinghy, all in the hope of starting a new life in Europe. He was far from being the first to perish in an attempt to make the hellish crossing, and is not even nearly the last to die. On reading about his final voyage, I was reminded of the haunting image of three-year old Syrian Alan Kurdi's tiny lifeless body lying faced down in the sand, having drowned in yet another gut-wrenching tragedy on the Mediterranean in 2015. His family had been desperately fleeing the war in Syria. All the options available to them were desperate ones and their gamble came at the most horrific cost. It is difficult to comprehend the terror of little Alan's final moments. How much did he understand the ugliness of his fate, the grotesqueness of the system that forced him into such danger. What we do know, however, is that Latinos was fully aware, even prophetically aware of the doom that awaited him. In his final poems, the translations of which are published in this issue of *Critical Muslim*, he seemed to predict his demise at the hands of a merciless sea that in the blink of an eye swallowed all dreams, hopes and aspirations of the dispossessed.

The pursuit of dreams does not magically end when the destination is reached. In Amro Ali's essay on Berlin exiles, we learn why 'hell' cannot be seamlessly exchanged for 'paradise'. Berlin is a destination like no other. Steeped in a history of violence and ideological scars, this palimpsest of un-beautiful brutalist beauty reinvented itself as a haven for counter-culture and non-conformity. Like many truly international capital cities, Berlin is an exception to the nationalist inward-looking tendencies that currently characterise more provincial areas throughout the world. The city attracts intellectuals, thinkers, drifters, hedonists, artists and activists, all looking for a place where they can fit in by not fitting in. When Angela Merkel declared there would be no upper limit on the number of Syrian refugees Germany, the wealthiest country in Europe, was willing to accept, her calculated decision was in the interests of her country. It also demonstrated the administration's commitment to human dignity. In recent years Berlin has witnessed a growing community of Arab exiles, disillusioned and shattered by the failures of the Arab Spring. In his essay Ali calls for the Arab diaspora to recover and rebuild their lives and continue to engage despite the trauma of exile: 'The procession of dislocation that materialised in 2011 has been viciously derailed since. Now, to coherently embark upon a regenerated starting point in this long journey of political redemption, a "we" is required: This feeds from new political ideas, collective practices and compelling narratives that are currently re-constructed and brought to life in a distantly safe city.'

Syria's hellish war rages on while Egypt's population buckles under the oppressive regime of General Sisi with human rights violations and surveillance routine. It is no secret that the entire region is utterly destabilised. We gain some historical insights with Zainab Rahim's review of the Channel 4 neo-noir series 'Baghdad Central', set in the aftermath of the US invasion of Iraq. Post-invasion Baghdad may be portrayed as hell, but we must be wary of dividing our world into the categories of hell or paradise for no place truly exists with a monopoly on either concept. In Paradise and Hell in Islamic Traditions, Christian Lange re-casts the concept of heaven and hell, suggesting the two worlds are far more enmeshed than traditional scholarship would suggest. There is hope of universal redemption from eternal hellfire, as articulated so well in the scholarship of the Andalusian philosopher Ibn Arabī: 'on the one hand Ibn al-ʿArabī makes room for hell as the manifestation of God's attribute of "majesty" (*jalāl*), which complements His "kindness" (*jamāl*). On the other hand, Ibn al-ʿArabī predicts that punishment in hell will eventually come to an end. However, instead of moving on to paradise, hell's inhabitants will remain in hell, attached to it, and in a certain way enjoying it, like natives prospering in their homeland.'

This brings me back to Iqbal's definition of heaven and hell as states of mind informed by our continuous present rather than far-flung physically located destinations. Life is, after all, essentially a negotiation of our circumstances, as illustrated by Shanon Shah's moving description of his Qur'anic voyage, and how his relationship with the sacred text continues to evolve as his life journey progresses. It is for this reason that Lange moves away from the commonly used term afterlife, and instead refers to paradise and hell as the otherworld. According to traditional Islamic teachings, to achieve a modicum of comfort in the otherworld, good deeds and exemplary moral conduct must be carried out throughout a person's lifetime. The realms of paradise, hell and earth are separated, Lange argues, not by impenetrable boundaries, but are instead porous states of mind, of existential presence, fuelled by religious symbolism, existing in the darkest corners of our imagination. It is difficult to stomach the extreme depictions of hell in Islamic tradition, characterised by the most macabre and brutal medieval punishments of the day, with particularly horrific torture seemingly reserved for women, religious minorities, and those who do not form part of the traditional establishment. In her 'Last Word on Patriarchy', Shehnaz Haqqani captures exactly why such a literal understanding of hell, among other more stagnant positions in traditional Islam, have come to prominence: '"Islam" as we know it is a process, and its teachings – besides the most essential, monotheism and belief in Muhammad as a prophet – is a matter not so much of truth but of power.'

Fear of the literal destination hell permeates through Islamic scholarship and continues to stagnate Muslim thinking, such is its vice-like grip on our psyches. Lange cites the poem 'Revolution in Hell' by the late Iraqi philosopher and poet Jamil Sidqi Al-Zahāwī, who dreams of his own death caused by consuming a dish seasoned with watercress. It is then that he ponders, 'hell is where the philosophers and rationalists are, that is to say all the forward-thinking, revolutionary spirits that traditionalist Islam condemns to eternal damnation: Ibn Sīna, Ibn Rushd, and Ṭūsī, but also Socrates, Epicurus, Voltaire', and questions which destination is for him.

Destination hell is a terrorising state of mind. A feature of traditional Islam many Muslims admit has led to them feeling alienated from the faith. Saimma Dyer writes of growing up in a Muslim tradition that many of us can relate to: 'my connection to God diminished as I was exposed to a dogmatic, rigid and fear-inducing Islam… The imam warned us about the dangers of hellfire and how almost everything in life seemed directed to lead us into that hellfire.' In adulthood, she discovered, just like Haqqani, that there are many ways of experiencing and 'being' in Islam. It was then that she embarked upon a spiritual path, an inner journey that would eventually lead to an awakening to an Islam that she could finally feel an affinity with. Whether the journey is one of ease or difficulty, the destination does not have to signify an end. Instead, it can be more than a culmination of what came before, as well as forming part of the process of all that is yet to be.

# NEW TERRITORIES

*Ebrahim Moosa*

These are tumultuous times. Talk of some goal, destination, direction and endpoint sounds vulgar. Yet, it's the only thing that keeps one sane: hope. Fervent hope for the pandemic to be over, for madmen to be out of power, for humanity to regain sanity. These are reasonable ends, yet they are unreasonable when the conditions we live in do not foster such hopes. Destinations might sound rational, but one has to wonder whether it is as evanescent as destiny. Why? Because the once solid pathways to ends and purposes have ceased to be pathways. They are as elusive as traces drawn on desert sands.

Linguistically we might cling to the word 'destination' or its plural, 'destinations' which holds out the hope for a plurality of ends, but I am afraid we are fated to face that old enemy: destiny. Destination derived from its Latin root contains within itself the elements of destining, appointing, foreordaining, purpose or end. Normally it is a concrete place, but not necessarily so. If humility was our strong suit, then we would regard every nanosecond as a destination. Live with it, enjoy it, savour it or fall with it. We are so habituated to seeing destination as a singular thing, that we forfeit its complexity. Hovering over destinations and destiny is the shadow of free will and human agency: are we the creators of our own fates in the age of technoscience or are we just bit players who are locked into larger systems of economics, politics and globalisation from which we are unable to extricate ourselves?

It is increasingly difficult to speak of any kind of future in concrete terms. Things are in constant flux, contingency is the order of the day. Once we discovered that our cosmos was neither fixed nor closed, but rather an open-ended and constantly expanding mass, then all the metanarratives we prized on earth, inherited from previous cosmological eras from the fixity of nature to the altering character of the divine begotten in earlier times, began to unravel.

German historian Reinhart Koselleck explained that somewhere in the middle of the eighteenth century the idea of a future that looked very different from the past become more pronounced. In previous eras, a person who mounted a horse on a journey could reliably expect to encounter the terrain ahead to look similar from the space left behind. It would be different in modernity. Now, mounted on a saddle one could no longer hold the expectation that the terrain that lay ahead would be similar to what had passed. No wonder uncertainty and anxiety are the familiar features of the human condition. Those solid ideas and concepts of justice, truth, love and compassion, while resounding with continuities from times past, no longer deliver and mean the same thing. Concepts are not static, they have a destination in the sense of *ṣayr*, becoming; to emerge to newness with creativity. New problems must be posed, concepts have to be adjusted, sometimes shaven, supplemented and sometimes they need a complete do-over. As Gilles Deleuze put it, 'of course, new concepts must relate to our problems, our history, and, above all, to our becomings'.

Yet, it is in times of uncertainty that faith and tradition are often viewed as resources of stability. Revivalist Christianity, Hinduism and Islam have for part of the twentieth and twenty-first centuries been offering its adherents strong doses of faith and quick-fix doctrines as elixirs to stabilise the uncertainty of the times and in doing so, pointing them to destinations and utopias. Strap on saffron robes, clutch to Biblical faith, imitate the Prophet Muhammad in all his Arab cultural redolence, and *voila* you have authenticity. Each religion fuelled by high-octane doses of faith rather than grappling with a narrative of understanding the human condition miraculously promises earthly salvation of some sort. Even though the turnover among such enthusiastic groups is high, the damage to the human fabric wrought is often irreparable, yet there is no shortage to converts to such causes in almost every decade. As many people join the ranks of the formal religions as the number of those who leave each religion daily.

Increasingly the symbols of the most ancient religions have come under severe pressure to provide the certainty that belief in a sky-God or faith in elaborate mythical deities once provided. A return to the older master narratives doling out certainties is superficially appealing but intellectually jarring. Absent is any literacy and practice providing depth and insight. Religions used to be about the otherworld, the beyond, afterlife and the place we cannot imagine: now it is all about the immediate and instant gratification, like fast food. Philosophers call this last-mentioned phenomenon immanence, meaning it only dwells in things or in us. Others, curse or lament the postmodern condition as a nihilism for giving up on the solid things, those certainties of old.

Globally we don't only face viral pandemics. Bigotry, racism and violence always stoked the embers of more fearsome fires of hatred. But global conditions around the world fired up the racists and bigots emboldening them to come out of their hiding places in the so-called advanced and not so-advanced democracies from Minneapolis in Minnesota to Kardampuri, a suburb of northeast Delhi. Everywhere black and brown human bodies are lynched by armed police, mostly white but not exclusively so. Or, brown mobs turn on other brown bodies and desiccate the bodies of their presumed enemies under the pretext of nationalist fervour or blasphemous outrage.

Talk about hell. For many of the wretched and not so wretched it is hell on earth. The Muslim scripture, the Qur'an promises to torment the bodies of disbelievers, malefactors of all types especially the arrogant for their ethical and other transgressions. They will be told: '"Enter the gates of hell, to abide therein." How miserable the abode of the self-important.' (Qur'an 39:72) Hypocrites, and those who defiantly trash the teachings of the prophets and thereafter pompously boast: 'Why doesn't God punish us for what we say?' The reply to their scoffing is swift: 'All they deserve is hell. Where they will burn; and what a miserable destiny.' (Qur'an 58:8) But the Qur'an also adjudicates with fairness. It promises those who try to live by ethical values that ultimately their 'destination is to God' (Q 24: 42).

One special term used for destination in the Qur'an, almost exclusively for those destined to hell is *mathwā*, meaning an abode or destination with permanence. This is bad news for the inmates of hell. Another term used for destination, is *maṣīr*, a term divided almost equally to identify hell for the miscreants and heaven as the end of the virtuous. *Maṣīr* as a term is intriguing. Derived from the verb *ṣayr*, to journey, does not signify a comfortable journey; rather it means a journey involving effort. To do *ṣayr* or, to reach a destination (*maṣīr*) involves effort, to furrow, to dig one's way out. And very interestingly, to do *ṣayr*, also means to *be*-come, the sense of an altered being. Destination thus is not a pre-given, but rather involves a journey of transformation. In Qur'anic parlance it is a journey towards the better and reaching God, abiding in God, as some possible meanings. The worst form of becoming is to turn into the anti-God polarity, where damnation and hellfire awaits. That too is another becoming.

Destination as a journey, rather than as some end that is foreordained appeals to me. But I have to quickly remind myself that I am too invested in my own agency and the agency of others because of the massive narrative of responsibility that Islam and other religious and secular traditions impose on adherents. Yes, we are invested with responsibility, otherwise why do we curse the racist bigots, violent terrorists and cruel human beings and prefer to see them behind bars and destined to some unsavoury place?

Responsibility does not only focus our attention on the things done and undertaken by unsavoury ones among our species. We also think of that colleague who was diagnosed with terminal colon cancer leaving behind five kids. The friend who will endure a lifetime of suffering because her young son or daughter committed suicide before reaching twenty. Or think of that family member who lost two adult children in less than a year, one to cancer and the other to Covid-19.

Destination as a journey is hard. Catechisms teaching predestination and free-will, in my view, just fail with their insoluble binaries: free-will vs. predestination. Nothing in life is that easy, left or right. Let's face it, sometimes life is just dismal. One can agree that life does not always go our way despite our most elaborate planning. Yes, we do despair. Faith teaches that it is okay to despair. What faith warns about is this: just don't go down the cauldron of despair to a point of no-return. Be like prophet Ayyub in the Qur'an and Job in the Bible who railed at God and finally recovered. In our happier moments, of course, we forget those painful agonies or we push them out of the way to see the sun shine and enjoy the smiling faces of people basking in the autumn sun in the park.

The last few years have been truly awful; and summer 2020 in America was truly abysmal. But the cause of my anguish was not only the virus or the virulent political bacilli dominating the country. Corruption in the bastion of law and order, safety and security became visible in all its fatal virulence. America's policing system still view brown and black people as runaway slaves, especially black people, folk of African-American heritage. Don't listen to Democratic politicians or Republicans who say there are bad apples among the police, the majority are good folk. No! The system is corrupt, it covers up its wrongs. It is not a system of public safety. The police force was invented to entrench slavery, not for community safety, but to return humans to bondage. An encounter with the police means your life is at stake as a person of colour.

In my native apartheid South Africa we feared the police for rough treatment and dehumanisation in ordinary encounters as black and brown people, but rarely feared for our lives in such conditions. Yes, we feared the security police who came after political activists often to thrust them into detention without trial if you were lucky, or to face a tortuous death. In America 2020 the police torture their arrested victims in open daylight and their vile acts are recorded on cellphones. And yet large numbers of people, including the president, remain unmoved, despite the national outcry and demonstrations against police brutality and injustice.

After protesting and agitating over the summer, I returned to reading. Toni Morrison (1931–2019), the Nobel prize novelist spoke to me in *Song of Solomon*. It is a powerful story that hovers between a past ancestor, Solomon, some of whose descendants live in Michigan in the early part of the twentieth century. It is a complicated story but I read it as an allegory – a veiled moral and spiritual meaning of black suffering in America. Unable to flee their bondage some of the African-American ancestors also told stories of finally flying away from slavery and to be liberated in the skies at death. But they leave their traces in the woods and rock formations in sounds and blooms for generations to hear their song.

Remaining on earth centuries later is a father with a curious name, Macon Dead, who in turn has a son by the same name, but the lad is nicknamed Milkman. Milkman is friends with a more wounded young man, called Guitar. His suffering, loss and experience as a black man witnessing injustice makes him join a clandestine vigilante group known as 'The Days' who avenges the deaths of black people at the hands of white authority. Milkman protests this kind of action and disagrees with his friend. Their exchange reveals the portrait of the black experience in

America and Morrison cunningly sketches the experience of everyone who lives in a white world. White people, Guitar says to Milkman: 'They want your life, man. … Look. It's the condition our condition is in. Everybody wants the life of a black man. White men want us dead or quiet—which is the same thing as dead. White women, same thing. They want us, you know, "universal", human, no "race consciousness". Tame, except in bed. But outside the bed they want you to be individuals.'

Morrison was an extraordinary commentator on American life and fully understood the nuances of black American life. To say she was prescient would be trite. What one learns and observes is that the conditions for several centuries have not changed for black people in America in any substantive manner despite civil rights, Martin Luther King Jr, and the first black president of the USA, Barack Hussein Obama. Milkman in his exchange with Guitar protests the revenge killing of a white person for every black life a white person had unlawfully taken. When forced to explain why he kills, Guitar is pressed and in frustration gives the most honest answer. 'It *is* about love. What else but love? Can't I love what I criticise?' Vengeance is about love, albeit a flawed mode. Black Love Matters as much as Black Lives Matter, one suspects Guitar would say. He would say, love is prior to life.

In the very year Toni Morrison earned her master's degree in American literature at Cornell University, a short-story writer and journalist, Saadat Hasan Manto (1912–1955) died in Lahore. Born in colonial India, Manto, barely 42, died in the newly-formed state of a divided subcontinent, Pakistan. A man frequently portrayed for lurking in the demimonde, writing about prostitutes and the forsaken, his mention in Muslim culture is associated with his hard drinking.

One theme Manto frequently portrayed in all its barrenness and nakedness in a few pages was the human condition. One question that tortured Manto's soul was this: is the human condition made and unmade in material conditions? Or is the human condition sometimes an unbreakable fate? Is it a destination? He leaves you with more questions than answers, perhaps because he played with fewer words than Toni Morrison, since she was a novelist and he a master of the short-stories.

So, thinking through the agonies of this summer of discontent, I also returned to Manto. Particularly to a short story that gripped me before, but now it made me reflect even more on our condition. It is titled in Urdu as '*Three-and-a-half annas*.' An *anna* is one-sixteenth of the colonial rupee, in short, a paltry sum. Using American currency as the benchmark of conversion, the title could be translated as '*Seven Cents*.'

Siddiq Rizvi, freshly released from prison overhears the narrator, Manto and his friends, converse in a coffee shop. The friends were debating whether prison actually reforms individuals. Uninvited, Rizvi yells over from the adjoining table before pulling his chair closer to their table: 'Why did I kill? Why did I soak my hands in the blood of a human being? That is a long story. Until I do not inform you of the consequences and passions embedded in the act, you will not understand anything – but at this moment you guys are talking about crime and punishment, a human being and prison – and because I was in prison, therefore my opinion will not be inappropriate.'

America has a prison-industrial complex. A stain on the character of a nation that promised to experiment in a new form of liberty and habitation, breaking from Europe. And, in Europe brown and black bodies fill the prisons in disproportionate numbers. I often shiver at the thought of being deprived of one's freedom and to be destined to a small cell, or forced to share a space without any choice with others for decades as punishment. Miscarriages of justice have kept so many innocent persons behind bars for decades. Prison like hell is an awful destination. And most studies show that prisons only further dehumanise in their current form.

Manto writes in the voice of Rizvi: 'Agreed, prison does not reform a human being. But this truth is repeated so frequently that it sounds like an oft-repeated joke, maybe a thousand times at social gatherings. Yet it is not a joke, for despite knowledge of this reality, thousands of prisons do exist – just as handcuffs, those shackles of a naked humanity – I too have worn these ornaments of the law.'

Manto the literary figure pokes a hole in the encyclopedic knowledge of criminal justice, theology and moral ethics. He re-stages the fragments of the political and the theological at once. These are questions encountered in real life as well as embodied in the lives of persons with whom we can relate inside and outside prison. In this prison story, it is not Rizvi who is the moral exemplar but rather someone most unexpected to be cast in that role. While it is typical of Manto to show us the moral lives of prostitutes, this time he picks from among that large mass of humanity who on the Indo-Pak subcontinent are marked as the 'untouchables' or, Dalits.

One of the most moving narratives is the plight of a Bhagu, who belongs to the *bhangī* caste among the untouchables, those who undertake the menial tasks such as sweeping and cleaning toilets. Rizvi narrates the story of this fellow inmate who received a one-year sentence for stealing seven cents, three-and-a-half *annas*. Why did he steal? Bhagu apparently told the court: 'For two days I was hungry and out of desperation I had to put my hand in the pocket of Karim the tailor.' In his naivety or honesty, he further tells the court, his goal actually was to take a sum of five rupees from Karim as these were his arrear wages for two months owed to him. As he confesses his guilt, he also mitigates the condition of his employer. Karim too was not at fault for not paying him, he explains, because many of the tailor's clients had not paid him for services rendered. Instead of finding the five rupees in Karim's pocket, Bhagu, it appears, could only lay his hands on three-and-a-half *annas* (seven cents) from the empty pockets of the broke Karim. Ironically, Manto does not omit to tell us that the paltry sum was safely repossessed and in the custody of the court's treasury because Bhagu was caught for the theft and the money was unspent. It must be obvious how Manto mocks the legal and political system by subtly pointing to the fact how the item a poor and desperate man stole is kept in custody. The question that comes to mind is, who is policing the ill-gotten gains of the rich and the powerful?

At his trial, Bhagu willingly confesses to a litany of prior petty thievery. He stole ten rupees from the purse of some rich woman for which he got a month-long penalty. Once he took a toy made of silver from the house of the deputy commissioner to defray costs 'because my child contracted pneumonia and the doctor demanded a huge fee for the treatment.'

'Sir,' Bhagu addresses the judge in mitigation: 'I am not telling lies. I am not a thief. Some conditions forced me to steal. And the situation was such that I got caught. There are bigger thieves around other than myself, but they have yet to be apprehended. Sir, now I have neither child nor wife. To my misfortune, I still possess a belly. If my belly dies then it will put an end to all these troubles. Sir, pardon me!' But as Manto's character, Rizvi explains, the court did not pardon Bhagu, but instead sentenced him to a year of hard labour for stealing seven cents.

Manto shifts the conversation to a philosophical and moral quandary. Why do we only think of truth and honesty in terms of the good? Why is good always the standard and yardstick? 'In the eyes of the law,' asks Rizvi, 'I do not know what the law views as honesty and integrity (*īmāndārī*)? But I know one thing: that I killed with great integrity. And I believe Bhagu *bhanghī* too stole three-and-a-half *annas* with great integrity.'

Integrity seems to be the driving force in Manto's narrative. But integrity is not only a moral virtue, but for him it is an affective virtue, tied to the human drives, something viscerally experienced. Integrity is a desire, an assemblage of multiple granular emotions and feelings. But integrity is not monochromatic and Manto, through Rizvi, challenges that once-revered teleological destination of right and wrong, black and white. The human soul is constituted by compositions of desire which in turn are directed and mobilised by the passions that bring the assemblages into play. There are no direct and fixed lines to a future, except through the experience of time, one which we embody.

Manto conceives of moral assemblages and desires of right and wrong, good and evil through Rizvi's eyes. 'Honestly speaking, I am now thinking to myself, what is good and evil after all?,' Rizvi poses a rhetorical question to the gathering of friends. Then almost philosophically he adds: 'One thing can be good for you and it can be evil to me. In one society something is deemed good and the same thing is deemed evil in another society. We Muslims believe that growing the hair under the armpits is a sin, whereas Sikhs are indifferent to such growth. If growing armpit hairs was truly a sin, then why does God not punish the Sikhs? If there is any God, then my request to the divine is this: for God's sake please smash these laws of humans and tear down the constructed prisons. And kindly build the jails in your heavens. You yourself can punish humans in your courts, after all, you are God!'

Echoes of Friedrich Nietzsche's subversive questions in Manto's narrative resound, in his bid to upend the standard narrative of morality. Fragmentation and singling out episodes from the immeasurable complexity of human life is one way for Manto to interrogate his social conditions. Morality, he seems to say, is not only the binary between right and wrong, but morality might want to explore multiple shades of the right and shades of the wrong.

And then when he turns his attention to the jails and prisons he acknowledges that he wishes to see movement, both literally and figuratively. Manto becomes a conceptual persona: he personalises thinking, he invests new energy in concepts. He not only proposes to move (deterritorialise) the prisons and relocate them to heaven (reterritorialise), but he also wants to move and relocate divine justice to the heavens and make it an affair of God. The idea of dispatching transcendent forms of justice to the heavens and delaying it to the afterlife is a transgressive and subversive idea. Perhaps there is an element of despair: humans cannot meet justice; the impossibility of realising justice on earth. Today we might say Manto tried to relocate old justice and old law to the 'cloud,' a metaphor for the paradise of information. Except that today the cloud is paradoxically everywhere, accessible and governs and monitors our minute movements, dictates our information and regulates our judgments with exacting speed and consequence. One wonders whether relegating things to heaven or the cloud is actually a good thing.

What I think Manto really wants to do is for good and evil to become immanent: one growing into the other, not easily separable and definable. Good and evil can be relative and relational, not absolutes. Good and evil can also hover outside of chronometric time. It can be a heterotopia, as Michel Foucault explained, beyond the reach of normal systems of law and political systems. Graveyards, hospitals, madrasas, prisons are all heterotopic spaces rebelling and challenging the utopias of the nation-state and neoliberal capitalism. Manto pushes good and evil into a heterotopic space, the unwanted space and thinks against the grain. Challenging the inviolable binaries of good and evil, which are yet to be broken, making both collide and clash in order to reveal something else.

In Manto's eyes Bhagu epitomised integrity. But human conditions made him resort to crime, an act he himself never desired. Survival forced him to perpetuate the wrong. To prove his case, Manto makes Rizvi narrate two incidents as a testimonial to Bhagu's character in prison. Bhagu frequently ran errands, acquiring a weekly stock of 20 precious *bidis*, leaf-rolled thin cigarettes, fetched from Rizvi's friend Jorji in another section of the prison. Bhagu dutifully delivered the entire stock, never cheating. In return for his services he received one *bidi*. But he was never shortchanged. A day before Bhagu was to be released, Rizvi sends him to Jorji with a note urgently requesting ten rupees. Bhagu again brings him the money with a note from Jorji. The reply note read: 'My dear friend Rizvi, I am sending these ten rupees, by way of this common thief. I hope by God, you get it, because tomorrow he is to be released from prison.' Staring at Bhagu the thought crosses Rizvi's mind, that if this guy got a one-year sentence for stealing seven cents, I wonder how much time he would do for stealing ten rupees. The motif shifts back to integrity *(īmāndārī)*.

I have been reflecting on these two portraits of Bhagu inside and outside of prison. Controlled conditions of human life. In bondage but with his belly fed; outside prison where his desperate poverty forces him to go against his better angels. There is very little difference in the sweep of these stories – the stories of people in other lands and times and the stories occurring in our neighbourhoods under multiple pandemic conditions. The viruses and the political bacilli that undoes the body politic, rendering us inert and frozen, are infesting our societies at a rapid speed. What is needed is to seek a mode of being and existence with new concepts and vocabularies that will ensure that we continue to seek integrity, albeit in different registers. Destinations need new territories.

# A STROLL THROUGH KL

*C Scott Jordan*

I am almost certain that the elevator which delivers me from my thirtieth floor apartment back to the Earth's surface would be one of the safest places to be in the event of global thermonuclear holocaust. The door's spring open after a firm, yet warm British woman's voice announces my ground-level arrival and one can almost see the sublimated haze that results from cracking open an airlock. A quick swallow pops my ears to the correct pressure calibration just as I am met by the aural bop playing in the elevator antechamber. The radio-over-the-announcement speaker in the space is a new adage. When the virus forced us into hermitage, our lockdown in Malaysia was announced as the Movement Control Order (or MCO, acronyms are a sort of hobby bordering on addiction here, so try to keep up). Perhaps the management felt benevolent in gracing us with this gift from above. Perhaps they thought this might distract us from their other numerous ineptitudes as a high-rise management company, little did they know the greater ineptitudes of the globe outside the complex gates would numb us to such small offences. Perhaps it is a self-fulfilling prophecy, but often times the speaker in that antechamber plays an all too familiar song that relates to some thought or thematic dressing the day desires to put to me. Of course, this is only about fifty percent of the time. The radio channel the speaker is set to, appears to float between fifteen second local news updates, Qur'anic verse interpretations set to a youthful, female voice with that most curious Malay-English accent, and super hits of the 1970s, 1980s, and 1990s. Such stark contradictions are par for the course in Malaysia generally, and here in Kuala Lumpur (KL for the initiated) especially. If I was so lucky, my evening descent from the high tower would begin with a snippet of what was once referred to as modern rock. Billy Joel, Queen, Madonna, Nirvana, and in this instance, Tina Turner's 1984 hit 'What's Love Got to Do With It?'.

An apt question indeed.

Each morning in KL begins with the songs of the cranes. Not the organic ones, but those mechanistic beasts which perch upon the numerous towers which make up the city's skyline that has the sort of elegance and style of Boris Johnson's hair. The twisting of cogs and popping up of modernity's 'development' might show the history of this dear town. A crescent of mountains in the Northeast gives the appearance of a chalice of mud dropped to the ground, two major cracks in the discarded cup are the two mighty rivers that slop the mud back and forth as the contents, whether they were once grand or banal, spill forth into the Straits of Malacca in the Southwest. The mightiness of the two rivers, the Klang and Gombak, are only revealed during intense rainy periods where they have been a historical menace for flooding. In their present latent state, glorified streams of the most unattractive hue would be a more fitting moniker. The colonial harvesting of Malaysia was not kind to the water quality and its postcolonial industrialism did rivers all across the country no better. Centuries of waste dump, industrial, human and otherwise; it is rather remarkable that even the slightest shade of blue can be found in these murky shallows. We are on the better end of a fifteen-year, billion dollar a year project to clean them up, but with the clock ticking towards the 2025 deadline, much is left to be desired. But fear not, you need not look at this environmental failure if you do not wish to, the Ampang-Kuala Lumpur Elevated Highway, the E12, hides it from the sky's view and a branch of the Klang Valley Integrated Transit System rides along the two rivers, post confluence so that passengers may look out either side of the speeding train, without having to look at the ecological disaster directly below it. It is a shame too, the rivers of Kuala Lumpur have been well set in concrete to the point where there is a rich potential for a very lovely river walk. Signs tell me that developments are underway, but we live in a time where contracts are only as stable as the government and well, the current 'government' if you shall call it that, leaves novel notions of confidence, integrity, and democracy somewhat lacking. The virus didn't help matters. Focus on upkeep and development in KL has the attention span of an ordinary house cat, and someone has seen fit to distract it with lasers on the wall, looking to only the new and fanciest of high-rise apartments while the past is left to its own devices and decay.

I was spoiled by the layout of American cities. My attuned internal compass never allowed to stretch its legs in such minor league urban explorations. American cities were always the easiest with their grids, running north to south, east to west, usually focussed on some natural border, be that a lake, river, mountain, or ocean. Numbered and lettered streets are common and make navigation kindergarten. Continue on this road for five miles and take a left at the tall lonely cottonwood tree, if you hit the megachurch, you've gone too far. Europe is a bit trickier, but they can't help but obey some sort of logic. Many of them are radial cities, emanating from some declared centre (often the locals believe their centre to be that of the very universe!), spiralling out like the arrondissements of Paris. Often these centres are churches or historically significant sites. One may learn a European city by playing a game of pinball, bouncing from café to café, monument to monument, or Starbucks to Starbucks. While the systems of orientation may differ, they have an inherent logic that is easy to get a hold of for those of us in touch with the alignment of our inner ear bones. Even strange places like Barcelona, can be cartographically conquered once one learns that directions are either given towards the sea or towards the mountains. While Asia is often a whole new world, my travels through China and Korea revealed the rules they play by. *Feng-shui* is not just a way to maximise your inner office peace of mind, it's a deeply cultural ordering. Literally meaning 'water-wind' to spare you a chapter of Chinese aesthetic philosophy, it is a need for harmonious balance. If you build a tall building on one end of town, something better match that on the far side of town. It's subtle, but once you've seen it, you can't unsee it and it leaves a rich beauty to these cities that are otherwise choked in clouds of pollution laden air. Aside from this, I see that many Asian cities followed the American and European fad that was sweeping the world. And to call yourself a worldly city, it appears you need a clock tower, a massive Ferris wheel, and a massive phallus. At some point in time, it would appear, that major urban centres agreed that they, seemingly definitionally, needed a large, oblong, erect tower as a symbol of status. It would appear the bigger the better, and the city with the biggest phallic building, I am told, wins a most important contest. Perhaps it is a sign of our globalised world that all cities must follow these rules. After all, them's the rules. Or so I thought. And then I found myself in Malaysia. Malaysia plays by all the rules and by none of the rules. Completely comfortable with this headache inducing dilemma where none of the puzzle pieces fit together, but somehow a piece or art is looking you back in the eye. And there are few examples of urban planning by abstract art than Malaysia's capital city.

One does not so much navigate Kuala Lumpur but, rather, one must negotiate it. And when all else fails, a prayer here or there can't hurt anything. Google Maps will show you clustered lobes of concrete towers tied together by what appears to be freshly boiled spaghetti. These are the roads of KL that twist and turn with less logic than the rivers that proceeded them. Existing on multiple levels of each other, diverging and converging whenever they feel like it. You may choose to turn left or to turn right, but fundamentally this is arbitrary. Yes, there is indeed more than one way to skin a cat. If you miss your exit, it was perhaps meant to be, and chances are the road will present you with another opportunity to find wherever it is you wish to go. This road here, it will take you to Singapore and Thailand and the Straits of Malacca, it can even land you across 110th St. in Manhattan. But that's the idea behind roads isn't it? All roads do lead to Rome, eventually. There is an international cry and many a clever capitalist has found a way to monetise it: 'build bridges, not walls'. But let us look beyond the dollars and donuts here. The point of these walls are to block paths or roads, after all, a sea to shining sea length wall is not only fantastical, but also laughably impractical. And bridges don't just exist, they serve to have roads where they physically cannot be. Other animals leave tracks in the sand, we leave roads. Ideally, they are like all of the collective silk of all the spider's webs, the endless wakes of whales in the ocean. They shift and change, decay and grow anew. Like all the running water on this planet they are connected. Usually when one focuses in on a segment of this grand network, the complexity is lost and unidirectional lines remain. In KL, this dynamism lives. The contradictions are rather startling, but I suppose if one proceeds forward with the grace of God Malaysian pedestrians presuppose, or even the direct forwardness of a Londoner's trot for which they know they are entitled to, that it is best to dive in. No need to waste time dipping a toe in to taste it. For you will never 'get used to it'.

The inherent contradictions of KL's roads are a match made in hell for the vehicular commuter. Insanity is the word that first and best comes to mind when I watch the driving patterns of Malaysia. Like sharks in the ocean, motion is the difference between life and death. Best get dying or best get cracking. Through my Western eyes it is aggression. But aggressive drivers are not what Malaysian drivers are. Aggressive perhaps in the way that a cobra or a feline postures before a strike. Though it presents with the spookiness of offence, it almost always is strictly defence. When a girl stands her ground against the Swedish parliament or the Bull of Wall Street, it is adorable or inspiring (depending on which side of those conflicts you find yourself), but when an apex predator is dethroned before an encounter with the truly most dangerous game, it's scary or, heaven forbid, evil. For that creature recoils to fight back, driven by fear, which lies at the heart of aggression. But 'fear is the mind-killer!' and it is not what propels a Malaysian driver. It is instead the black sheep of the emotional family – respect. A fundamentalist follower of respect. Respect for time, space, speed, and the forward motion a road demands. Pedals are meant to be placed before the floor, this is in respect to time, life is for living, not joyriding. If I need to turn right in 100 metres, but the right lane is overflowing, I will get into the left lane and force my way back over almost instantaneously. This would get you a honk and a proudly displayed finger in the States, but here it is a respect for, space, fill the roads, and the forward movement of roads, for if time is to be delayed, then spare no space and let the mental math do itself. Motorbike conductors spare no space or speed, shattering the imagined lines that divide lanes. Why pick a lane when you can have it all? Yet respect of the other must be upheld. If a car wants it, it must be let in, even if it is travelling at an insufficient speed and your acceleration would leave it to the dustbin of history. Only the ever ignorant, hopelessly lost youth don't let others in. An old timer may click his teeth at such an egregious error of driving tradition. Of course, I may add anyone who thinks that the relatively new advent of automobile driving demands a tradition, grossly undermines what tradition is all about. Yet, if I am accelerating at a rate that could reverse the monsoon winds, then you must in accordance with this seemingly whimsical law of respect, get over and let me pass. The contradictions compile, but motion and progress are life. And it all adds up to the greatest contradiction of all, that patience is no virtue on the roads when it is a necessary evolutionary step forward for anyone hoping to make a life in Kuala Lumpur. Just as the roads are as fluid as time itself, they have changed the landscape of KL in its relatively short history.

Where the Gombak and the Klang rivers meet is where KL takes its name sake, at least this is the most popular theory. *Kuala* roughly translates as a meeting of two watery bodies, an estuary, a confluence, a marriage. *Lumpur* means mud. Feel free to run wild with the metaphors one can take from a muddy confluence. Of course, what is a theory without a few competitors. Malaysia likes its theories that make unlikely bedfellow with uncertainty. This point is made resoundingly clear when one examines the digitisation of KL's rumour mill via WhatsApp or attempts to navigate the second city, the digital lives of Malaysians on Facebook. Another possible origin states that KL was originally named Pengkalan Lumpur, or 'muddy landing place' as Klang used to be known as Pengkalan Batu, 'stone landing place'. Typical linguistic deterioration gets us to Kuala Lumpur, then to KL. A third theory holds much intrigue. A Cantonese word 'lam-pa' may have been a part of the settlement's original name, meaning 'flooded jungle' or 'decaying jungle'. After all the first major residents of the confluence were Chinese miners. But a revelation like that could have as drastic an effect as if Americans figured out how many of their city names came from first-nation languages. Shutter. Of course, be careful with your use of the word *lampa* as the local Hokkien language equates this slang term to bullocks. I suppose the etymological progression makes sense as I'm told the flood waters could easily get that high. Again, let all the beautiful metaphors for this city's nomenclature sink in.

Uncertain origins such as these make for wonderful dinner party discussion. But it takes an impressive level of acceptance to be so nonchalant with uncertainty. Even the original arrival of the nation's predominant religion, Islam, in the archipelago is open to debate. A common theory holds that Islam travelled to Malaysia along the silk road line via India and the old Persian Empire. As if ideas can only travel by land. Another theory says one of the Prophet's own men carried the message directly to the Archipelago, a tale that has been mythologised in a way that could rival America's brown haired, blue-eyed Jesus riding a bald eagle with a sign of peace on his left hand and the Star-Spangled Banner in his right. Another provocative, and currently quite popular theory, holds that Islam ironically came as a gift from none other than China. Some of the oldest Islamic recordings date back to the state of Terengganu where its earliest mosques bear striking architectural similarities to those built in a China lost to history.

At the muddy confluence, where a national capital would arise, a practical obstacle would make it the edge of civilisation. It was the furthest point up the Klang River boats could transport supplies and men. From there, they'd have to trek by foot to establish what would become highly lucrative tin mines. The point of confluence was an old Malay burial place and what a beautiful place to lay your loved ones to rest, where two rivers become one? Today, the oldest mosque in KL, Masjid Jamek, stands in its place. Built in 1909, the mosque was constructed in that all-too-Malay style which marries the height of Mughal India and Moorish Spain. An impossible meeting by way of both time and space, made wonderfully possible in the eternal KL. Chinese businessmen and Sumatrans looking for a place to make a living journeyed to the gateway into the great beyond. Of course, with opportunity comes sacrifice as malaria and all the dangers of the jungle accompanied those first settlers of KL at the dawn of the nineteenth century. The modern-day megametropolis started as a neighbourhood of miner's homes built of wood and thatched palm (commodities found in aces in the jungle), which unfortunately made them prone to devastating fires. The backwater where disposable labourers were sent to make a living or die trying gained immense value as the tin mines began building the state of Selangor into a source of wealth for whom so ever could hold it. Chinese businessmen and gangs partnered with Malay princes and rajas to fight each other. Multicultural army against multicultural army, a purse of tin to the victor. It boggles the mind what brings people together and tears them apart. KL was captured and burned to the ground a couple of times before its strategic importance would forever alter the future of this little mining town. And who would suspect the British Empire. Seeing KL as a strategically more ideal foothold for controlling the tin industry, but also most business running through the Western part of the archipelago, it was made the seat of colonial administration in Malaya. And to minimise the fires, they order construction in brick, bricks made in what is now the modern district of Brickfields.

As KL had been a predominantly Chinese town since its early days, the head of the Chinese community, the Kapitan Cina was one of the most powerful positions. Its early office holders both maintained good relations with neighbouring Malay community leaders and seized the economic opportunities by monopolising the tin mining industry and leading the way as the rubber industry rose to prominence along with the latest technological advancement of the automobile. It also didn't hurt the coffers to hold the keys to the opium, prostitution, and gambling industries either. No doubt, corruption and greed were a part of KL since the days of mud. But despite the controversy behind the early leaders of KL, if it were not for the Kapitans, KL would have gone the way of the wood and atap houses. But then the railroad came to town and off it stepped the British. The British found the Kapitans a great tool, as long as they were useful, and once they weren't, well the British Empire did not become one on which the sun never sets by hanging onto tools it deemed useless. And British Malaya was spared no expense from the full onslaught of colonial tactics. Institutions that both elevated and entrapped sprung up throughout the land. And the divide and conquer methods made famous in British India, rippling into contemporary events of xenophobia, were no stranger to Malaya. While precolonial Malaya was not without its tensions between people, there is little argument that the frying pan was not exchanged for the fire when the British came to town. Greater importations of Chinese and Indians from other branches of the Empire came to KL and not only through ghettoisation, but also a strange career/class based social categorisation kept divisions intact without the potential for boil over should one catch wind of such notions as a diverse and plural society. It should also be noted that when the British took a quick recess from Malaya rule, the Japanese did not help the rising racial tensions in the country, especially as they could pit some of these races against their mortal enemy the Chinese. By the end of Britain's long summer holiday in Malaya, all their divisions remained, a loose collection of only some of what was the ancient Malay world was given its independence and a 'best wishes' from the former colonial administration. Sultans came together cautiously with deep historical memories of wrongs and debts, Singapore and Borneo hung by a thread and the jungles were not just filled with zoological monsters and *hantus* (the Malay jungle spirits) but this new spectre known as the Communists, and of course they looked strangely familiar to the Chinese. The Malays got political power; the Chinese found themselves holding the purse. And the monsoon winds showed no signs of slowing. It was time to come together.

My residential complex spits me out on the historic Jalan Raja Muda Abdul Aziz. My weekly shopping-for-essentials destination is KL City Centre (KLCC). Geographically, it is straight ahead approximately three kilometres. But to go straight ahead would be to dive into the labyrinthine Kampung Baru (Kampung being the village and *Baru* the Malay word for new), a take on the traditional Malay village, right in the heart of the towering capital city. So, I am stuck with left or right. The left is quicker, but more treacherous. The Jalan itself bares more in common with its river ancestors, changing on a whim, and indeed, everyday it is a new road as they work tirelessly to build an MRT station that runs beneath it. Signs will line my journey depicting a shame filled man, his head down as he pleads to embrace the discomfort now so that the future may be prosperous. Ah yes, the wonderful lie of progress. If we keep building, then everything will work itself out. We don't think about what we are building or how it will change things, what history may be lost. We just carry on, head down. This has driven Malaysia since the late 1970s. And indeed, Malaysia has almost every year appeared to become a new land, KL itself changing drastically through the years. But we beg, has it gotten better. At times, it appears my intended simple journeys to the grocery store have me walking the perilous and ever-changing path laid out by Hades for Orpheus.

So, to the right I journey. Jalan Raja Muda Abdul Aziz from the look is rather unassuming. The North side of the street is a collection of residential complexes and various elements of what I'll call a medical city block. Hospitals, research centres, clinics, even teaching and training facilities. If I look towards where the sun will inevitably set, I see a series of towers from this vantage point, but one in particular sticks out to me. It doesn't even need to be the coolest or tallest building to command my respects. It has an overt brutalist influence, matching a certain speckling of other towers, *Menaras* in Malay, built in the 1980s. Each bearing the oppressive base of concrete, but with some arching, a certain Malayness is conveyed and healthy use of sweeping glass windows give the error of something wanting to look to the future, but not in a creative way. Whenever this tower catches my eye on a commute, I cannot help but hear Howard Shore's beautiful compositional theme for Sauron and the forces of evil used throughout Peter

Jackson's *The Lord of the Rings* trilogy. Marching drums and bass-filled brass accompany the letters U, M, N, and O which perch high atop the tower like Sauron's all-seeing eye. Long banners of the Malaysian flag are liberally strung about the tower. I am told that during an election, the whole tower is made into a lightboard advert worthy of the famous Las Vegas strip. The Tower is the height of a sprawling PWTC (Putra World Trade Centre) complex which features an elegant campus with a convention centre built in the style of the Malay long house. PWTC is within walking distance to some of KL's oldest premiere hotels and a sophisticated canopy of air-conditioned elevated walks sends pedestrians to all the wonderful places they may desire without having to face the reality of the ground level. This is the HQ for UMNO, the political party that has held onto power in Malaysia since its independence from the British, all the way up to the historic elections of 2018. The Barard-dûr-esque tower is ironically named Menara Dato Onn. This particular Dato Onn was Dato Onn Jaafar who following the Japanese defeat in 1945, met with other Malay nationalists concerned with the Malaya's future after the departure of the British. It all began as a movement. An organised union of Malay nationalists which took on the apt name of the United Malay Nationalist Organisation. Malays from all over British Malaya came together in a series of congresses to agitate for the creation of the Malayan Union. The new British satellite protectorate threatened the position of Malays as it was seen in the British system. The Malayan Union first gave citizenship to anyone born on the land and required equal rights for all. The threat came in that the British system had shoehorned Malays into the civil service sector which, when opened up to all would take away one of the few methods of upward bound social movement for Malays. While most of the state power was in British hands, what little power remained would slowly be ceded from the Malays as they would be condemned to rural poverty and their culture and way of life would fade into memory if they were ruled by the others. UMNO declared itself a political party in 1946 after the third Malay congress in Johor and Dato Onn Jaafar would be the party's first President.

Although the young UMNO could easily have been a thorn in the side for British Administrators of the Malayan Union, the two found a common enemy in the menacing Communists during a period known as the Emergency. In 1949, the Malayan Union was swapped for the Federation of Malaya and a bit more autonomy was granted by the British. Then the idea of independence was tabled in return for British support of UMNO's rise. Dato Onn, upset at UMNO's refusal to allow non-Malay's to join the party withdrew. He formed a new one, the IMP (The Independence of Malaya Party), and began the cry for 'Merdeka', a term originally attributed to a freed slave which came to stand for freedom and independence. Dato Onn's IMP was unable to hold wider Malay support and he even went on to try and form one more party which could not escape the eclipse of UMNO, especially after they made the critical coalition with the MCA, Malayan Chinese Association, to form the Alliance, a coalition which would rule until evolving into Barisan Nasional (BN), (a former ruling coalition, that still exists today). Malaya would get its independence in 1957 (a little over a decade late for many). And history, by its nature, making comedies of tragedies as it does, now had Dato Onn's name on the hallmark of the party he fought against in the end and Merdeka is one of the first of Malaysia's gallery of public holidays.

My eyes avert from the all-seeing UMNO to see a deserted school. I adjust my face mask slightly. When will kids be allowed to again play freely about this yard? A painted mural shows a diverse collection of students, stereotypically emphasised in their Malay-ness, Chinese-ness, or Indian-ness to make the point without being offensive. The early days of an independent Malaya were not without their troubles and as with any fledgling democracy many are left to simmer under the surface. One of the saddest parts of these troubles was the break-up of Singapore and Malaysia in 1965 another is the famous incident of 13 May 1969.

Approximately where this school house sits, once stood the special residence for the Menteri Bensar (Chief Minister) of Selangor, the state in which KL finds itself (although now it stands as a federal territory within, but outside of Selangor). The general election of 1969 came as the climax to a decade of racial tensions all across the country. The day of the election, 10 May, a rather peaceful funeral procession took place for a young Chinese boy who was shot dead by Malay police in KL. As the polls closed it was revealed that the Alliance had won less than half of the popular vote after facing tough opposition by the newly formed Chinese dominant parties: DAP (Democratic Action Party) and Gerakan (Parti Gerakan Rakyat Malaysia). It was reported that non-Malays gathered at the residence of Selangor's Chief Minister asking him to resign and give the position to a Chinese. Provocative non-Malay-on-Malay taunting was reported all across the country. Seeing the rhetoric coming out of the election as a slight on Malayness, members of UMNO Youth planned to organise a small victory parade for the Chief Minister Harun Idris. The rally would take place on the evening of 13 May, a Tuesday, but since Sunday, Malays from all over Selangor and other neighbouring states coalesced in Kampung Baru to rally the Malay victory, despite how close it all came. In the afternoon, on their way to the rally, a band of Malay travellers ran into harassment from non-Malays in Gombak. The squabble was described as a fist fight that escalated to the point of casting empty glass bottles and stones back and forth. With half an hour to go before the procession would begin, word of the scuffle reached what is now Jalan Raja Muda Abdul Aziz.

As you walk along the Jalan, another major Jalan, intersects, forming the Northwest corner of Kampung Baru. Today this seemingly innocuous street houses a regular evening jam as hungry mouths look to eat at the finest eateries in KL. In 1969, this road was the thin red line dividing the Malay Kampung Baru from the Chinese Chow Kit. It was the embodiment of the racial divide. Enraged by the news from Gombak, many of the Malay masses gathered at the Chief Minister's residence broke off, seeking revenge on the unsuspecting Chow Kit area. It would later be found that Malays from out of town came not just with political spirit but also parangs and kris (traditional Malay bladed weapons). Like the fires that used to burn down the wooden city in its precolonial days, hate and riots spread throughout Chow Kit and quickly over took over the city as Malay and Chinese struck back and forth. Cars and shops were burned, looting ran rampant and just as the scheduled victory procession would have begun eight Chinese were dead. In less than an hour, the whole city had fallen into madness. Mobs and gangs ran riot, cinemas were burned, a police station was besieged and an attempt was made to burn down the UMNO headquarters of the day. A curfew was instated, but poorly announced. The Inspector General of the Police gave a shoot-to-kill order for violators. By 5am the next morning, eighty people were dead. The number of Malay dead was equal to the number of dead Chinese. Equality never tasted so rancid. Before the sun would rise, police and military munitions would tip the death toll on the Chinese side significantly. As the roads sprout from KL, so too did the violence and chaos. Indian Malaysians would also find themselves entrapped within the race war. Parliament was suspended for over a year as the NOP (National Operations Council) took the reign of the country to reinstate law and order. The deputy prime minister, Tun Abdul Razak would direct the NOP until he was made the next prime minister following the resolution of the state of emergency. The NOP's final report named 'racial politics' as the primary reason for this tragedy, alongside the Communists, because why not.

The thin red line between Kampung Baru and Chow Kit is now called Jalan Raja Abdullah. It is a nicely kept road, yet the sidewalks are both slanted and elevated to a comical proportion. This mixed with the segmenting and random fencing that makes walking the relatively straight road a weird play on Tetris for the pedestrian. It is no wonder most elect to simply walk along the road's edge joining the anxiety inducing egalitarian ecosystem that exists here between humans, motorbikes, cars, buses, and stray cats and rats. There are no trees on this road and thus the sun is allowed to shine upon it unadulterated. Every inch of the road side is developed a few roads lead you into Kampung Baru, while every block is an eatery, but this order has been disrupted as seemingly random high-rise towers have found their way into Kampung Baru and Chow Kit equally, like weeds left to overtake the garden. Maybe these colossi can provide the shade desperately desired on this street. Shrieking car horns, and less than distant ambulance sirens wail to fill the atmospheric sounds occasionally silenced before the commanding calls to prayer radiating from the ornamental Kampung Baru Jamek Mosque. The gutters are deep not just for the high volumes of rain water accumulated in this part of the world, but to swallow up bad memories. How should anyone remember what happened here only fifty years ago? But what greater reminder is there than the toxic racial tensions that have grown deep roots in this society. You don't notice it unless you look below the veneer of warm empathy and adherent hospitality that constitutes the cultural normal of Malaysian society. A normal I hope does not fall victim to the post-Covid desired new normal. A normal we could all benefit from aspiring to. It is a light in which one could not think to find racism or hate, but who ever said hate was weak and lacking of cunning as an adversary. And these sorts of contradictions are ontological to Malaysia. The ultimate lesson is that utopia is a fantasy. The good doctors on the far side of this street will tell you, a disease is never cured. To properly cure a disease would be to render the organic inorganic. It is the nature of biological process that nothing is really gone, a fragment must always exist, if only to remind of what came before.

How might we enculturate such transcendence? A bridge could do it. I find that I have slid off Jalan Raja Abdullah into the southwest corner of Kampung Baru. Whispers tell of this place or that having the greatest *nasi lemak* in Malaysia with the frequency of pizza joints in New York City claiming to have the world's finest slice. Except here, the whispers may speak to truths. It is in these tasty dishes that true Malay traditional culture has a good chance of living on. My vision is obscured by a massive towering apartment complex, what truly is the textbook antithesis of kampung. Although it is interesting how Malay families can make high-rise flats into rather convincing faux kampung. It's enough to break your heart if it wasn't already broken by the systematic dismantling of Kampung Baru that has been occurring in waves over the last two decades and with such patience that one day you wake up and it's gone and you have no idea how it all happened without greater awareness. Yet beyond the abomination of a monolith to modernity, climbs a bridge that reaches over the interstate that constitutes Kampung Baru's southern border. The actual border is the Klang River which I assure myself does still exist below the elevated motorway. While the apartment complex is most certainly awkward and ill fit for the two or three story kampung bungalows that typically constitute the neighbourhood, it is not necessarily beyond one's imagination to find, they have become a stable of Malaysian architecture and not without being to the dismay of many. But as I steer around the dark tower, in pursuit of the bridge, which in its majesty seems more fit for the uber-modern architectural anomalies appearing, say, in Singapore or Hong Kong. More out of place is the sudden park I find myself in at the northern leg of the bridge. It is one of those artificially green and groomed patches. It is a locale more fit for a north London suburb, those green breaks from the monotony of terraced houses. Technically they are natural and one could argue of nature, but every inch of them is a planned imitation. Benches are a staple along with some contraption for children to climb upon and perhaps some modern art and a tree here or there to keep up the illusion. I feel like I have fallen off the face of Malaya into a René Magritte painting.

Pinching myself to prove I am awake I proceed past an escalator entrance that seems as though it just materialised from below the ground, it was one of the ways into or out of the subterranean Kampung Baru LRT (Light Rail Train) Station, towards a massive cement square pillar. Within the pillar rises and falls a lift, around the tower's circumference wraps a tiered stairway, presumably to heaven. Electing exercise, I climb the steeper-than-they-look stairs, and begin to sweat. It starts to rain; or rather, in KL it always pours, in spontaneous and overly dramatic fashion. As I reach the top of the pillar, I cannot tell rain from sweat but I'm not bothered because even the few prepared umbrella wielders were no match for this torrent of water. At the top of the pillar a thin ledge provides about the width of an average Malay body's worth of protection from the constant rain. Not surprisingly, the ledge is filled with those hoping for a reprieve from this uninvited downpour. And I must say I am impressed by the effort to socially distance that is at least being attempted. I, along with the others unable to find a place decide to make a mad dash for the bridge, it is hard to tell how porous the roof is in its design, but it is at least some cover. A few brave souls run out on a platform that allows for a nice picturesque background of the bridge and the commanding twin Petronas Towers that demands a quick selfie.

The bridge is called the Saloma Link. Its purpose is to get folks from Kampung Baru to KLCC and at first glance you may be tempted to think it represents the bridge all civilisations must cross from tradition to progress into modernity (what some confuse for 'the future'). And maybe this is wishful thinking, but I like to think that maybe there is a devilishly wonderful subversion at play here. Yes, on the south side of the Klang River, or the E12, stands the stereotypical vision of the megacity. From New York to Shanghai. Skyscrapers and busy streets. Lights to keep such cities from ever sleeping. It looks like money is made here. It looks like this is the life we all desire. But that's the adverts talking. Every day the cranes make it look like more towers are built. Construction never ends, yet over sixty percent of these spaces are empty. There is an addiction to development on that side of the bridge. My going theory is that the buildings are showered in external lights so you don't have to see the lack of internal room lights as these spaces remain unoccupied. Development for development's sake. But I prefer to see the Saloma Link as something a bit cleverer than this: a testament to the one thing that may get us out of the messy present into a truly better future. Love.

The Saloma Link is named for Salmah binti Ismail, the Singaporean entertainment icon of the 1950s and 1960s, who took the stage name Saloma. Renowned for her singing career as well as her acting, she was known as the Marilyn Monroe of Asia. A trendsetter and an idol. She was also married to the famous Malaysian film maker and singer, P. Ramlee, for whom the street you fall out onto on the south side of the bridge is named after. Love's eternal bonds, as seen on Google Maps. The link itself is quite a beautiful work of art, it almost feels a violation to walk across it. Its ornamental roof is designed in the fashion of the pointy betel nut leaf which is used for the floral arrangement called a *sireh junjung* that is often a centre piece for Malay weddings. Lining the pointy roof of steel bent in lovely displays of Islamic geometry are dazzling LED lights capable of making rather stunning images. Mostly they fade between solid colours, blue gives way to purple and on down the rainbow to green which is traded for gold and silver which run as weaving interlocking streams before an elegant pattern of green and gold flow in a lovely design. Occasionally, the various leaves are coloured yellow, red, and blue for the Malaysian flag. But at its height an image is projected of the Malaysian flag, appearing to wave in the wind, red and white stripes as well as a crystal-clear crescent moon holding the fourteen-point Malaysian star against a blue sea background. A convenient throughway and romantic lookout point. And it's exactly sixty-nine metres long. Perhaps there is an architectural sweet spot to a sixty-nine metres in bridge construction to which I am unaware, but I'm hard-pressed to not believe this is yet another element of the ongoing joke this bridge wants us all to lighten up and laugh at. And dear architect, you command my respectful, immature chuckles.

In accordance with contradictions and the sentiment of the local expression '*okay-lah*', which side is the 'from' and which is the 'to'? The bridge is more attractive than either destination and you can see how it brings people together, young lovers, families, friends, staring up at the wonder of the lights, or down to the quiet sci-fi look of the E12 which never seems to be terribly occupied with traffic. Or out to the mountains beyond the looming towers that beg for your attention with their stale and stagnant lights. Even the neon red static illumination of the all-seeing UMNO in the distance has the majesty of a motel's vacancy sign. As the rain continues to fall, the sun now beyond the horizon, for a moment I see an ideal of civilisation. Underneath the beautiful canopy of the Saloma Link children run about as if in paradise. The various groups under the long bridge all respect each other's space and face masks are mostly properly affixed to all our faces. Individuals strike a pose as friends move about to get the perfect angle that will give a unique snap shot of this new landmark and garner the most likes and comments once posted to Facebook and Instagram. At the midpoint of the bridge, at just the right angle, one could take a selfie that captures the puritanical light of the Petronas Towers under the arch of the bridge's canopy as a nice background. A boy and girl stand face masked with eyes expressing joy, their arms locking their necks together, as the boy's long arm adjusts for the perfect shot. The girl pulls down her face mask to steal a peck on the cheek. We can only hope they captured an adorable candid shot.

It was in this spirit Saloma is so fondly remembered. One of her more famous roles was as Mastura, the surprise heroine of P. Ramlee's *Ahmad Albab* (1968). Mastura is the third and youngest daughter of a wealthy man looking to see his daughter's continued prosperity through their marriage to other wealthy numb skulls so the great wheel can keep spinning. As the black sheep of the family, Mastura is shunned and married off to a pathetic poor goat herder, played by none other than P Ramlee himself. The films twists so that Mastura's other two sisters find themselves in seemingly happy relationships with wealthy men who lead them into a life of corruption and crime to win their 'happiness'. In Mastura and her husband's devotion to God and each other, they come to be the truly happy couple preaching the method to their success as the story ends with a hope for us all, a hope that cannot be found in gems and designer products. And some still claim this bridge, with its namesake, is meant to lead away from tradition towards blind progress. I think not.

The south side of the Saloma Link seems disparaging, as if sliding down the throat of a great beast. On the left, the Australian Embassy looks like a concrete Soviet inspired fortress and then the high skyscrapers, a shadowy salted Earth looking patch marks the controversial future home of Trump

International Hotel, KL. For now, it is just foundational rebar and tilled Earth. Maybe this one won't get off the ground. We'll see, oh but wait, what is this on the right. Trees and an old gate. It appears tradition found a way to cross the river. But who ever said tradition had to ever be bound by time or space? As the Indian intellectual, Ashis Nandy, has noted. Tradition must change as everything else changes. If not then you truly allow the future to leave you behind. The Jalan Ampang Muslim Cemetery looks like the central park to KLCC (Kuala Lumpur City Centre). And there Saloma lies in eternal rest. Here grave lies between P. Ramlee's, her beloved, and her ex-husband Aman Ramile. I wonder how Saloma would feel about her final position, but then I remember, this is KL, so how could something like this be out of place. As we say, 'okay-lah!'

As the footpath to the Saloma Link gives way to the vast intersection of Jalan Ampang and Jalan P. Ramlee, despite one's opinion on the structure, one cannot help but stare in awe at the Petronas Twin Towers, especially lit in their standard blinding white light. It must have been more so when the towers pierced the sky for the first time in 1997. Now the skyline around it has somewhat enveloped the structure which ruled the sky from 1998 until 2004, when Taiwan won that oh so important contest with its Taipei 101 tower. But this is what comes with progress for progress's sake. Onward and upward, never look down and certainly never look back. You wouldn't want to learn anything along the way! The Petronas Twin Towers should be seen as a beautiful testament to modernity, influenced by tradition. The shape of the two towers is based on the *Rub el Hizb* the octagonal illusion produced by placing two squares upon each other so that their corners don't overlap. A wonderful contradiction that results in a geometric beauty. At the base of the towers is one of KL's many malls, Suria KLCC which is shaped interestingly like a water molecule, where the two outer lobes of the mall are bent slightly. That bend makes water a polar molecule and because of that little detail, life is possible. At the beginning of the MCO (Movement Control Order), my weekly trip to KLCC was surreal. It was like spelunking an ancient ruin. All the levels of the mall were black and blocked off, only the subterranean level was open where a few like me, dressed protectively in a new take on what post-apocalyptic raiders might appear like (essentially less BDSM leather attire and hockey pads, more facial coverings), scavenged the shelfs of the essential services, a grocery store, a pharmacy, and a post office. Today, the light lives again in KLCC, and the people are back in droves. I've never been one for anxiety, but I suppose now is as good a time as any to give into that millennial stereotype I somehow missed out on. Sure, everyone is wearing a face mask, for the government has mandated it and few of us have an extra 2,000 RM (1,000 RM if you are an MP in the ruling coalition it would appear) in our pocket to pay that fine. But only so much can be asked of a people, especially after they have been locked up at home for the last five months. Social distancing, something that was less than an idea a year ago, has gone out the window from whence it came. The government recommends at least two metre's distance between yourself and others, for those who care to read the signs in this mall, they recommend three metres. But who carries around a ruler? Yet escalators are chalk full, children run about unmasked, and face masks have a tendency to slip under one's chin and seem to have trouble covering people's noses (for perhaps they forget that is also an airway). Thankfully my own mask keeps my jaw from hitting the floor, I just hope that my eyes are not revealing too much of my deeper thoughts. I move quickly trying not to touch any one or be touched along the way. The booby traps Indiana Jones endured are nothing compared to navigating a mall in KL. And it seems every tower has one in its base and they are all connected. Essentially KL today is a city composed of loosely connected malls rather than districts. Once my goods are acquired, sick of people, society, and civilisation I elect to use Grab, the ride sharing service to make my way home. Thanks to what the forty-fifth President of the United States has done to that verb, I never verbalise this term. I refuse such linguistic devolution. It is always 'I will take Grab' or 'I shall use the ride sharing service known as Grab', and I'll attempt to end any traditions of 'Grabbing my way across town'. As I crawl into the back seat of my designated vehicle, remembering I am in KL, the quickest way home is to begin by driving in the opposite direction.

Now that construction had kicked back into over drive, with more high-rise condos needing building, the heavy-duty vehicles work overtime and in so doing decimate the roads around KLCC. My ride home is not smooth. If I wanted that I'd be better off riding in an all-terrain steel trap through an uncharted jungle or in a military vehicle through a war-torn city. Things only somewhat stabilise once we turn onto the road that leads to home. Jalan Tun Razak. I have often quipped that it is the worst road in KL and I have not received much resistance to such a truth claim. In the GPS's effort, which is worthy of a few extra RM tip, to get me home as quick as possible, we have zigzagged to the Southern end of town. The environment is an elephant's graveyard of scaffolding and orange barricades. The only thing more common than Malaysian flags in this moment might be the black scrip on orange AWAS signs (the Malay equivalent of Caution). Howard Shore's orchestra erupts back to its *Lord of the Ring's* themes as we pass the navy blue, glassy exterior square tower, crowned with a metallic *songkok* to give it that, not-quite-enough extra few metres on the top. The Exchange 106 stands like Isengard on a ringed plane of cultivated land, every tree in sight struck down, presumably by orcs, to feed the ever-hungry machine. It is the glory of the TRX (Tun Razak Exchange) what was poised to be the next global financial centre to rival Wall Street, Canary Wharf, or Lujiazui. It is often mistaken as the tallest building in KL, but actually it sits below the Twin Towers and both will be surpassed within a year or two, the way the crane flies, by the blue bent straw of a building rising up which is currently known as PNB 118, but will reign supreme in South East Asia as the Warisan Merdeka Tower. The Exchange 106 is the only completed part of the planned financial district, whose fate lies in a flood puddle of uncertainty as its prime source of income was the scandal hit 1MDB development fund.

Across the street lies a mega scaffolding structure, looking like a prise hidden under a sheet waiting to be revealed. This is the next great mall/residence/hip socialising centre/everything you ever need in one place complex to be called Bukit Bintang City Centre (which will be inevitably referred to as BBCC, which I recommend people really take the time to annunciate so as to not send the wrong signal). The only thing that can be seen is the seemingly torn from history front gate of the former Pudu Prison. Originally built at the turn of the century by the British administration, once on the edge of the jungle, with tigers and *hantus* as effective guards as anyone. This prison is a famous execution site for many drug and arms traffickers and housed many a Malaysian being held under the imperial vestigial law known as the ISA (Internal Security Act), a piece of anti-sedition legislation to help you imprison enemies you didn't want to have to go through the trouble of giving due process to. In 2009, the now abandoned prison was destined for demolition. Many consider this an act of historical erasure. To that, then Deputy Minister of Finance Awang Adek Hussain (an UMNO man), responded that in his opinion, this piece was not something for Malaysians to be proud of. So why not just be done with it? By 2012, only the main gate remained standing proudly at the edge of Jalan Tun Razak. But fear not, shame is not so easily buried in muddy slop. Soon it will stand alive again as the gate to a new prison. The prison of the colonised mind and the colonised future!

I am not the first to say Malaysia has too many holidays. It apparently needs two separate holidays to celebrate its independence. Add in all the Sultan's birthdays and coronations, the two Eids, boom – a month of the calendar gone. But I find a great significance in Malaysia's two holidays: 31 August's Merdeka, the celebration of the end of British rule and 16 September's Malaysia Day, the day Sarawak and Sabah (and Singapore, but, uh, that's complicated) joined what we today refer to as Malay-s-i-a. The fourteen-point star on the Malaysian flag signified a unison between the fourteen states of Malaysia, which included Singapore, yet even after Singapore's 'expulsion' the star remained unaltered. When in the 1970s, KL was made a federal district, the federal star again seemed appropriate. So perhaps it is fitting that fifteen days stand between the two holidays for celebrating Malaysia.

Sitting at Merdeka Square in KL, my eyes are distracted from the beauty of the Mughal/Moorish fantasy all around to a small monument outside the Kuala Lumpur City Gallery. It is a sign that reads 'I Love KL' where love is replaced by a heart. This symbol is perhaps one that unifies many cities the world over, even though it is a violation of the copyright New York City holds over the emblem (and has sought prosecution to uphold). But KL's heart is tilted to the side, in a profoundly simple solution. I watch as face masked peoples of all walks of life pose and contort themselves and their loved ones in pursuit of the perfect Kodak Moment. Apathy and despair cannot win in this world. At the entrance of KL, a sign welcomes you saying 'City of Contrast and Diversity' And I would be the last person to disagree with that. But perhaps I may suggest an addition: '... and one in which contradictions reveal that hope never dies.'

# WANDERER

*Hafeez Burhan Khan*

My first ever trip abroad was to Bhopal in India, to visit relatives. I was 21 years old, skinny, long-haired and ready for adventures. I travelled alone and by the time I returned home, three months later, I was a changed man. I had well and truly caught the bug, my world had physically, mentally, and emotionally expanded. From a young age I knew I wanted to travel but my wanderlust took some time to be realised. My parents wanted me to complete my education before travelling anywhere. Perhaps they had an inkling of how much I would be transformed by the experience. They themselves hadn't been back to India since the mid 1960s so while I was growing up we had never visited India as a family (we would go the year after my inaugural trip thanks to my insistence). Also, unlike today where travel is considerably cheaper, the expense had been too prohibitive.

I would read about far-off destinations, poring over our much-treasured complete series of *Encyclopaedia Britannica* that took pride of place on our bookshelf. But more than anything travelling is in my blood. My father's influence led me, almost inevitably, to follow his footsteps. As a young man, he was the first in his family to go abroad. He quite literally jumped onto a ship in Mumbai, on a whim, when he was a teenager, and sailed around Southeast Asia. Later, when India and Pakistan became two separate countries, he divided his time between Karachi and Bhopal. In 1955 he arrived in the UK, and in 1962, after a brief trip back, drove a VW Combi from Bhopal to England (the drive of choice for every hippy on the flower power trail in the 1960s).

A huge photo album full of black and white photographs from his jaunts was kept in our living room cabinet. I would often leaf through the album wondering about these far-off places. Despite containing images that were utterly alien to me – a set of strange images with no reference point – I was transfixed by them. My father would tell me about the events and characters in these pictures and regale me with stories of the places he had visited, bringing the images to life. Not only was he passionate about travel, but my father loved history and geography, all of which rubbed off on me. One of his most prized possessions was a collection of maps ranging from local to world maps. I would spend hours studying them. It was all so random, yet an enriching learning experience as I began to understand how to use maps in different ways. There were physical maps, there were economic maps and there were maps showing the population of different places. Maps helped me to appreciate maths, history, geography, politics and economics at a very young age. Yet these maps were abstract because I couldn't actually visualise what they looked like, these places that I knew so many statistics about, so it was left to my overactive imagination to daydream. By the age of eleven, I knew the capital cities of most countries and could probably point out any country in an atlas.

Another of my father's books that intrigued me was about the fourteenth century Moroccan wanderer Ibn Battuta, described as the greatest traveller in history. Though the book was in Urdu, my father would read me the exploits of this intrepid seeker, who, for three decades criss-crossed the Islamic world as well as India, Southeast Asia and China. I would listen with rapt attention and my mind attempted to imagine these places of wonder with their strange customs. Not only was he a traveller, but he also offered his services as an Islamic Judge in the various countries he found himself in. Ibn Battuta travelled nearly 120,000km compared to Marco Polo's 20,000 km. Despite this, at school we were taught only about the auspices of Marco Polo's travels. It is almost incomprehensible that a person could travel such great distances when 95% of the population at that time almost never ventured more than five miles from their village. Just as my father was, Ibn Battuta has been a source of inspiration for nearly all of my adult life. Unlike the great traveller, however, I am probably a little more discreet in my opinions about the places I have encountered than he ever was.

Before my first trip to India I had only been abroad in the recesses of my imagination. However, I had visited places in the UK with my family. We didn't have a car but we'd go to the Lake District, the Yorkshire Dales, the seaside and London on coaches. In today's age of multi-purpose travel this may not sound like a great accomplishment but for a child from inner city

Bradford, it was quite a big deal. During the holidays, my parents would put me and my sister on the bus and my cousins would pick me up in Blackburn. I must have been nine or ten when I first did this. Imagine any parent doing that now. And I may have been twelve or thirteen when I went on the coach alone to Tredegar in South Wales. It's almost unthinkable for a mother or father to put a child, alone, or even with a similar-age sibling on a coach at Bradford Interchange at 8.50am, with the destination Cheltenham. The coach would stop at Leeds, Wakefield, Barnsley and Sheffield to pick up passengers. I would spend the entire journey looking at the scenery in wonderment outside, while reading the road signs and making a mental note of where I was. It was so very exciting. We would circumvent Birmingham via the M6 and M5, where you can see the tall buildings of central Birmingham a few miles away and imagine what type of place it might be. What I did know was that it must be a huge city because it always seemed as though we had spent ages driving through it and it never seemed to end. Eventually, we would arrive in the Worcestershire countryside, which was so stunning with rolling hills as far as the eye can see. At 2.20pm we would reach a huge sprawling complex, where hundreds of coaches would be filling up the bays and would all leave at 3pm to go to destinations in the South West of England and South and West Wales. The other half would go back up north. Upon disembarking from the coach I would, for a few moments, feel lost and anxious in such a vast place, but I would do exactly what my parents instructed. Nobody would bat an eyelid when I, a child, would go up to the information desk and ask for the coach to Aberdare. They would ask me where I was going and I would tell them Tredegar, then they would give detailed directions because so many coaches are parked in long rows and columns. I would walk past coaches going to Bournemouth, Poole, Weymouth, Exmouth and Torquay. It was so easy to get lost. And if I did feel lost, I would always ask a bus driver or an official, just as my father had told me to do if I was unsure about anything. I actually rarely felt lost in this huge maze because the bays were numbered and I eventually would find my coach. It was always behind the coach for Swansea. By 2.45pm, excitement and anticipation would be building, people would be bustling, getting on the coaches, and there always seemed to be a frenzy of activity as lost stragglers looked for their coaches with just minutes to go. The driver would take a final tally of all passengers. The engines would be switched on and revved as if we were in a grand prix. My heart would beat faster as I imagined I was on the cusp of some great race. Then at 3pm, a horn would sound, we were not yet moving but you could feel the ground shaking, the coaches at the front would begin leaving. Then, finally, I would feel the coach gliding out of the station. At this point I'd crane my head to look ahead and look behind, at the convoy of coaches, nearly all heading towards the M5. Coaches as far as the eye can see and eventually most coaches turning off onto the motorway and I'd imagine where they are going, while my coach headed to Gloucester. By 6.30pm my coach would arrive at Tredegar and my uncle and aunty would be there, waiting to pick me up. Back in the 1970s and the 1980s, Cheltenham was the coach hub for people from the North of England going on holiday to the South West of England and South Wales.

So in essence, I began to travel way before I ever set foot out of the UK, my young self consumed by curiosity about different places. Curiosity is a driver, it compels me to wander. I'm drawn to places so far away from what I'm accustomed to, to cultures and contexts that I don't know, to people who live a very different life to me. I'm always driven by a thirst to learn more about different ways of doing things, by the history of a people, by their physical landscapes, to greater appreciate the diversity of our planet. I reach into these experiences and memories particularly in this age of increased nationalism, parochialism and othering. I can't deny that when I was in my twenties and early thirties, I was driven by thrills just as much as seeking knowledge and wonderment. Now that the thrill factor has declined, perhaps in no small part due to age, I feel drawn to the internal as well as external dimension travel elicits. I came upon the concept of psychogeography some years ago and felt a resonance with it. It describes the effect that geographical environment has on an individual's emotions with reference to the place they are in. It is the phenomenon of drifting and losing yourself in the city. Cynics may call it strolling. For the uninitiated, *London Orbital* by Iain Sinclair introduces the idea well. Travelling has never been a tick box break for me, where you visit a place and whizz through a list of 'must-see' sights and 'bucket-list' things to do. Psychogeography explores the emotional journey of presence in a new environment, the expanding of my world, deriving some meaning or feeling or even the experience of profound emptiness upon arriving at a new place. I was already an unwitting psychogeographer as a child when I would walk through the streets of Bradford, which at the time were dominated by the huge wool and textile mills that would be pulled down in the 1980s. But then, whether we like it or not, we've all been psychogeographers one time or another.

A few years ago, I was in the city of Dalat in Vietnam. I'd been in Vietnam for some weeks and was gradually making my way north to south spending an inordinate amount of time tasting the amazing food that Vietnam had to offer (I accidently ate dog but that's another story). Dalat is a city unlike any other in Vietnam. Situated in the central highlands at an altitude of 1,500m, it is ringed by pine forested mountains and is known as the city of eternal spring. The scenery itself seemed like it wouldn't be out of place in northern Europe. What had the most effect on me was the sky. It wasn't an Asian sky but resembled the skies of Britain with the very same hues of blue and cloud form. As I gazed upwards, I was moved by a sight so different to anything I had seen on the rest of my trip in Vietnam. I checked into a hotel, not in the traveller's area, but in a commercial part of town. I am just as much enthralled by the shops and businesses of any place than had I stayed in the touristy part. It may sound ridiculous but I felt butterflies in my stomach as I surveyed this normal street. Why was my spirit soaring at such an unremarkable scene? I wonder if it was the mundanity, the minutiae of life, that made me feel so alive. This wasn't a panorama manicured for me as a tourist, picture postcard landscapes contrived for my pleasure. Instead this was real life – working life that you could find anywhere in the world. Just a normal street. And in the midst of it I felt incredible. I left all trace of guidebooks and maps back in my room and I let my instinct for drifting take over. I remember seeing a grassy hill behind some houses so I decided to wander over. The grass and the green had a positively Andean effect on me akin to Quito in Ecuador and for a few seconds I found myself strolling around Quito as pleasant memories flooded back. What was it about Dalat? Why do ordinary streets spark such joy within me? I had let myself become a part of the beating heart of the city instead of looking at it from afar. The locals reacted to me as another person, not as a tourist. Going into shops, places to eat I felt accepted for just being me.

The dynamics of travelling change with age. It's different whether travelling with a friend or with my wife. Age and the weight of life experience have made their mark and I must concede that I'm not in my twenties anymore and don't feel the energy in the same way as I did before. I don't always need those big moments. Simply walking from one place to another can be so rewarding. One of my favourite walks in London is from Stamford Hill down towards Dalston. Not the most picturesque amble but the street life, the urban environment is so evocative it has a truly uplifting effect on me. There is so much to see, yet it is the ordinariness of the streets that makes it so extraordinary.

I enjoy travelling with my wife and with friends, but in all honesty I've always preferred travelling alone. Travelling solo is when I really have time to think deeply, to breathe, to be able to make decisions that don't affect anyone else, to be spontaneous and free. In most of my travels, I've had a general idea of where I'm going then suddenly and for no logical reason have veered off to go somewhere else. That in itself is a delight because you really have no idea in which destination you may end up. One time I'd just landed in Buenos Aires and my intention was to stay a few days in the city. The shuttle from the airport stopped at the coach station. Twenty minutes later, I was on a huge South American cross-country coach to Cordoba which was over 400 miles away. But it's more than that, I prefer the loneliness, there's something almost romantic about being solitary in a strange place. It allows me the opportunity to be consumed by my internal chatter and my imagination. It's as if my brain suddenly becomes wired and I approach thoughts with a lucidity that I'd hitherto been unable to achieve. The journey becomes equally inward as much as outward. I can only speak for myself though, it's been therapeutic and I come back home fighting fit with batteries recharged. It's not surprising, but weeks of waking up early to catch trains or buses, the physical endurance of lugging round my backpack, walking for hours or engaged in different forms of activities, leave me invigorated. At night, when my head hits the pillow, I have the most restful sleep. I've never been the kind of person where the hotel has to be perfect. For some, the hotel is just as important as the destination because if you're on holiday then you will be using the hotel for relaxation but if you're travelling from day to day then you just want a place to lay your head.

When travelling with my wife, these days she insists on a modicum of comfort. Nothing fancy, just not slumming it anymore, as she says we're too old to be backpacking like a couple of teenagers. I'm happy to stay in dormitories because they are considerably cheaper. Alone in Amman in Jordan I spent £4 to sleep in a dormitory, which was the most comfortable and restful sleep of my entire trip. The next night, I was in Irbid in Northern Jordan, not a tourist hotspot and the price of accommodation was ridiculously cheap. I ended up slumbering in a luxurious king size bed in a huge hotel room with a sofa and dressing table, more in keeping with the style of five star luxury holidays. The bathroom was so large I feared I would get agoraphobia. The rest of my journey in Palestine was spent in dormitories. Travelling alone is the ultimate expression of freedom. You are beholden to no one.

For the discerning traveller the journey to the destination is half the fun, whether it's by plane, train, car, foot or husky. I don't enjoy air travel for obvious reasons. Train travel is fun depending on which train you're on. Indian trains are great for striking up conversations with locals and fellow travellers alike. Someone will always chat to you whether it's to practise their English skills or just to be friendly or offer you food. You can also stand up and walk around on the train plus the seats can turn into beds. However, trains are limited by where they can go to. Unlike buses, which can get you to places trains can't and some of the drives can be spectacular. The downsides are that there is less room to stretch out and some of the night buses leave you cramped and groggy when you reach your destination in the morning. The buses in South America and Mexico are a whole different class, however. Some coaches have seats that become virtually horizontal, in some services, you get a blanket and food and drink. I remember a journey where I was on a coach for twenty hours from Patagonia to Buenos Aires. I stayed three hours in Buenos Aires before getting on a coach for another twenty-hour journey to the Iguazu Falls. I felt no weariness as I got off the coach. Both coaches provided meals and the seats became beds more or less.

Having said that, the most terrifying bus journey I've ever been on was in the mountains in Peru in 2010. We were in Cuzco and were going to Huaraz, the mountain climbing centre of the country. The normal journey would traverse around the mountains before winding along the coast to

Lima, then onwards to Huaraz. Considering we'd done that journey from the opposite direction, we decided to go through the Central Highlands, which until recently was off limits due to the insurgency of Shining Path, which had been rumbling on since 1980. This route would knock a day off the journey plus in the spirit of adventure, we'd be going through spectacular scenery and visiting areas that had been isolated for decades, and were only now opening up. It certainly was an adventure - we traversed roads, dirt tracks, got bogged down in a muddy track where our double decker bus almost toppled over and held our breath as the driver disregarded any notion of a speed limit. South America is notorious for road traffic accidents and we were less than reassured when before we set off, each passenger was photographed for identification purposes in the event of a mishap! This was compensated by the scenery which was breath-taking as we crossed gorges, fast flowing rivers, and meandered around huge mountains. There was one dirt track which was only wide enough for one vehicle and wound up to the top of the mountain pass around U and V bends. At times, the driver crept around the bend where the tyres were so close to the drop that any error by mere centimetres would have had our coach tumbling down the ravine which was over 300 metres down. This was scary but the driver was so calm and composed, we never felt like we were going to meet our maker. Not so the next day, in a different bus with a different driver, where the tyres had no treads, the driver hurtled up and down winding roads increasing speed as he came to a turn above raging rivers with drops of hundreds of metres. During this madness, if you looked out of the window, it seemed that we were suspended in mid-air but that was because the tyres were literally driving over the air. The scenery was again stunning yet I hardly noticed as I kept my head down reciting various suras from the Qur'an and praying for safe passage. I was frozen in terror as I was sure the bus would be flying off the road or smash into a rock wall at any moment. I looked up from my feet to see my wife fast asleep and oblivious to our inevitable annihilation and the locals in the coach chatting cheerfully and nonchalantly looking out of the window, while bone-crushing heavy rock blasted out from the speakers. 'Nobody's gonna slow me down, I'm gonna reach the speed of sound,' so sang Deep Purple. Bonecrushing indeed! Six hours later, I emerged from the bus shaking uncontrollably blathering to my well-rested wife of our close brush with doom. I've been on some hair rising journeys in my time but this time I was convinced we were going to die. It's no surprise that there are so many bus accidents in Peru. But I don't regret it, because we lived to tell the tale and the experience was completely unique. It gave us the opportunity to visit isolated towns such as Ayacucho and Huancayo. Far from being backwaters these once cut-off places were thriving cultural centres for the Aymara Indians.

There are many reasons why we choose the destinations we travel to. Does 'travel broaden the mind'? That in itself is a meaningless expression, designed to embody a phenomenon bereft of significance. Some people choose a destination to deepen their understanding of the world and themselves, others go to relax, get a bit of sun and enjoy. There are those who actually come back with more prejudice than before, finding that their superficial engagement with their destination serves to reinforce pre-existing stereotypes and questionable views. I can only speak for myself as I'm driven by an insatiable sense of curiosity about the places that I visit. I like to quietly observe and interact as meaningfully as I can, whatever that means and in whatever manifestation it takes, with people I meet. There is something about being 'on the road' that causes my senses to be assaulted by a variety of stimuli and my thoughts lucid as the cogs in my mind whir like clockwork. It is one of the rare moments I feel synchronicity in motion. I am travelling in both mind and space, exploring externally and internally.

The destinations I've chosen are not just based on aesthetics but are an attempt to challenge myself. In 2019, I went to Palestine. My base was Ramallah a place I had formed an impression of years before, when I watched images of Yasser Arafat, embattled in his compound, under attack from the Israeli Army. I stored in my mind a scene of a dusty shambolic place. At first this seemed quite accurate, as the bus from Jerusalem drove past ramshackle buildings and trundled jerkily over potholed roads of a refugee camp. A few minutes later, the bus was driving through smart residential areas, shopping plazas with giant computerised screens that wouldn't look out of place in a European city. The centre of Ramallah was bustling with people, young people were hanging out with friends, families were shopping. I took a sharp intake of breath as I surveyed gleaming malls, designer outlets, cafes and restaurants with international cuisine and sleek offices. There was plenty of bling too, with Mercs, BMW's and other flash cars a common sight. My expectations had been totally blown out of the water. Ramallah is 'The Emerald City' I joked to myself as I was sure there must be a catch. So, I walked around the city looking for a less than desirable neighbourhood but the city was impeccable. I struck up conversations with residents of the city who were full of optimism but gave a word of warning. Sometimes people may tell you what they think you would like to hear. Regardless, with a healthy dose of cynicism, I endeavoured to find out if there was a dark underbelly. What I learned was that the citizens of Ramallah are living in a gilded cage, increasingly surrounded by Israeli settlements and under tight restrictions imposed by the Israeli government as to where they can travel within their own country.

I've been extremely fortunate, I've been on several 'holidays of a lifetime'. I've mountain biked down the 'world's most dangerous road' in Bolivia, I've crossed mountain passes high up in the Himalayas while simultaneously freezing and having the back of my head burning in the sun. I've sailed the felucca up the Nile from Aswan to Luxor, I've lived in a hut on an island in Laos, I've stayed in a cave in Turkey, I've hung out from a milk van while careering around the mountains of Ecuador, I've lived in the back of beyond in a village with no electricity in Nepal, I've tasted the finest pizza in Naples (I didn't have another pizza for the next three years), I've visited the seven ancient cities of Delhi, I've seen the sun come up over Machu Picchu, I've white water rafted down the raging rivers of Chile, I've played hopscotch going back and forth over the line that separates Chile and Argentina whilst the border guards looked on incredulously, I've sang Led Zeppelin songs amongst a group of young Arabs on the streets of Damascus, I've had a private tour of the Kremlin Museum in Moscow, I've spent a whole day eating non-stop in Penang before throwing up, I've got lost in the forests of Bulgaria, I've got adrift in the Tatra mountains in Poland, I've roamed the deserts of Morocco on a camel, I've seen the horrors of Auschwitz and torture camps of Cambodia and Bosnia, I've seen armed members of Hezbollah jogging in Levi's, I've sneaked into The Forum of Ancient Rome past a snoozing armed guard, I've snowboarded down the slopes of the Andes in Chile, I've slept in the U-Bahn the entire night in Berlin, I've raced a bus down a mountain on my mountain bike outside Kathmandu, I witnessed elderly ladies storm a government building during an attempted coup in Bangkok, I've had Welsh cakes in Patagonia in Argentina, I've been shot at by the IDF in Palestine, I was almost the victim of a scam in Ho Chi Minh City in Vietnam, I've played cricket in Quito, I've gate-crashed a wedding in Mexico, I danced with a belly dancer on stage in Alexandria before being thrown off the stage into the audience for a joke, I've snowboarded on a bin bag with locals in the Bronx in New York and I've bought an Iranian rug from a Pakistani in Paraguay.

But this all pales into comparison to when I visited Uzbekistan, Kazakhstan and Kyrgyzstan twenty years ago. To say it was an ordeal is an understatement, I came back both mentally and emotionally exhausted and spent the next few days in bed sleeping. Independent travellers were almost non-existent in Central Asia, people travelled in tour groups back then. Firstly, it took me a month to get the visas at a cost of over £500. These places had still not escaped their communist past as I was about to find out. Taxi drivers everywhere saw me as a potential goldmine. Now, having to pay a little extra is accepted. It's part of the deal when you go travelling. Several times, I was pulled into police stations and interrogated on the pretext that I might be carrying uranium or plutonium. Then they would ask me to present my money, while several officers crowded around me, some even attempting to grab the money out of my hands. Sometimes, this would continue for up to forty-five minutes before they got bored and sent me on my way. I acted dim-witted most of the time. I knew that I had to stay calm as they just needed an excuse for me to get angry. It got to the point that I would duck into a side street if I saw any police. I was lucky, I met a couple of German travellers who had $500 taken from them by police in Tashkent. Then there was the time in Kyrgyzstan when I had a knife pressed against my stomach twice. Firstly, when I'd come back from a tour. The tour operators wouldn't give me back my belongings as they wanted more money which wasn't part of the agreement. I almost came to blows as they attempted to grab my rucksack from me, then one man put a knife to my stomach which I pushed away. A couple of days later, a similar thing occurred. A coach driver wouldn't give me back my rucksack because he wanted more money. I went and retrieved it, and again, he put a knife to my stomach which I just knocked away. If you think I was being brave, I wasn't. On both occasions, I had severe stomach ache and needed the toilet fast. During a wedding in Samarkand, a drunk wedding goer told me he loved me, then he threatened to shoot me. Luckily for me, some people dragged him away. Nonetheless, I met some wonderful people, a student in Samarkand who allowed me to stay with his family for almost a week and looked after me when I fell ill. Ordinary people, without whose help, I wouldn't have had the amazing experience that I had.

I must finish with what is probably the most astounding thing I've ever done. I spent a week living with nomads in yurts cut off from civilisation in Eastern Kyrgyzstan, high up in the lush green pastures, surrounded by the Tien Shan Mountains. A life unaltered through centuries. I would spend the entire day on horseback exploring the different valleys under the massive azure sky, where I wouldn't come across a person for hours on end. Sometimes, I'd pass by a handful of tents and wave to the inhabitants, I would chance upon crystal clear lakes, where the snow tipped peaks were a stone's throw away and the air was rarefied. I'd return late in the afternoon where the family I was staying with cooked a meal that would meet a King's approval. At night, I would sit outside my yurt gazing at the star encrusted sky above. It didn't get much better than this. It was the closest thing to 'magical' that I've ever felt. There's so much to say about that trip. But that's for another time.

# A QUR'ANIC VOYAGE

*Shanon Shah*

Maybe it was the price of trying to lead a double life, but I was left broken after three consecutive Fridays – the year I turned nineteen. It was in Melbourne, 1997, not long after the start of the academic year. I was psychologically destroyed by a hat trick of khutbahs during weekly Friday prayers in the rooftop Muslim prayer room on my university campus. Each of these Fridays, I sat cross-legged on the wall-to-wall patchwork of prayer rugs amid the pong of freshly bared male Muslim feet. I tried not to make eye contact with the bearded male khatib preaching from the pulpit, whose testosterone-soaked Australian-accented English was punctuated by rapid-fire Arabic quotations from the Qur'an. The first sermon promised hellfire and gory punishments for Muslim women who did not cover their hair. The second, hellfire and eternal damnation for the Jews and the *kafirs* and all the Muslim 'hypocrites' who associated with them. The third focused on homosexuals. 'They need to be thrown off a tall building,' said the khatib, with relish.

These three consecutive Fridays, I returned to my room afterwards to sulk alone. It never occurred to me to evaluate any of these claims or even cross-check them with my own copy of the Qur'an. I never considered exposing my unease to anyone else who attended those Friday prayers. And I had no reason to question the accuracy of the verses quoted or their interpretations – I never had and never did. But after the third khutbah in the series, something snapped. I stopped attending the mosque altogether. I stopped praying, even on my own. I stopped reading the Qur'an. I couldn't fathom why a sacred Book would promise such damnation and hatred towards the people who cared for me, delighted in my company, and were becoming like a surrogate family to me in Australia – 'free-hair' women, 'kafirs', and 'homosexuals'.

My elder sister, brother and I were raised in a middle-class Malaysian family by a mother and father who were both teachers and hardened disciplinarians. My siblings and I were academic overachievers at school and university, but this scholarly prowess was undercut by a constant insecurity about our mixed ethnic identity. We were officially classified as Malay but were of mostly Pakistani and Chinese ancestry. We spoke good Malaysian English, bookish Malay, a smattering of Chinese dialect, and non-existent Urdu or Punjabi. When we spoke English or Malay, our accents immediately exposed us as 'fake' Malays to other Malaysians. We weren't very observant Muslims and often revised the truth when quizzed by our Islamic religious instructors – there was, shall we say, a gap between the *reported* number of times we prayed daily and the *actual* number of prayers performed. Still, we were semi-observant and aspired to be better Muslims when we grew up. When I got a scholarship from Petronas, the state-owned oil-and-gas company, to study for an engineering degree in Australia, my family blessed my journey and reminded me to seek Allah's protection and guidance always. As a rite of passage, I was gifted with my own travel-sized Qur'an, the kind my sister and brother received when they started university in Kuala Lumpur.

But I was on a collision course with the Qur'an the day I set foot on Australian soil. Within the first few weeks of arriving, my inner flibbertigibbet wiggled loose. It all started with a gentle knock on my door by Boontree, my Thai neighbour who had an innocent, sweet voice and, I would soon discover, a filthy sense of humour. 'Dinner?' she asked, and we quickly became dining hall buddies. From there, I made fast friends with a gang of non-Muslim international students – non-Muslim Malaysians, Singaporeans, Indonesians, Koreans, even a few white Aussies. We binge-watched American sitcoms and dramas in the TV room or played Doom (that '90s first-person shooter game), went to the movies on weekends, and often hung out in each other's rooms to study whilst listening to music.

In between these social gatherings, I would rush to the on-campus Muslim prayer room or my own room to pray the five daily *solat*. Weekly Friday prayers on campus were followed by plans to go nightclubbing – sans booze, of course, at this stage. This was my way of observing all the Islamic obligations I was meant to – at the same time, I repressed any questions I was starting to have about my true religious beliefs and my sexuality. I was becoming an expert compartmentaliser. Or so it seemed.

One night, one of my Petronas friends rapped on my door after dinner. She didn't come inside – that would have been immoral. Hovering at my doorway, her head wrapped in a tudung, she pointed out a verse in the Qur'an from Surah Al Imran (the Family of Imran): 'The believers must not take the disbelievers as friends instead of the believers' (3:28). Although left unspoken, I knew exactly why she was directing my attention to that verse. It wasn't entirely a *j'accuse* moment because I could tell she was also troubled. After all, she and our other Petronas friends had fallen for Boontree's impish charms, too.

'What are we doing here?' she asked in Malay. I replied that we had received good scholarships that would enable us to get good degrees from good Australian universities.

'But this is *darul harb*,' she said, alluding to another layer in the interpretation of the verse.

'You think Australia is an abode of war?' I asked. 'Then why would our government let us study here?'

She wasn't persuaded, and would remain unpersuaded. Months afterwards, she and her friends would be abused on the streets of Melbourne in broad daylight by Islamophobic thugs screaming for them to take those 'tea towels' off their heads and 'go home'. I was numb when she told me. I had no idea how to carry the weight of the pain of racism and Islamophobia we faced alongside the Qur'an-bashing I was desperately trying to escape.

There were some glimmers of hope, such as when I discovered Ziauddin Sardar's *Introducing Islam* in a Lygon Street bookshop, or when I came across a decent Australian television programme about Sisters in Islam, the Malaysian women's rights organisation. It was refreshing to be exposed to the heavy intellectual lifting these Muslims were doing with the Islamic tradition, showing people like me that there were other ways of being Muslim. But these discoveries were still rare and isolated and, by the time I had graduated and returned to Malaysia in early 2001, my soul was destroyed and I felt exiled from the Qur'an. I was also resigned to having to work with Petronas, even though I made some last-ditch attempts at freedom. I dabbled in independent journalism and won a patriotic song writing contest mere weeks before I had to report for duty at the Twin Towers in Kuala Lumpur (which I recounted in *Critical Muslim 32: Music*).

And then the 9/11 attacks happened.

If the trio of violent Friday sermons marked the exilic phase of my journey with the Qur'an, 9/11 brought me back kicking and screaming. Love it or hate it, my journey with the Qur'an would never solely be a personal spiritual quest. It was entangled in global geopolitics and the politics of being Muslim – or, in my case, an angry misfit Muslim. I was mad as hell, and I wasn't going to take this anymore. Nobody – Muslim or not – was going to push me out of Islam.

I rolled up my sleeves and decided, like the Pulitzer prizewinning historian Garry Wills, I had better acquaint myself with the Qur'an. Wills' book, *What the Qur'an Meant and Why it Matters*, resembles my journey of having to unlearn internalised stereotypes and to shed lots of personal and political baggage regarding Islam. Ironically, this is what makes the first part of the book so depressing. My unlearning took place at the dawn of the twenty-first century, when I thought that George W Bush was as imbecilic as an American president could possibly get. This slim book by Wills was published in 2017, a year after voters handed the keys to the White House to Donald Trump, an even bigger imbecile. *Plus ça change....*

It's not that Wills' analysis or intentions are suspect. What is exhausting is that, after all these years – close to two decades after 9/11 – a well-meaning defence of the Qur'an by an American public intellectual must still introduce it as a 'problem'. The silver lining is that at least Wills owns this as *his* 'Qur'an problem' as a practitioner and scholar of Roman Catholicism.

The book's first part can therefore be excused as necessary context-setting – to be fair, this is where Wills skewers Dubya and The Donald – but it is in Part Two that things come to life. Here, Wills engages in a deep reading of the Qur'an that is creatively enriched by his Roman Catholic spirituality. Take, for example, his personal exegesis of 45:18: 'Now We have set you [Muhammad] on a clear religious path [*shari'ah*], so follow it. Do not follow the desires of those who lack [true] knowledge.' Like many Muslim commentators, Wills points out that whilst the term shari'ah denotes Islamic Law, in Qur'anic language it refers to a pathway to a water source. For the Prophet Muhammad and his followers in the Arabian desert, this meant that the shari'ah was essentially a passage away from death and decay into life. But Wills goes further and compares this Qur'anic moral path with the path of righteousness referred to in the New Testament. According to him:

In the Gospel of John (14.6), Jesus says, 'I am The Path [Hē Hodos], and The Truth, and The Life. No one can reach the Father but by way of me.' In the Acts of the Apostles, Christianity itself is called simply The Path (Hē Hodos). Saul, before becoming Paul, persecutes 'followers of The Path' (9.2, 22.4), but after his conversion he follows The Path (24.14). Converts were catechized in The Path (18.25-26). Nonbelievers attack The Path (19.9, 23), though a Roman procurator was lenient toward The Path (24.22).

In other words, Jesus Christ *is* the shari'ah. There is, according to Wills, concordance between Johannine and Pauline Christology and Islamic Divine Law. While I find this synthesis of scriptural exegesis appealing, as I explore further below, I wonder who else possibly would. Admittedly, Wills is trying to make a point about Islam to a non-Muslim, probably white Christian American audience, which is of course salutary of him. Me? I cannot imagine attempting this logic on the many Muslims in Malaysia who argue that Christians cannot use the world 'Allah' to refer to God and that Malay-language Bibles need to be banned. I can just hear the indignation and incredulity in response. 'You expect us to follow what a Christian is saying about Islam?' 'He has an agenda to distort the Qur'an!'

Throughout this book, Wills relies on the translation of the Qur'an by Muhammad Abdel Haleem, Professor of Islamic Studies at the School of Oriental and African Studies (SOAS). Serendipitously, Abdel Haleem's *Exploring the Qur'an*, also published in 2017, analyses the Qur'an's text semantically and thematically to rescue its interpretation from the distortions of both 'anti-Islamic polemicists and propagandists' and 'Islamic extremists and terrorists'. Abdel Haleem is not afraid to disagree with prominent opinions in traditional tafsir and to put forward his own suggested translations. His mastery of Arabic means that these are, for the most part, authoritative and convincing. For readers who are expert in neither Arabic nor tafsir literature, this can be comforting *and* intimidating.

Yet, erudite as it is, this book opens in a way that might be just as exasperating for some readers as Wills' book. After all these years, a book by a Qur'anic scholar still needs to open with a series of chapters debunking the idea that the Qur'an promotes war, violence and terrorism? Granted, Abdel Haleem's opening chapter will help many a reader to negotiate the linguistic intricacies of 9:5 – the so-called 'Sword Verse' – more clearly and confidently. But, in a way, it's still apologetics against the enduring Orientalist hangover about Islam's supposed propensity for violence. And, as with Wills' book, the question is, who exactly would find Abdel Haleem's book appealing? Would anyone who was already intent on joining Al Shabaab, the Taliban, the Islamic State, or Jemaah Islamiyah stop to pick it up, consider its arguments, and miraculously revise their understandings of the Qur'an?

To me, the true gems in this book are revealed in its latter pages. Against the popular neo-Orientalist idea that the Qur'an is void of narrative coherence, Abdel Haleem implores paying attention to the intricacies of *balagha* (Arabic rhetoric), which informs the Qur'anic voice. For instance, the chapter which systematically analyses the divine oaths found in the Qur'an provides much food for thought. An example of a Qur'anic oath – this one specifically on the oneness of God – is: 'By those ranged in rows, who chide forcefully and recite God's word, truly your god is One, Lord of the heavens and the earth and everything between them' (37:1-5). According to Abdel Haleem, these oaths and other stylistic elements were very much tied to the audience that the Qur'an was trying to reach:

The Qur'an was clearly very much interested in having its message listened to by those who doubted or denied it. It did not state its message with no interest in how it is received, but tried hard to convince those who rejected it by using oaths, other arguments and by persuasion and dissuasion, known as *targhib* and *tarhib*.

The severe language of the Qur'an has often made me feel nagged, ambushed, or damned, especially when Qur'anic verses are spat out in icy judgement or heated anger. But if, like me, you're a relative latecomer to the party, it is a relief to discover that the Qur'an's rhetorical features – *targhib* and *tarhib*, namely – are creative responses to particular literary genres. The implications are therefore straightforward, aren't they? We just need to separate our analysis of the merits of the Qur'anic text itself from the ways in which Qur'anic verses are subjectively and selectively interpreted in different contexts.

Are things really that simple?

I was thinking along these lines, my pen racing ecstatically on my notepad, while I listened to amina wadud's address at the Second International Muslim Leaders' Consultation (IMLC) on HIV/AIDS in Kuala Lumpur. It was 2003, and I had taken time off from Petronas to volunteer as a rapporteur at this conference, co-organised by the Malaysian AIDS Council and the Malaysian Department of Islamic Development (Jakim). It was like I had walked into a parallel universe. Masjaliza, my friend who at that point had just started working with Sisters in Islam, subtly pointed out the who's who of the progressive Muslim world the first morning. amina, Farid Esack, Ebrahim Moosa, and of course some of the founders of Sisters in Islam – Zainah Anwar and Norani Othman – all were there, mingling and chatting in the pre-conference hubbub. I was particularly awestruck by the quiet confidence exuded by Marina Mahathir, President of the Malaysian AIDS Foundation back then and daughter of then Prime Minister Mahathir Mohamad.

Still, I remained somewhat ambivalent. Moments before commencing our rapporteur duties, I told Masjaliza that Islam didn't seem to have a place for Muslims like me. As we took our places next to each other, Mas replied, 'Maybe it's up to you to claim that space.'

And then amina spoke.

In her presentation, 'Vulnerabilities: HIV and AIDS', amina argued that irresponsible interpretations of the verse 'la taqrabul-zina' (do not approach adultery) from, the seventeenth surah, Al-Isra (The Night Journey), had the effect of killing obedient Muslim wives:

With regard to the eighty per cent heterosexual women who contract AIDS in monogamous relations, a direct look at Islam and sexuality is called for. According to *shari'ah*, if a Muslim man desires intercourse with his wife, she must comply. If she does not, she is guilty of *nushuz*, recalcitrance.... In the face of this, the vast majority of Muslim wives... open their legs to their men as they are not only expected, but commanded to do by that which is most popularly understood as 'Islam'. Women turn towards men who have contracted AIDS and open their legs to their own death and destruction.... The consequences for the *muhsinat* and *qaanitat* are the same: they will die because they are 'good'.

The specks of my exploded brain can probably still be seen on the high ceiling of the Hotel Istana grand ballroom. I was mouthing 'wow' to a beaming Mas when the pin-drop silence after amina's talk was broken by Majid Katme, from the Islamic Medical Association of the UK. 'You are a devil in a hijab!' he stood up and screamed from the floor, jabbing his finger at amina while she sat silently on the stage with the other panellists. 'I will round up one hundred people to shut you up,' he went on, his voice becoming hoarse. 'All the rest of the Muslims here, if you stay in this room and listen to this filth, you are all apostates!'

Amid a growing chorus of jeers at amina, Katme was joined by Nazleen Umar Rajput from Kenya, who exclaimed repeatedly, '*I* am the perfect example of the Muslim woman, not you!' She added that she would have expected the kind of arguments that amina was making from 'a Christian or a Jew', but never from a Muslim.

Rajput, Katme, and several other enraged Muslims then stormed out in unison. The next speaker, a Malaysian trans HIV/AIDS activist, went to the podium hesitatingly and tried to pretend that nothing had happened even after this earthquake, but still struggled to choke back the tears. Before I knew it, I was crying – loud sobs of anguish, hot tears streaming down my cheeks onto my notepad. Mas was in tears, too, and gave me a packet of her tissues to wipe my snot – we giggled a bit at this and continued crying together.

Later that night, we visited amina in her room, along with Salbiah, a mutual friend of amina's and ours who was the conference's chief rapporteur and who had roped us in as volunteers. 'Call me a devil when I wear a hijab, call me a devil when I don't wear hijab,' amina fumed. 'Well it's off!' I didn't know it then, but that's the moment I turned into an activist. I began strategising on the side-lines with Sal, Mas and all the other Muslim and non-Muslim delegates and volunteers who had silently taken amina's side. Some of the youth decided to put together a declaration calling for respect for diverse voices and opinions in Muslim communities' responses to HIV/AIDS. I was tasked with presenting it during one of the plenary sessions. While I read the declaration aloud, Rajput prowled around, slowly and deliberately taking flash photographs of me from different angles, and of the other youth delegates and volunteers flanking me.

One night, Mas and I stood chatting in front of her hotel room before I went back to mine. We were both bleary-eyed and powdery-skinned from another long, air-conditioned, tension-filled day. 'And after all that vitriol, amina's still Muslim!' I said. 'Yes,' Mas said. 'And do you know why she became Muslim? She says it's because she read the Qur'an.'

She read the *what*? Or, perhaps more accurately, she did *what* with the Qur'an?

I sat on this information for a while. After the conference, my quotidian commutes to Petronas were, for a little while, filled once again with reading light fiction – Harry Potter, Terry Pratchett and the like. No one in my family knew about the transformation I had gone through, and neither did anyone at work. Only Mas and my newfound friends at Sisters in Islam could appreciate what was happening. One day, I took the plunge – I bought a copy of Abdullah Yusuf Ali's translation of the Qur'an.

At age 25, for the first time in my life, I was going to read the Qur'an in English translation from cover to cover. Of course, I had completed a full recitation of it in Arabic as a child, but I never knew what the words meant. Sure, I had been exposed to Malay translations of selected surahs and *ayats* in school and, of course, I was familiar with the more oft-repeated verses from Friday khutbahs and other Islamic talks and lectures. But this was the first time that I had decided to read the Qur'an *by* myself and *for* myself, in entirety, for its meaning and sense. I was arrogant enough to have a proviso, though – if I found anything that undermined my sense of fairness, justice, and kindness, I would stop reading and I would renounce Islam, if only in my heart. But when I got to the end of the translation, I thought, 'This isn't so bad. So maybe I am Muslim after all.'

'This isn't so bad.' Sounds like an anti-climax, doesn't it? I knew, though, that I was only reading the Qur'an in translation – a turgid one at that. And if even a turgid translation of the Qur'an couldn't put me off, perhaps I was on solid ground. This adventure with the Qur'an led me to one of the most exciting discoveries I made in this phase of my journey – translations matter. A staple Sisters in Islam activity in its public education workshops on gender and Islam is to compare different translations of the first verse of the fourth surah, An-Nisa (the Women). The activity begins with the following excerpt projected for all participants to see:

...He created you (humankind) *min* a single *nafs*, and created *min* that *nafs* its *zawj*, and from these two He spread (through the earth) countless men and women... (Qur'an, 4:1)

The words in italics are deliberately untranslated transliterations of the original Arabic – 'min', 'nafs' and 'zawj'. A different translation of the Qur'an is given to different clusters of participants. Usually, the Malaysian groups that sign up for these workshops are multi-faith, so Muslims and non-Muslims sit alongside each other poring over these translations. For many people, it is their first time handling the Qur'an and looking up specific references within it. They are asked to locate the verse themselves and to identify how their particular translation treats these three keywords.

Muhammad Marmaduke Pickthall's translation gives 'min' as 'from', 'nafs' as 'soul' and 'zawj' as 'mate'. His is basically a creation story that says we were all created from a single soul and its mate. Muhammad Asad's translation has the same mystical quality, but with a subtle difference – he translates 'min' as 'out of' (rather than 'from'), 'nafs' as 'living entity', and 'zawj' as 'mate'. Yusuf Ali says we were created 'from' a single 'Person' and *his* 'mate', which is also how the Shia scholar Mir Ahmed Ali translates these terms. But look what happens when we come to Muhammad Muhsin Khan and Muhammad Taqi-ud-Din Al-Hilali:

O mankind! Be dutiful to your Lord, Who created you from a single person (Adam), and from him (Adam) He created his wife [Hawwā (Eve)], and from them both He created many men and women…

What begins as a poetic, unadorned and non-gendered creation narrative in the versions by Pickthall and Asad acquires more solid corporeality via Yusuf Ali and Ahmed Ali and ends up with sex, marital status and individual names, according to Khan and Al-Hilali. (For the record, Abdel Haleem's choices with 'min', 'nafs' and 'zawj' agree with Pickthall's.) In my early years as a zealous returnee to the Qur'an, whenever I led these workshops, I would pause deliberately before asking, 'And which translation do you think is endorsed by the Saudis?'

This was my proxy revenge on my Australian tormentors – flinging *my* knowledge of translations of the Qur'an back at *them*. 'You suckers thought you could weaponise the Qur'an against me? Hasta la vista, baby!' In hindsight, I cringe that my newfound smugness was founded upon a mere droplet of knowledge about the historical, political and doctrinal nuances of the Qur'an in translation. Thank goodness for the scholar of religion, Bruce Lawrence, who has produced a brief albeit rich and riveting exploration of this very subject – *The* Koran *in English*.

The contours of Lawrence's argument will be familiar to many Qur'anic scholars. For centuries, Muslims were reticent about producing translations of the Qur'an. This was largely, of course, because of Muslim belief in the infallibility and inimitability of the Qur'an and the sacredness of the Arabic in which it was revealed. Translations would be tantamount to human interpretations that reduced the semantic richness and divine purity of the original. Lawrence summarises this position in a three-step syllogism: 'If you don't know Arabic, you cannot understand the Qur'an. Without understanding the Qur'an, you cannot become a Muslim. Unless you become a Muslim, you cannot be saved. Therefore, you must know Arabic to be saved.'

Christian scholars and polemicists took the opposite approach. A succession of Christian thinkers and writers, including Martin Luther, insisted that their co-religionists read translations of the Qur'an – the better to know the enemy. A summary of Orientalist translations is provided by Lawrence (and Abdel Haleem), and includes some key figures and turning points – the first Latin translation by Robert of Ketton in the twelfth century, the first English translation by Alexander Ross in the seventeenth century, the landmark eighteenth century version by George Sale, and the influential nineteenth century translations of John Medows Rodwell and Edward Henry Palmer.

The gradual growth of this Orientalist canon unleashed a succession of English translations of the Qur'an in the early twentieth century by *Muslims* with ties to the Indian subcontinent. From the start of the century until the outbreak of the Second World War, the following translations of the Qur'an into English appeared throughout the British Raj – Muhammad Abdul Hakim Khan (1905), Mirza Abul Fazl (1910), Hairat Dihlawi (1916), Maulana Muhammad Ali (1917), Ghulam Sarwar (1920), Pickthall (1930), and Yusuf Ali (1934-37). As Lawrence puts it, 'in less than forty years seven Muslims, including a British convert who lived in India (Pickthall), produced more *Koran* translations than all of the British Orientalists from the preceding three centuries…'.

And there I was in the months after 9/11, humble-bragging at Sisters in Islam workshops that I regularly consulted four or five translations, as though this was proof of my deep Qur'anic immersion.

I am not, however, the first Muslim to take a politicised and activist approach to the Qur'an. But that depends on how 'Muslim' is defined. One significant Muslim translator of the Qur'an into English, Maulana Muhammad Ali, was an Ahmadi – the sect that is banned and persecuted in Pakistan and other Muslim countries because they believe their founder Mirza Ghulam Ahmad (d. 1908) to be the Messiah. Mirza Ghulam and his followers engaged in vigorous debate with Christian missionaries whilst adopting Christian proselytising strategies. If Christians tried to win converts in the East, the Ahmadis went to the West, sending emissaries and books to the UK and the US. It is this milieu that informed the work of Maulana Muhammad Ali, whose Ahmadi identity has led many contemporary lay Muslim commentators to deride or dismiss his translation. Yet, according to Lawrence, it is undeniable that this translation's 'historical value exceeds its sectarian origins', paving the way for other translations to emerge, including Yusuf Ali's and Pickthall's.

Meanwhile, the ambivalence of Muslim authorities about translating the Qur'an ran deeper than mere sectarian concerns. Pickthall journeyed to Al-Azhar University in Egypt to consult its ulama about his translation so that he would avoid mistakes and breaches of orthodoxy. He was aware of the furore about Muhammad Ali's translation, but thought that the Egyptian scholars had issued a fatwa against it because it was a product of the Ahmadi heresy. He soon learnt that the ulama were divided over a more fundamental issue – whether *any* translation of the Qur'an was allowable. There was also an element of condescension by the Egyptians towards Muslims who were not Arab, and Pickthall even contemplated abandoning his project and leaving for Damascus. He persevered, however, and gained Al-Azhar's endorsement, albeit with some crucial caveats. His translation is known as *The Meaning of the Holy Koran*. The word 'meaning' in the title and the rendering of 'Koran' were the result of the ulama's decision not to permit fallible, human translations of Islam's Noble Book to be titled 'the Qur'an'. It was also stipulated that translations must be called 'a translation of an interpretation of the Qur'an' or 'an interpretation of the Qur'an in language X'.

In the latter half of the twentieth century, the pronouncements of the ulama became increasingly entwined in sectarianism and politics. It was merely a matter of time that this culminated in the Saudi juggernaut and the Wahhabi-endorsed ascendancy of the Khan-Hilali translation, introduced above. But it hasn't stopped there, of course. New translations keep emerging, with the oft-stated ambition of achieving greater authenticity and clarity. In *The Majestic Quran: A Plain English Translation*, published in 2018, the Al-Azhar-trained translator, Musharraf Hussain, asserts, 'Mine is an authentic translation, neither liberal nor free, however, I have used interpretation to join ideas together….I have used plain English: simple words and avoiding archaic words and turns of phrase.' The parallel Arabic text is presented in clear, beautiful calligraphy, which would satisfy readers who value this aspect in their translations. For the record, Hussain's rendition of the first verse of Surah An-Nisa has 'nafs' as 'person' and 'zawj' as 'his partner' – choices that align him with Yusuf Ali rather than Pickthall or Abdel Haleem, and definitely not Khan-Hilali.

Ultimately, the glut of translations we now see – from scholarly, sectarian or proselytising endeavours, or different permutations thereof – has provided fertile ground for a phenomenon that reminds me of the American poet Billy Collins' 'Introduction to Poetry':

I ask them to take a poem
and hold it up to the light
like a color slide

or press an ear against its hive.

I say drop a mouse into a poem
And watch him probe his way out,

or walk inside the poem's room
and feel the walls for a light switch.

I want them to waterski
across the surface of a poem
waving at the author's name on the shore.

But all they want to do
Is tie the poem to a chair with rope

And torture a confession out of it.

They begin beating it with a hose
To find out what it really means.

Of course, traditional Muslim scholarship maintains that while the Qur'an is poetic, it is certainly not poetry. It can only be verbatim Divine Speech. The point is, I have not only suffered the effects of the Qur'an being tied to a chair, its verses being tortured for their 'true' meaning – I've been guilty of doing this, too. I can't speak for anyone else, but in my case, I wonder if this has to do with my own feelings of inadequacy as a Muslim. It's a kind of impostor syndrome that is difficult to overcome. The wounds of Australia and my Malaysian upbringing have never fully healed.

Grief is what dragged me through the next phase of my journey with the Qur'an. In my thirtieth year, I endured the death of my beloved Toni Kasim – my best friend, mentor, confidante, and a loving and passionate member of the Sisters in Islam family. When Toni was admitted into hospital in early 2008, I fell onto my prayer mat in tears, praying for it not to be anything serious. When she was diagnosed with cancer, I fell again in tears, praying for it not to be fatal. When she died three months later, my world fell apart. I had just started a new job and began overworking to cope with my loss. I overate, gained a copious amount of weight, developed insomnia, and fell ill at least once a month. Mutual friends of mine and Toni's were a comfort, as were my siblings, but for a while, nothing could fill the Toni-sized hole in my heart.

Until one day, when I just decided to pray again. I didn't know what I was praying for, or why, but I just started. All I know is that the same God who took Toni away started giving me back my life. My effort at praying five times a day was organically followed by an effort to take care of my physical health and, yes, to read the Qur'an again.

The inner activist still hadn't deserted me. In my newly revived visits to the mosque on Fridays, I was yet again incensed by some of the khutbahs I was hearing. They triggered memories of Australia – except Malaysian Friday sermons are written by the state Islamic bureaucracy and delivered monotonously by state-appointed imams to thousand-strong congregations, many of whom nod off to sleep after the first five minutes.

Not me, though. I would stay alert and, for the most part, accept the normative, benign preaching. At times, however, I would bristle at the usual crap that would surface whenever there was a political crisis brewing. This is when state machinery would be invoked to demonise the usual suspects – Shi'a Muslims, lesbian, gay, bisexual and transgender (LGBT) people, Ahmadiyya, feminists, secularists, Jews or Christians, or different permutations thereof.

One day, after a particularly egregious khutbah decrying the supposed evils of Christianity, I decided enough was enough. I rang up a few of my Christian friends and started arranging appointments to attend Sunday services in solidarity with them. Over the coming weeks and months, I visited Lutheran, Roman Catholic and Syrian Orthodox churches in Kuala Lumpur. And I have attended countless Anglican services since coming to the UK in 2010. This engagement with Christianity has transformed me profoundly, not least by making me fall in love with the Bible. I love all the books in the Old and New Testaments – the Gospels, Paul's Epistles, the minor epistles, the Prophets, the Psalms, the Pentateuch, you name it.

This love often feels dangerous and I have often wondered whether I am now betraying the Qur'an. In wondering this, I am dealing with centuries of Christian-Muslim baggage that I have internalised, from the early polemical anti-Muslim tracts of the Syriac Fathers (who often recycled anti-Semitic material to use against Islam as the 'new' quasi-Jewish heresy) to the hardening of the Muslim charge of *tahrif* (scriptural distortion) against Christians and Jews. This long and continuing history of counter-accusations of scriptural distortion and falsification is, frankly, exasperating. For a long time, I have just chosen to ignore these Christian-Muslim tit-for-tats. As a corpus, I see the Abrahamic scriptures as an intricate interplay between the agency of the Divine and the human, albeit with different degrees of emphasis between the two. What has continued to vex me, however, is the nagging idea that the Qur'an contains ignorant mistakes in its recounting of Biblical episodes, for example, the Annunciation of the Virgin Mary and the birth of Jesus.

The most delicious surprise for me, amongst recent scholarship about the Qur'an, is therefore Karl-Josef Kuschel's *Christmas and the Qur'an*. Kuschel, a Catholic theologian, begins by analysing the discrepancies in the Gospel accounts of the birth of Jesus. Only two of the four canonical

Gospels – by Luke and Matthew – contain this story, and both differ in setting, chronology, and other important details. However, Kuschel skilfully demonstrates that within this genre of writings that have come to be characterised as early Christian, the primary social and theological message is clear. Despite their differences, Luke and Matthew show the disruptive power of the spirit of God, for whom nothing is impossible in the cause of love, justice, and liberation of the oppressed.

Kuschel uses this comparison as a starting point to analyse the birth narratives about Muhammad in the Islamic tradition and the birth narratives of Jesus in the Qur'an. What emerges is that the supposed 'discrepancies' between the Qur'anic narratives of the birth of Jesus and the canonical New Testament accounts are not arbitrary mistakes. Qur'anic elements that do not appear in the canonical gospels – Mary's withdrawal after learning of her pregnancy, her labour pains under the palm tree, and the baby Jesus's ability to speak and later bring clay birds to life – are not fanciful inventions or deficiencies. These are rather distillations of key 'plot points' in other apocryphal Christian texts, including the Gospel of Pseudo-Matthew, the Protevangelium of James, and the Gospel of Thomas. Similarly, there is an argument that the 'discrepancy' between the Qur'anic narratives involving Abraham and accounts in the canonical Hebrew Scriptures are distillations from other apocryphal sources – the *Testament of Abraham*, the *Testament and Death of Moses*, and the *Apocalypse of Abraham*, to name a few.

This argument is different from polemical Orientalist claims of the Qur'an being an inferior derivative of the Jewish and Christian scriptures. As Tarif Khalidi, also a renowned modern Qur'an translator, argues, the Qur'an's engagement with canonical and non-canonical Jewish and Christian scriptures demonstrates a creative synthesis and improvisation of these texts. This is how the Qur'an produces its own argument about the nature of the Divine, and humanity's quest for justice and redemption. The Qur'an engaged with versions of Christianity and Judaism that were alive and evolving, and it took an active stake in key doctrinal developments within these traditions. According to Geneviève Gobillot, modern readers lose so much when they ignore this rich ecosystem of canonical and apocryphal texts that inform the Qur'an's rhetorical strategy and style.

It is fitting to rest here, for now, in my destination with the Qur'an. Perhaps another time I will have the courage and expertise to write about journeys and destinations narrated *within* and *through* the Qur'an. For now, I have sought healing by recounting my adventures *with* the Noble Book. The narrative of the birth of Jesus and the life of the Virgin Mary, oddly, remind me of what the celebrated mystic, Jalaluddin Rumi, said – the Qur'an is a shy and veiled bride and we are advised to approach her not directly but through the guidance of her friends. It's a heteronormative and patriarchal image by modern standards, but still tender and profound. Modern readers can perhaps substitute 'bride' for 'groom' or even 'non-gendered spouse', if that makes the analogy more palatable. Either way, be careful what you wish for. In *Balti Britain*, Ziauddin Sardar recalls his trepidation about his arranged marriage in Pakistan until he gets to confront his bride-to-be directly when he spots her carrying a bucket of water. 'Oay,' he shouts. 'Do you think I would make a reasonable husband?' 'Probably,' she shouts back, 'but not for me.' Then she throws the water over him. Zia is smitten and the wedding is a goer.

My journey with the Qur'an has been slightly darker. It hasn't been linear. It has involved lots of pain, anger, and disputation, as well as wondrous excursions into Christian and Jewish scriptures. In other words, it has strangely emulated the Qur'an's enigmatic and elliptical narrative structure. I am still rediscovering other ways of enjoying the Qur'an – through calligraphy and listening to melodic recitations, for instance – but the journey remains long and winding.

When my older brother died in a tragic accident a few months after my fortieth birthday, the first two things I packed before rushing for the first available flight back to Malaysia were my travel Qur'an and my pocket-sized Surah Yasin. It felt like the longest flight I ever had to take in my life, interspersed with outbreaks of crying and repeated recitations of Surah Yasin. Before he died, my brother had started developing misgivings about Islam, which led him to regard my constant search for spiritual meaning as a bit deluded and infantile. But I thought, 'Sorry, *bhai jaan*, you are getting Surah Yasin from me, whether you like it or not.' As I washed his fingers, his hair and his face lovingly in the mosque, in preparation for the *jenazah* prayers, I silently and repeatedly dedicated Surah Al-Fatihah (the Opening) and Surah Al-Ikhlas (Purity of Faith) to his soul. In my terror-filled and sleepless nights afterwards, I recited the words of Psalm 23, 'Though I walk through the valley of the shadow of death, I will fear no evil.' And I constantly recalled two verses from Surah Al-Sharh (Relief), 'Truly with hardship comes ease, with hardship comes ease.'

This second and more dramatic encounter with grief has shattered me, but it has also cleansed me of even more emotional baggage, insecurity, fear, longing and arrogance I have attached to the Qur'an. The Noble Book has finally become medicine for my body and soul. I honestly feel God reaching out to me and speaking to me through it. My feelings about the Qur'an are perfectly captured by the psalmist: 'O God, my God, eagerly I seek you. My soul thirsts for you, my flesh also faints for you, as in a dry and thirsty land where there is no water.' And, as God assures even a misfit Muslim like me in verse 153 of Surah Al-Baqarah (The Cow), 'Believers, find strength through patience and prayer – God is with those who are patient.'

# BERLIN EXILES

*Amro Ali*

'These streets lose themselves in infinity ... a countless human crowd moves in them, constantly new people with unknown aims that intersect like the linear maze of a pattern sheet.'

Siegfried Kracauer on Berlin, 'Screams on the Street' (1930)

Dislocating the Arab future from the grip of the political bankruptcy and moral morass in the Arab world might appear remote and relegated to the domain of quixotic dreams. But does it need to be that way? As communities are unsettled, resistances triggered, a chorus of voices fired up, waves of bodies set in motion for justice, and a range of emotions roused even when they no longer have an appetite, can the continued onslaught on reality not also reinvigorate political thought? The procession of dislocation that materialised in 2011 has been viciously derailed since. Now, to coherently embark upon a regenerated starting point in this long journey of political redemption, a 'we' is required that feeds from new political ideas, collective practices and compelling narratives that are currently re-constructed and brought to life in a distantly safe city.

Berlin is where the newly-arrived Arab suddenly (but not always) recognises that the frightful habit of glancing over the shoulder – painfully inherited from back home – gradually recedes. All the while, a new dawn slowly sets in among the meeting of peers in this new city. As such, Berlin is not just a city. It is a political laboratory that enforces a new type of beginning, one that turns heads in the direction of matters greater than the individual; and it generates a realisation that the grey blur that nauseatingly blankets the future can actually be broken up.

Following the 2011 Arab uprisings and its innumerable tragic outcomes, Berlin was strategically and politically ripe to emerge as an exile capital. For some time now, there has been a growing and conscious Arab intellectual community, the political dimensions of which to fully crystalise is what I wish to explore.

When the storm of history breaks out a tectonic political crisis, from revolutions to wars to outright persecution, then a designated city will consequently serve as the gravitational centre and refuge for intellectual exiles. This is, for example, what New York was for post-1930s Jewish intellectuals fleeing Europe, and what Paris became for Latin American intellectuals fleeing their country's dictatorships in the 1970s and 1980s.

Against those historical precedents, the Arab intellectual community in Berlin needs to understand itself better, moving away from an auto-pilot arrangement, and become actively engaged with political questions that face it. In effect, there is a dire necessity for this community to acquire a name, shape, form and a mandate of sorts. With a vigorous eye to a possible long-term outcome, this may include a school of thought, a political philosophy or even an ideational movement – all cross-fertilised through a deeper engagement with the Arab world.

This is certainly not about beckoning revolutions and uprisings, nor to relapse into the stale talk of institutional reforms. If anything, there needs to be a move away from these tired tropes of transformation – away from quantifiable power dynamics that do not address matters that go deeper, into the existential level that shores up the transnational Arab sphere. This is the very area where the stream of human life animates a language of awareness and the recurring initiative helps to expand the spaces of dignity for fellow beings. Yet, this area is currently ravaged in a torrent of moral misery and spiritual crisis.

## *Freedom as Wanderer*

So here we are. Between Berlin's spirited idiosyncrasies and an Arab community maturing away from 'ordinary' diasporic pathways lies the foment of the politically possible.

'I was born in Tunisia, lived in Egypt, and gave my blood in Libya. I was beaten in Yemen, passing through Bahrain. I will grow up in the Arab

World until I reach Palestine. My name is Freedom.' This popular streak, and variations of it, could be heard throughout the Arab world in February 2011 when hope for revolution was at its peak after the fall of Tunisia's Zine El Abidine Ben Ali and Egypt's Hosni Mubarak. Within it, freedom is a wanderer that carries contagions as it roams across Arab borders.

Syria was not yet in the verse. The revolutionary moment there would launch in March 2011 and it would be the Syrians that would pay the highest price of an ephemeral euphoria that evaporated into the terrestrial orbit of actual change. Instead, wandering freedom turned into a dystopian monster as hundreds of thousands became themselves forced wanderers. The Mediterranean Sea, long celebrated for its grace and splendour, became a morbid burial ground of people fleeing for safety.

Buttressed by the refugee waves, an intellectual flow of academics, writers, poets, playwrights, artists, and activists, among others, from across the Arab world gravitated towards Berlin as sanctuary and refuge. This took place against the backdrop of a long-established Turkish presence, initiated by the 1961 Guestworker Treaty, and Chancellor Angela Merkel's 2015 refugee intake that partly shaped the post-2011 Arab transition.

A unique Arab milieu began to take form as new geographic, social, and cultural conditions necessitated a reconstruction of visions and practices. The exile body built on the embers and mediated on the ashes of a devastated Arab public left burning in the inferno of counter-revolutions, crackdowns, wars, terrorism, coups, and regional restlessness. It was that public that authoritarian regimes had worked so hard to contain and that everyday people battled courageously to reclaim. Tunisia's Mohamed Bouazizi set himself ablaze at the close of 2010 and, ever since, opened possibilities for claims and struggles.

The newcomers to Berlin were thrown under the weight of newfound political obligations to their countries of origin. They did, after all, depart with a guilt-ridden sense of unfinished business. Yet in this gap of historical time, individual greatness and the passion of public freedom blossomed while a new character formed through the tear gas, streets, protests, and coffeehouses. In a marvellous transformation, they could 'no longer recognize their pre-2011 self'. Hence, the arrival in Berlin not only came with an incomplete political consciousness, but an anxiety to resist a return to the 'weightless irrelevance of their personal affairs', as the German-Jewish philosopher Hannah Arendt conveys it.

On the one hand, this new community navigated between the support and collaboration of German institutions, civil society, universities, cultural spaces, left-wing politics, churches, mosques, the large Turkish community, and a fluctuating German sense of responsibility to the refugee crisis. On the other hand, the Arab community is menaced by local racism, a growing far-right movement in the form of the Alternative for Germany (AfD), Arab embassies, foreign security agencies and reactionary sections of the diaspora. Moreover, its members are thrown down and disoriented by the modern malaise of the 'Inferno of the Same'. This is how Berlin-based South Korean philosopher Byung-Chul Han aptly describes a world of unceasing repetition of similar experiences masquerading as novelty and renewal. Consequently, we are seeing love – with all its earmarks of commitment, intimacy, passion, and responsibility – struggle to swell through the ranks from relationships to community-building in a world of 'endless freedom of choice, the overabundance of options, and the compulsion for perfection'.

Not only is fragmentation fomented by the upheaval caused by exile and transition, the individual in general struggles to flesh out a position towards a world that has become increasingly noisy and blurred. A world that has scrambled the once-relatable relationship between time and space, now under the neoliberal storm is turning responsible citizens into hyper-individual self-seeking consumers, discharging a plastic one-size fits all repetition of behaviour that precludes deeper forms of unity and a communal spirit.

Nonetheless, even with the challenges it confronts, the Arab community is unfolding in the shadow of complex socio-political ecologies and wide-ranging entanglements that are arguably unprecedented in modern history. Hitherto, most forced Arab migrations have happened on a country by country and era by era basis, such as Libyans fleeing Gaddafi's regime in the 1970s, or the Lebanese fleeing the civil war in the 1980s. Moreover, transnational Arab relocation to the Gulf was primarily spurred on by economic factors, to say nothing of their residency that hinged on the shunning of any hint of politics. In contrast, we are currently witnessing the first ever simultaneous pan-Arab exodus consisting of overlapping legitimacies – beyond culture, religion, nationality and economics – born of the Arab Spring.

This new exile marvel is brewing in a cultural flux with questions that are only beginning to be raised. Exile is meant here, as Edward Said writes, as 'the unhealable rift forced between a human being and a native place, between the self and its true home'. Additionally, exile transpires irrespective of one being banished from the homeland, living in legal limbo, studying at university, or even one who recently acquired German citizenship. We are talking about exile as a mental state, where even if you faced no political persecution and chose to return to your country of origin, you would still feel alienated by a system that can no longer accommodate your innate or learned higher ideals. As Palestinian poet Mahmoud Darwish once put it: 'Exile is more than a geographical concept. You can be an exile in your homeland, in your own house, in a room.'

For example, in late 2015, I attended the screening of a Syrian film in Kreuzberg titled *True Stories of Love, Life, Death and Sometimes Revolution*. During the question and answer session, a fellow country man in the audience asked the film's co-director, Nidal Hassan, 'What can we Syrian artists even do now given that we are in exile?' Hassan replied entrancingly: 'We were in exile even in Syria…we just have to continue to change the world through our practices.'

From another angle, Dina Wahba, Egyptian doctoral researcher at Berlin's Freie Universität, evocatively pens the exile consciousness: 'I get out, look around, and realize how beautiful it is. I feel guilty that I'm here, while some of my friends are in dark cells. I also feel guilty that I'm here and not enjoying all this beauty. Crippling fear has crossed the Mediterranean and taken over my mind. Fear is a strange thing. I cannot go home, but neither can I make a home here.'

As such, the sense of exile in Berlin is deepened by a wide-ranging emotional spectrum, from an all-consuming survivor's guilt vis-à-vis those that stayed behind down to a pleasant stroll through Tiergarten Park in which a nagging thought might arise that whispers, 'if only back in Cairo we had such large free unmolested spaces to breathe in'.

## *Converging Points Into Lines of Meaning*

Arab Berlin, since 2011, has sprang a swathe of energetic pockets of creativity and thought. Yet, there is something missing in these hyper-present moments: the dynamic spaces from theatre to academia to civil society volunteering are fragmented and rarely talk to each other, not to mention the disconnect from the wider Arab community. You cannot help but sense that the creative and intellectual efforts are hurled into a void rather than being taken up by a greater political current that can extract these experiences and marshal them towards a pre-eminent narrative.

The strength that makes up the Berlin tempest that unleashes the creative and intellectual Arab energies, also happens to be its dissolution as its intense present breaks with past and future. That is to say, the exile might pursue the present as a way to escape or numb the trauma or crippling melancholia haunting the past, and anxiety saturating the future. But this can often mean the self is reduced to individual interests with the exciting present acting no more than a euphoric smokescreen of collective advancement.

How does one obstruct the trap that enmeshes the Arab Berliner? How does one interrupt this endless fluidity and 'recycling' of presents? How can one address an animated present that seems somehow ruptured from building up on the past and navigating into the future? How does one obstruct the trap that enmeshes the Arab Berliner?

The cultural and political dynamics that materialise in Berlin, backed with intensity and creativity by wide-ranging institutional and grassroots support, summons Berlin and the Arab exile body to be assigned into a shared conversation. If one listens closely, the hoofbeats of Arab history are reverberating out of Berlin more than any other western counterpart.

Unlike London, Paris, and New York (vis-à-vis the US) which cannot claim historical 'neutrality', the function of Berlin works strangely well as it is linked to a peculiar backdrop: the contemporary Arab approach towards Germany is premised on the notion that it was never a coloniser or invader of Arab lands. The 1941-43 *Afrika Korps* is given little attention in Arab historiography, although this should not detract from the dark ties that some Arab elites pursued with Nazi Germany.

In other words, Germany was never a coloniser like France or Great Britain, nor does it have an aggressive foreign policy like the US. The idea of Germany rarely arouses a divisiveness and antagonism that would aggravate Arab security officials or activists. The paradox of its power is that the savagery Germany committed in the first half of the twentieth century skirts around the Arab world. While German orientalism is not alien to Arab scholarship, this is not what is usually or immediately deplored in Arab scholarly circles and the Arab imagery regarding Germany – to that country's stroke of luck. Even strong German support for Israel does not elicit the same degree of Arab anger towards it as with the US and UK, partly because of the sound popular view that Germany is coerced by historical guilt. So, in a sense, Germany is conditionally, if not grudgingly, let off the hook.

## *The City Above All*

Themes of liminality strongly resonate with the self-perception of the growing Arab intellectual community's idea of rebuilding, transforming and becoming. Berlin's imperfection, sketchiness, and incompleteness, furnish a sense of freedom and growth which the compact beauty of London and Paris can never provide. If every space is 'perfectly restored', this then can lead to exclusion and a sense that all spaces are occupied. Berlin's grotty pockets and incompleteness electrifies you with the truth about the world as it is. While the post-war Berlin story – that saw Cold War divisions, reconstruction, and reunification – is anything but straightforward, we can come, as a result of such past tensions, to appreciate the current political and intellectual landscape of Berlin in the way it accentuates the idea of human value.

The marriage between city and thought is critical in understanding the exiled Arab body politic undergoing a collective soul-searching struggle, beyond the initial wandering of freedom, which is evident in the intellectual and everyday subtext. There will need to be a deeper gaze into *maghfira* (forgiveness), *tasalah* (reconciliation), *inikas* (reflection) on past mistakes, as well as the notion that the nation-state that brought many ills to the Arab world no longer makes any sense. Therefore, the concept of the city will need to spearhead the decolonisation of nation-state models and replace it with more humane ways of governance. As such, the Arab community's exploration of forgiveness, reconciliation, and reflection comes with the aid of complementary themes embedded in Berlin's code.

### *Reassembling the Political*

Towards that end, Berlin will need to be actively thought of and treated as one critical hub and safe space to reconstruct alternative narratives and futures– a space that will require a physical presence and minimal reliance on the digital sphere of social media and communication technologies. Coming from the Arab world where the physical public sphere is repressed, social media makes much sense. However, it is quite a sight to ponder when I look at my digitally-immersed (which I am not always innocent of either) Arab colleagues and the privacy-obsessed Germans.

To re-emphasise, this is about Berlin. A gifted Syrian poet in Hamburg or a lustrous Moroccan film director in Munich are of little use unless they physically make the trip to the German capital, disclose their identities and make their presence felt. Better put, 'meet, merge, emerge' as Australian author Stuart Braun pithily states in his aptly named book, City of Exiles: Berlin from the outside in. No digital mechanism can ever be a viable substitute to the world of shadows. There needs to be a resistance to the levelling effect brought on by the digital topology that deceives with its pseudo-egalitarianism and smooth open spaces yet fragments responsibility. It does this, Han states, by promoting arbitrariness and non-bindingness that undermine promises and trust that are required to bind the future.

This stands in contrast to the real world's nooks, corners, crannies, and alleys that filter and impede the information pollution and the armies of trolls, and permit slowness, mediation, and trust processes back into the collective fold. The orderly and measured disengagement from social media is one way to avoid the recurring problem of disintegration of one's efforts, scattering of thoughts, and inability to hone in on matters down to their essence.

The political should thus not simply be understood as a destination where a Syrian has to wait for that momentous day to return to a post-Assad land (if the obvious needs reminding, even sinister dictators and their regimes cannot cheat mortality and the laws of history). Rather, it is to think and engage politically in the present and be tested within the society of Berlin.

I remember a few years ago, a group of Syrians started a charity 'giving back to Germany' which handed out food to the homeless. While charity is always to be commended, justice needs to be at the forefront of one's goals of becoming better acquainted with the political problem that not only leads to homelessness, but also to understand it in much more nuanced ways than what the political can popularly imply. To illustrate this, the German population is suffering from a loneliness scourge. The communal capital stored within many Arab spaces can be unloaded into these German voids. Loneliness, a growing phenomenon in this hyper-individualised world, and one that is making inroads into Arab cities, has political implications from the way people view minorities to voting patterns, and therefore it needs to be treated as a political problem.

### *A Conference in Perpetual Motion*

There is something unsettling about attending a brilliant symposium on Middle East studies in Berlin, only to leave with the predictable knowledge that it will fall into a black hole. Even if publications and podcasts were produced, it reaches only a few, and certainly not the wider Arab civic body in question. A continual dialogue with the public needs to be fostered. Think of it as a conference in perpetual motion: To widen the net to young Arabs to engage in political thinking without the need to enrol them in formal structures of learning; to translate complex academic theories into digestible intellectual gems, which could be as simple as rewriting or summarising conference notes to be pinned up on a board in an Arab café in Neukölln. The intellectual exile body will need to forge an intimate relation with café staff, barbers and other occupations critically-positioned within common social spaces.

It would be a delusion to think that the mosques and churches have no place in this endeavour. Any project to live out one's secular fantasies is doomed. There needs to be a move beyond the spaces of smoke-blowing chatter over Foucault versus Deleuze and the echo chamber it entails. This is not a matter of merely tolerating faith because it is deeply rooted in the

Arab community. Rather, it implies coming to terms with the constructive role faith can play in an increasingly alienating environment and, therefore, that it needs to be better framed and understood rather than overlooked by intellectual currents.

It must be remembered that whether one identifies as intellectual, activist, dissident, artist, filmmaker, and so on, one has chosen to operate more vividly within, what Czech thinker Václav Havel describes as, the 'independent life of society'.

The Arab barber and Arab author in Berlin may have developed from the same background that brought them various shades of pain, except the latter is disproportionately more noticeable, given a special title, and a de facto voice to speak for others. The barber's expression of truth is demoted as it is seen to fall below the boundaries of societal 'respectability' and creative norms. The practice of faith might not only be his attainment of truth, but his coping mechanism. However, attaining truth can materialise in numerous other ways. If a Syrian barber is tending to a Palestinian customer, they might get into a conversation of a common struggle, evoking sympathy, empathy, and kinship. He might not let the patron pay if he sensed financial hardship. He could decide to put up a picture of Aleppo before the war as a reminder of what was lost but will someday be regained, even with its rubble. What looks like the everyday mundane is, in actuality, the desire to incrementally expand the spaces of dignity wherever one traverses.

The Arab author is simply one manifestation of the same political spectrum that produced that barber. The author just happens to be one of the most visible, most political, most clearly articulated expression of Arab grievances. Yet the author should not forget that he or she developed, consciously or not, from the same background and reservoir as the rest of society and the upheavals of the Arab Spring. This is where they draw their strength and legitimacy from; and this society has a very large reservoir of pain, unhappiness, confusion, and uncertainty. But when the intellectuals and activists not only recognise the futility of separation from that background, but also return to and engage with it, not as shawarma-buying customers but as citizens-in-exile in an ever-expanding conversation with moral obligations, the securing of a steadfast future is aided.

Arab Berlin would need to build a reciprocal relationship with Arab cities, beyond the institutional level. Currently, the two candidates most receptive to new ideas are Tunis and Beirut. These would form the intellectual bridgehead cities to the Arab world. It should not be presumed, however, that Tunis and Beirut will be painless to engage with simply based on the appearance of liberty. Nevertheless, there is a reservoir of latent possibilities in this novel relationship with these two cities that needs to be explored.

This arrangement is needed, or is perhaps a first step, until Cairo, the only Arab city that can move ideas by its sheer weight, is someday restored back onto the path of political maturity and intellectual openness. Perhaps this approach is also a modest attempt to address a deeper problem: One of the causes of the tragic downward spiral in the region was the historical shifting of the ideological Arab gravity centres to Riyadh, hauled away from Cairo, Damascus, and Baghdad. It is not that these three cities lost their cultural capital as much as their clout was reined in by the reckless vision of Gulf oil money. The ageless beauty and humility of Gulf Arab culture – one that was at the forefront of environmental care – was ripped apart as it descended upon an accelerated hyper-modernity devoid of politics, and the region keeps on paying the price in countless catastrophic ways because of the Gulf's ineptitude and irresponsible adventures.

This whole endeavour is under no illusion with regards to the obstacles faced. The cynics will assert the spectre of the far-right and xenophobia will hamper the efforts of the Arab exile body. Perhaps. But rather than being spectators on the sidelines, the idea is to merge the stream of evolving Arab politics with German progressive politics, as well as to actively hold a mirror up to official German hypocrisy that preaches a human rights discourse yet sells deadly weapons to dictatorships (Egypt being the top importer of German armaments). Moreover, the world's problems are interconnected more deeply than we could ever imagine and addressing this needs to be realised on a city, as opposed to national, level which is within human grasp.

The other evident challenge is the visa regime. To avoid being consumed by the consular labyrinth, a focus should not be placed on importing more intellectuals into Berlin, but rather, to make do with who is available, who is able to move there, and who is able to visit or pass through. More crucial even is to gradually raise a generation that thinks in new political ways. In this, the greatest challenge I believe will be the absence of a global momentum – that only shows up in rare cycles – to galvanise the community. Momentum versus little of it is the difference between a packed public lecture with audiences sprawled across the stairs and floor, sacrificing thirst and inconvenience, to feel part of something big, as opposed to a dozen regular attendees subjected to the speaker's voice echoing in the room. The painfully long intervals between momentums will need to be filled with thinking, reading, writing, and gatherings, geared towards slowly building up the community. Because when the momentum arrives unannounced, there will be no time to finish reading a book or stay seated to the end of a theatre play.

The manipulation of identity will be another obstacle thrown by the Arab sceptics, particularly in official capacities, as well as their supporters, who might insinuate that something coming out of a Western city is not as authentic as an Arab or Muslim one – despite the political currency emerging from an Arab body. Remember, we are dealing with Arab regimes that decry Western human rights as not applicable to them all the while, for some 'inexplicable' reason, granting exceptions for Western arms, neoliberalism, consumerism, torture methods, higher degrees and so forth. The same regimes that sing tone-deaf nationalist rhetoric and loyalty to the homeland, and yet it is not unusual to see a growing number of the elite's children studying, working, and living in places like London and Rome with no intention of returning home.

The identity neurosis underpins the same mentality that accepts being vomited upon by Gulf capital that turns the thriving Arab cultural realm into vast wastelands simply because, as one of the superficial subtexts hold, the finance is coming from a Muslim country, and therefore something must be going right. As if the insertion of an air-conditioned sleek mosque in a mega mall rights the wrongs of the eviction of local communities, destruction of age-old mosques, and state appropriation of their lands under the flimsiest of pretexts to build that mall. Progress does not come off the back of cement trucks. The shredding of a political value system in the Arab world is why Arab Berlin exists in the first place. In any case, the bridgehead cities partially address this identity concern by repelling the superficial charges that will potentially unfold in the future.

### *What is the Contemporary Zeitgeist? What is Our Ruh-Al Asr?*

We live in an era that is mostly nameless, faceless, and spiritless – compounded by the very neoliberal forces that strip people stark naked before the monster of mutant capitalism. This beast of anti-politics has, not surprisingly, been eagerly adopted by liberal democracies and authoritarian regimes alike. Undoubtedly, much worse for the latter as the deliberate weakening of political pluralism, civil society, institutions, and freedom of speech, incapacitates the ability to hold back the deluge of socio-economic dehumanisation. This is a crisis without the shrill dramatics of a crisis because it is quiet, smooth, seamless, and well internalised. But as with any crisis, only by naming it and giving it shape can we attempt to limit the formless threats that have yet to come.

Perhaps one way to approach this is to return to an obscure article written in 1870 by Syrian intellectual Salim al-Bustani in the *al-Jinan* journal. Titled *Ruh al-Asr* (Spirit of the Age), it was most likely formulated as a response to the well-known German equivalent, *Zeitgeist*. *Ruh al-Asr* was a literary and philosophical theme that was constituted by a 'metaphysical force in terms of its moral imperatives of liberty, freedom, equality, and justice'.

Like many of his Arab contemporaries, al-Bustani was clearly seduced by the 'liberality' and 'human progress' blowing from the West, yet he implored his readers to defend local traditions and values as encroaching abstract principles would not make a tenable replacement. Specifically, he disdained Arabs selecting European customs for no other reason but simply because they are European (a phenomenon that still protrudes its long arm into the post-colonial era). He grew concerned at the West's peripheral extremes of nihilist and anarchist violence, a precursor to the modern Islamist variant, that would violate the moderation and disruption of the momentum of *Ruh al-Asr*. As illustrated through the role of heroines in al-Bustani's stories, the momentum of *Ruh al-Asr* largely centred on intelligence, common sense, and decency, with the aim of helping and lifting the individual through reading and learning, and refining society away from corruption. *Ruh al-Asr*, hence, is a phrase we might need to revive and imbibe with new meaning.

This endeavour to breathe new life into *Ruh al-Asr* could have been better facilitated had Germany, or Berlin specifically, still had a strong altruistic Zeitgeist – a term which has regrettably been reduced, in a best-case scenario, to fashion trends and fads, and, worst-case, the purview of the far-right. I say this because a compelling Zeitgeist could ideally provide a backdrop and soundboard to its Arabic counterpart.

Zeitgeist, since the early nineteenth century's era of romanticism, has often guided some sort of enlightening or dark spirit in the German public sphere. With Berlin at the epicentre of the Cold War, Germans could identify themselves, or sympathise, with ideological markers – Marxist, anti-Soviet, pro-US – that may have clarified where they stood regarding political matters. A Zeitgeist came in various incarnations. For example, in the 1970s, the left-wing Red Army Faction (Baader Meinhof) terrorist group could, despite the violence they inflicted, draw sympathy from large sections of West German society, particularly the intellectual and student scene. But Zeitgeist could also propel the same strata of Germans into supporting peaceful measures like the anti-nuclear protests and environmentalism of the 1980s.

While viewing a 1970s documentary on Berlin long ago, the English commentator's closing words etched into my mind: 'This is West Berlin. A city that feeds on its nerves, a town that has learned to live in isolation, to flourish under tension. In spite of Detente, still a frontier post, living in some sense from day to day. Truly a phenomenon of our times and a lesson for our generation.' That Berlin no longer exists. The welcomed removal of the existential threat, however euphoric, has diluted collective forms of political spirits. A one-off massive demonstration against neo-Nazis is not a sustained political spirit as much as it is a political culture reactive against Nazi encroachment. The latter, however, should not be trivialised, as such a massive protest and discourse still puts Berlin ahead of the Western pack who still struggle to build up a meaningful response to the wave of xenophobia and an angry far-right.

Ask a German with non-immigrant roots in Berlin as to what inspires or moves Germans today, and you will be surprised not at the answer, but how long it takes to get an answer. As if the question is something that has not crossed their minds before. Understandably, the hesitancy seems to be governed by historical wariness of Germans being inspired in murky directions. But it is also because many will sincerely confess that individual self-interest has assumed the helm. When a worthy response does come out, it is usually akin to battling climate change or helping refugees. Consequently, the inability to mould a coherent and compellingly humane narrative has partly thrown Zeitgeist to the mercy of a resurgent far-right.

At times you do see flickers of a beautiful human spirit. In the summer of 2015, there was an upsurge against the increasing dehumanisation of refugees and many Germans came on board to support the mass refugee intake; also revealing a transitory leadership quality in Merkel who proclaimed *"Wir schaffen das"* (we'll get it done). Yet, this revived altruistic Zeitgeist barely lasted six months, it was ripped apart in the early hours of the new year 2016 in Cologne by drunk refugees who reportedly attacked German women. This, however, raises the hindsight point: there is something very problematic about a Zeitgeist and ideals that welcomes the refugee only to easily dismantle the whole endeavour upon being tested by one, albeit serious, incident.

Even if Arabs were to somehow reanimate *Ruh al-Asr*, they will still feel intellectually orphaned in a Europe that has lost its political imagination. Nevertheless, rather than being spectators, the Arab exile body needs to envision itself collectively engaged with the forces that are holding back the far-right tide. Together, they aid in reviving, however modestly, the better nature of the German imagination, contribute to battling the global depletion of political thought, and push out parallel democratic narratives against the germination of Arab authoritarian ones.

But before all this, it needs to be ultimately asked: What is our *Ruh al-Asr*? There is no easy response. In the revolutionary honeymoon days of 2011 and 2012, this could have effortlessly been answered heterogeneously, but today, it is wanting. It certainly is not to accept the continued drive towards entrenched repression in the Arab world. To engage with the question, we would need to go deeper, way beyond discussions of solutions to the Palestinian problem or Egyptian authoritarianism.

It needs thinking at the existential level of our moral quagmire. Not only are our publics duped into cheering massacres or muted over the killing of a journalist in a consulate. The normalisation of their lives toward biological and work processes also robs them of any higher attainment of the common good. We thus need to go back to basics and redefine every single word that permeates the lives among us: citizen, city, state, Arab, Muslim, Christian, Jew, Sunni, Shiite, exile, justice, happiness, education, Inshallah, and so on. To also ask, why do they matter? Questions need to be raised on the region's Christian, Nubian, Berber, Amazigh, and other non-Arab and non-Muslim minorities, and how they can be raised to a dignified equality. It is not lost on me that an Arab exile body is already inherent with tensions that dislodges voices who do not easily subscribe to the Arab label. It will require the ability to shed light on the refugee not simply or only as an object of sympathy, reform, or potential terror, but to elevate him or her as an intellectual producer. To understand what constitutes the better parts of our *Ruh al-Asr* is to delineate a new way of framing the world. To fight the freak reality of *maskh* (shapelessness) and be salvaged from the terror of the same.

Rather than a prescription for an Arab utopian future, it is better to consider present realities to build a new manual of thought, drawn from the lived veracities of the Arab world along with the experience of displacement, migration, movement, exile, alienation and settlement in Berlin into the narrative.

Facing similar transcendental questions of his time, al-Bustani struggled to make sense of the Arab future in the shadow of colonialism. From his 1875 short story, *Bint al-Asr*, 'Daughter of the Age', he invokes the spectre of uncertainty following the influx of European influences: 'these things are taking place at a time whose meaning, like the uncertain light of dawn, is yet unclear. Therefore, the minds of many people, too, are not clear. Even strangers (Europeans) are in the dark, like the natives. This state of affairs shows that the country is suffering under the burden of a cultural situation whose values are in an uncertain state of transition.'

Al-Bustani faced a different moment of truth in which he wondered and wandered, as to what will eventually come out of this confusion for his fellow Arabs. Nowadays, we face that confusion again, just as we have faced it numerous times since al-Bustani's day. For God knows what tomorrow brings, but the journey will draw from and humanise the symbolic capital that was born in 2011, as well as to reinvigorate it in novel ways that opens up new pathways. The galvanising moments of 2011 was when desire and the imagination were given free reign until they were torpedoed by blood, remorse, despair, and exhaustion. More than ever, what is needed is to judiciously rekindle desire and imagination but, this time, to reign it in with knowledge and discipline.

We need to produce new personalities and thinkers who will further aid in tapping into the curiosity, relentlessness, inventiveness, and ingenuity of a heartbroken community; to adopt emerging texts as guides, imbibe philosophical thinking into the heart of upcoming ventures, and to produce books worthy of inheritance to the generations yet to arrive; and we need to encourage not only the learning of the German language and refining our approach to the Arabic language, but to be constantly conscious that political thinking is inescapably structured by the words we use and evade, and therefore a revitalised vocabulary is needed to question and discuss the taxonomies of power. But above all, we need to come to terms with our mortality that humbles us into the awareness that our milestones are heirlooms of past struggles, and the fruits of our efforts might only sprout beyond our lifetime. One is not expected to do everything, but nor should one relinquish one's responsibility to do something worthwhile for others.

By breaking through Siegfried Kracauer's words of anonymity and aimlessness at the opening of this essay, we need to find ourselves, and each other, on the streets, from human to human crowd to an animated body-politic, becoming that new people on the Berlin scene with names, aims, and voices, that intersect with what is just and good. The surge of different rhythms harmoniously complementing the other will reveal larger than life meanings, sounding off a special melody that will be worth listening to.

# STRANGERS IN A STRANGE LAND

*Robert Irwin*

> 'The East', i.e. Asia, had the reputation of being vast, rich and full of marvels. The wealth and fertility of India was fabulous. William of Newburgh, discussing the situation of the Holy Land, mentions that the Bible asserts the special place of Palestine, but considers that this cannot mean it is the richest and most fertile part of the world, 'unless what is recorded about India be false'. If God had wished the Chosen People to enjoy the most fertile land on earth, that would have been where he would have placed them ... The East was also where Nature was most playful, producing oddities and wonders of all kinds ... They include two-headed snakes, men with dogs' heads, elephants, cannibals, centaurs, black men, unicorns, and parrots who can say 'hallo'.
>
> Robert Bartlett, *England under the Norman and Angevin Kings* 1075–1225 (Oxford 2000)

Although the Western imagination tended to locate the strangest and most improbable marvels in India and points further east ('The Cannibals that each other eat, The Anthropophagi, and men whose heads Do grow beneath their shoulders', as Othello put it), the Arab lands provided enough of the marvellous and the strangeness for medieval European pilgrims, traders, adventurers and spies to be going on with. Francesco Suriano, a Franciscan pilgrim who was in Egypt and the Holy Land in the 1460s, wrote of the Muslims that he had encountered, 'I conclude that, if they could, they would walk backwards just to be different from us'. He had prefaced this remark with a long list of the contrasts, including the following: the women only wore one dress, whereas the men wore three or four; Europeans took off their headgear in a sign of respect, but Muslims took off their shoes; Europeans liked dogs, they liked cats; Europeans wrote from left to right, they the reverse; Europeans despised imbeciles,

Muslims reverenced them as saints; slaves in Europe were servants, with them lords. (Regarding the last remark, Suriano was commenting on the rule of Egypt and Syria by the Mamluk military white slave elite from c.1250 to 1517.)

Quite ordinary aspects of everyday life in Cairo struck visiting pilgrims as weird. In our globalised world we are, almost all of us, familiar with street food. This seems not to have been the case in medieval Christendom. Many pilgrims noted that the Arab townspeople never or rarely cooked at home. Indeed only a few had kitchens, but instead bought their cooked food from stalls in the street. If they needed baking done, they took the stuff to a bakery with a furnace. According to the fifteenth-century German pilgrim, Arnold Von Harff, the cooking and baking was done on camel dung, for such was the shortage of wood, and the baths were heated the same way. The fourteenth-century Franciscan pilgrim Niccolò da Poggibonsi remarked that 'they eat at any and every hour and Saracens must have stomachs of iron'. The adventurer Lodovico di Varthema observed goatherds bringing the goats into people's houses to be milked before the eyes of the purchasers of the milk. (More on Varthema shortly.) Felix Fabri found it remarkable that the Saracens cooked eggs in a frying pan. He also claimed that women never enter kitchens, 'for Saracens loathe food cooked by women like poison'. (The fifteenth-century, pilgrimage-loving Dominican Felix Fabri has been described as 'the Proust of pilgrim literature'. This is not because he was sensitive, subtle or gay, but simply because he was so prolix.)

The Arabic sources for the Mamluk period—chronicles, biographical dictionaries, poems, fantasies, chancery encyclopedias, satires, panegyrics, mystical treatises, shadow-play scripts, occult treatises, erotica and so forth—are extraordinarily rich, yet I guess that one could read them for a hundred years without coming across any references to street food or to goatherds visiting peoples' houses. The inhabitants of medieval Egypt and Syria were the unassuming experts on their way of life. But why should they write about the way they ate, dressed, built their houses, enjoyed themselves and buried their dead, for a readership who was already perfectly familiar with these things? Their way of living was how it was and, as far as they knew, it had been so pretty much the same since time immemorial. As the brilliant Middle Eastern historian, Ulrich Haarmann

(1942-1999) observed: 'The geographic and cultural distance from which Western visitors to the Nile, the Sinai or to Palestine came again and again permitted a conscious awareness of, and reflection on, structural differences in the everyday world that they found there. The inhabitants of this world, on the other hand, were not capable of this, at least not without conscious effort . . . the milieu within which they lived was close, intimate and taken for granted'. After reading so much in the annals about embattled sultans, strangled viziers, feuding emirs and deceased ulema, it makes a welcome change to read about cages of singing birds outside the houses, polo matches and moonlit picnics in the cemeteries.

The word 'pilgrim' derives from the Latin '*peregrinus*' which means 'stranger', and medieval pilgrims in the Middle East were aware not only of being perceived of as strangers in that region (and sometimes therefore spat upon, stoned, or treated with extraordinary kindness and hospitality), but also conscious of the strangeness of the places they visited. One of the few handbooks available to them as a guide to the region was the Bible and, to a significant extent, the holy text filtered and explained what they encountered. Nineteenth-century travellers in the Middle East were to be guided in what they saw by their reading of *The Arabian Nights* and consequently their travel narratives are peppered with tedious and pointless references to Aladdin, Ali Baba and Sinbad. In somewhat the same manner the pilgrims took the Bible as their *Rough Guide* to the Mamluk Sultanate.

Von Harff traced the origins of the Mamluk slave Sultanate back to Pharaonic times for 'it was never questioned since the time of Joseph, who was sold by his brothers in Egypt, that a Sultan should be a heathen born, and always an elected renegade Christian . . .' Von Harff believed that Joseph had ruled in Egypt after Pharaoh's death, and, because of his just and good rule, 'they will have no Sultan who has not first been sold'. Most pilgrims believed that the pyramids were Pharaoh's granaries, built after Joseph had interpreted Pharaoh's dream and predicted seven lean years. The fourteenth-century lawyer and pilgrim Nicolas de Martoni believed that the Arabs were under a curse because they were the descendants of Pharaoh. Opinion was divided about the origins specifically of the Bedouin, but most believed that they were the descendants of Israel's ancient enemies, the Midianites.

Obviously Jerusalem and the Holy Land was the chief destination of Christian and Jewish pilgrims. But Egypt was also a Holy Land, sanctified not only by Joseph's sojourn there, but also by the confrontation of Moses with Pharaoh's sorcerers. Moreover, the balsam garden of Matariyya, a little way outside Cairo, was visited by almost all pilgrims. This was known to be the place where Mary and Joseph rested on their flight into Egypt. Specifically they had rested under a fig tree in that garden which had survived into Mamluk times. Oil was extracted from the balsam or balm plants that grew only in this garden and this was sold to pilgrims for huge sums of money, since this oil was the cure for a large and improbable list of medical complaints. The fourteenth-century pilgrim Giorgio Gucci accused the Saracens of bulking out the expensive balsam with their saliva.

Travel to the east was a dangerous adventure. Fabri asked Eberhard, the Duke of Wurttemberg, for advice about going on pilgrimage, but got this reply: 'There are three things one cannot advise upon, one way or the other, marriage, war and the pilgrimage to the Holy Land. They all may begin well and end badly'. Fabri also quoted the ancient philosopher, Anarcharsis: 'Those at sea cannot be counted either among the living or the dead'. Once they had landed, pilgrims and other travellers were careful to dress scruffily in the hope that this would protect them from theft or harassment by officials, and, according to the learned Fabri, Osiris was the first traveller to grow long hair and a beard. The fifteenth-century Rabbi Meshullam of Volterra, listed some of the difficulties to be faced by pilgrims heading to Jerusalem from Egypt. They would need to take all their food and drink with them, not forgetting lemons to repel insects. The soft sand made it difficult to travel fast. One needed to be dressed like an Arab in order to avoid being identified as an infidel. It was necessary to sleep in one's clothes lest they be stolen. The horses were liable to die from the brackish water they had to drink, and the desert was littered with the bones of horses and camels.

The Bedouin were a particular menace: 'you will always find people lying in wait on the road who are hidden in sand up to their necks, two or three days without food or drink, who put a stone in front of them, and they can see other people but others cannot see them'. When they spotted a caravan that seemed vulnerable, then they mounted their horses and launched an attack with lances and maces. It is understandable that the threatened pilgrims formed no favourable opinion of the Bedouin. The fourteenth-century Irish Franciscan, Simeon Semeonis remarked that, though the Bedouin dressed like Cistercians, they lived like animals. Though many thought the Syrian Bedouin were Midianites, some, including Fabri, believed them to be the gypsies who had been driven out of Egypt. (Gypsies were beginning to be a familiar sight in Western Europe in the fifteenth-century.) The Palestinian Bedouin rode bareback, had no armour and were only lightly armed. Suriano and others attributed this to Bedouin fatalism. They would die only on the day that God had decreed their death. It did not occur to Suriano that it was stark poverty that forced the Bedouin to fight in this fashion.

Apart from danger, there was of course boredom—days becalmed at sea, days crossing arid deserts, delays at customs posts, and, after a while, a deep weariness with one's travelling companions. As Malcolm Muggeridge once observed, 'Writing about travels is nearly always tedious, travelling being, like war and fornication, exciting but not interesting'. Fabri, though he travelled out to the East twice, would have agreed. While waiting to embark on a ship at Venice, as a matter of piety he visited numerous churches in the city and was bored rigid by how much alike they were, and later he also confessed 'I am weary of writing' (but, of course, he still kept going). The Holy Land, vaunted by Exodus as the land of milk and honey, offered little in the way of spectacular memorials to its biblical past. Much later, after visiting so many nondescript shrines in Palestine, Mark Twain remarked in *The Innocents Abroad* (1869) how odd it was that most of the individuals mentioned in the Bible appeared to have lived in caves that had been successfully identified by the locals.

Though piety or greed took most Westerners out to the East, a few were just looking for strange sights and adventure. Ludovico di Varthema was such a one. He was young and the Orient was a natural place to seek out such things. As Varthema wrote, 'When we came to Alexandria, a city of Egypt, I was longing for novelty as a thirsty man longs for water . . . ' His *Itinerario,* published in 1510, gives an account of his travels in Egypt, Syria, Hejaz, Yemen and as far as India and Moluccas. He gave a painstaking account of the *hajj* rituals in the Hejaz. But he also gave a no less meticulous account of the two graceful unicorns (sic) that he had seen in the temple enclosure in Mecca. A little later in his journey he was brought as a captive, a suspected Christian spy, to Aden. But he thereupon feigned madness and tore off all his clothes. His naked state aroused the interest of the black sultana of the Yemen, since the women in that region were allegedly very keen on white men, and she ordered baths and food for him and regularly visited and caressed him. 'Entering where I was, she called me "Ludovico, come here, are you hungry?" And I replied; "Yes," and because of the hunger I had coming to her, rose on my feet and went to her in my shirt. And she said: "not in that manner, take off your shirt." I replied: "O, madam I am not mad now." She replied that she knew that but she still wanted to gaze on him as if he were a nymph. She went on to offer him great riches if only he would sleep with her and with tears and prayers, though Varthema valiantly resisted the dusky temptation. One can if one wants, regard this as a sober account of the sex life ofYemeni sultanas, yet it seems more plausible to regard it as fiction inserted to entertain.

Western travel narratives dutifully logged the necessary stopping points on the holy trail (and some of these narratives were hardly more than the medieval equivalent of t-shirts that boasted of one's trip abroad), yet very few of these narratives were entirely free of fantasy. Von Harff located the islands of men and women a little way beyond the Arab island of Socotra. The women visit the island of men only once every ten years and Von Harff, who claimed that he had visited Socatra, was privileged to see some of these Amazonian women on that island. They were identifiable because they each had only one breast, the other having been cut off to facilitate their archery,

It is not clear where the Castle of the Sparrow-Hawk was located, but, from Johann Schiltberger's account, it was obviously worth a visit. Schiltberger was taken captive at the Battle of Nicopolis in 1396 and, having been made a slave in the service of the Ottoman Sultan, he was subsequently acquired as a slave by Timur. Later he travelled extensively in the Islamic lands. 'There is on the mountain a castle, called that of the sparrow-hawk. Within there is a beautiful virgin, and a sparrow-hawk on a perch. Whoever goes there and does not sleep but watches for three days and three nights, whatever he asks of the virgin that is chaste, that she will grant to him.' When the three days are up the sparrow-hawk shrieks to summon the virgin. According to the fourteenth-century Franciscan pilgrim Simone Sigoli, the Sultan had to pay annual tribute to the powerful, though entirely legendary Christian king, Prester John lest that king prevent the flooding of the Nile. Not all the mirabilia were entirely imaginary, for travellers marvelled at the sight of pyramids, giraffes, crocodiles, ostriches and hitherto unknown fruits. But, according to Meshullam, the crocodile could not shit, but a bird turns up and eats the shit out of its mouth. Crocodile skin was sold in the West as that of a dragon. The fourteenth-century pilgrim William von Boldenseele had his Christian faith confirmed when he discovered the image of the cross inside a banana. One of Cairo's mirabilia was remarked on by several pilgrims and, as Martoni had it: 'In Cairo they have a wonderful invention which is so hard to believe I am afraid of being called a liar. I certainly would not write about it if I had not seen it for myself. They build ovens, I don't know how, with walls made of jars all round, and put in hens' eggs, twenty or thirty thousand of them, depending on the size, with a carefully tended slow charcoal fire. Chicks hatch after a few days.... '

To return to more mundane aspects of the medieval Near East, Fabri commented on Arab dress: 'the Saracens, contrary to the ordinance of Mahomet have readopted many customs they were wont to use in the days of idolatry, as in the matter of garments; for they wear hermaphrodite garments which do not distinguish men from women, such as we read Queen Semiramis wore of old'. (According to Diodorus Siculus, an ancient Sicilian Greek historian, Semiramis was a princess who cross-dressed in order to rule as a king in ancient Assyria, and Fabri, who was remarkably well read, often cites Diodorus.) Semeonis described women's costumes in great detail: 'All of them adopt a strange and wonderful fashion of dress. They are dressed in linen or cotton mantles whiter than snow, and veiled and covered up to such an extent that their eyes can only be perceived with difficulty through a very narrow veil of black silk . . . These trousers, boots and other ornaments give them a close resemblance to the fictitious devils seen in miracle-plays'. As for the men, the Arab way of pissing attracted comment. According to the fifteenth-century bishop, Louis de Rochechouart, the Muslim men pissed like sailors and they never spoke while urinating, or if they did it was a great insult. When Suriano claimed that Muslims reverenced imbeciles, he was clearly referring to the *majdubs*, or holy fools, familiar figures in Sufi belief. According to a fifteenth-century pilgrim source, the first house a holy fool entered in the morning was blessed.

Varthema claimed that the Turkish and Circassian mamluks treated the Arab women as they liked. 'If they accidentally meet two or three ladies, they possess this privilege, or if they do not possess it they take it: they go to lay in wait for these ladies in certain places like great inns, which are called khans, and, as the ladies pass before the door, each Mameluke takes his lady by the hand, draws her in and does what he will with her. But the lady resists being known, because they all wear the face covered, so that they know us, but we do not know them.' Varthema claimed that he knew of several instances where mamluks raped their own wives without being aware that they were doing so. Arab men were bastinadoed if they did not respectfully salute a mamluk encountered in the street. According to Von Harff, the mamluks habitually carried sticks with which to beat those who offended them. Within the cities, only mamluks were entitled to ride horses.

Despite the arrogance of the mamluks, they were widely despised by their Arab subjects. Bertrando de Mignanelli was a long-term resident of Damascus in the late fourteenth-century and a friend of the Bedouin sheikhs of the northern Syrian desert. According to him, the paramount sheikh of the Bedouin despised the Mamluk Sultan Barquq, because he was a slave of Christian origin, whereas the sheikh was of 'old Saracen stock'. Similarly, Emmanuele Piloti, a Venetian merchant resident in Alexandria in the early fifteenth century, reported that the Arabs despised the mamluks as dogs and renegade Christians. (Arab chroniclers of the period sometimes mocked the mamluks for their inability to speak Arabic properly.)

The mamluks usually provided pilgrims with escorts to protect them from Bedouin attacks and in general the pilgrims, particularly the aristocratic ones, got on well with the mamluks. Although most mamluks were of Kipchak Turkish or Circassian origin, the pilgrims were quite likely to encounter mamluks who were of German, Italian or Hungarian origin, and those mamluks were usually keen to get news of their homelands. Moreover members of the mamluk elite and the pilgrim elite shared common interests in fighting, hunting and estate management, as well as in drinking the pilgrims' wine. Arab interpreters hated mamluks and pilgrims in equal measure, and in Palestine Arabs were hostile to the foreign visitors, despite their dependence on the pilgrim trade. The main pilgrimage season in Jerusalem was around Easter and Arab traders came from as far away as Damascus to benefit from it. Nompar de Caumont, who was in Jerusalem on a pilgrimage-cum-shopping spree in 1419, gave a long list of his purchases in the town – much too long to be fully listed here, but they included a Damascus textile of red and gold, an ivory chaplet, four white silk belts, thirty-three silver rings that had touched the Holy Sepulchre, five 'serpentines' that were efficacious against snake venom, two pairs of gilded spurs that had touched the Holy Sepulchre, five Turkish knives, six pairs of chamois leather gloves, twelve more Turkish knives, a bone of Saint Barnabas and a bone from one of the eleven thousand virgins. Fabri was shocked by the practice of selling embalmed corpses of babies, supposedly the victims of Herod's Massacre of the Innocents. In Egypt ground-up mummy powder, *mumia*, was sold to Europeans as a medicine, as well as a painter's ingredient, mummy brown. It could be awkward if the pilgrimage season overlapped with Ramadan and according to a late fifteenth-century source, the Muslims in Jerusalem were so noisy during this month that the Franciscans used to issue new arrivals with leather ear plugs.

Not all pilgrims were what they seemed. Some were spies. Ghililbert de Lannoy and Bertrandon de la Brocquière had both been sent out by the Duke of Burgundy to report on the quality of the troops and the fortified defences of Egypt and Syria in preparation for a crusade, which in the event was never launched. Moreover, even genuine pilgrims were likely to make notes on the ruined state of the old crusader ports on the Syro-Palestinian coastline, as well as of the martial qualities of the mamluks and their auxiliaries. Varthema was most impressed with the mamluks whom he observed to be constantly exercising and improving themselves. But Semeonis was not so impressed. Having watched mamluk cavalry playing polo outside the Citadel in Cairo, he commented that 'they never play in a military manner. Nor are the horses and their riders tested as to agility, bravery, and the other military virtues, as is done in the case of the jousts, tournaments, and other military performances of Christian knights'.

But, even within Semeonis's lifetime, cavalry manoeuvers, lance play and archery were ceasing to be the be-all and end-all of warfare and, contrary to what some of the older scholarly studies and hack histories have suggested, the mamluks were not so infatuated with a cavalry based ethic of chivalry that they disdained the deployment of artillery, and, though Arab chroniclers were slow to register the new technology and find a vocabulary for it, the evidence indicates that the mamluks started to use cannons in the early fourteenth century, though they were only commonly used in the fifteenth century, which was when handguns also started to be used. Brocquière, who was in Syria in the 1430s, states that arquebusiers (men carrying handguns) protected the *hajj* on its return to Damascus. Brocquière also watched Greek fire being let off in Beirut (and during the same celebration cannons were also fired), and he took notes on its recipe and purchased moulds for the Greek fire to take back to Burgundy. Since he was interested in all aspects of warfare, Brocquière also took careful notes about the manufacture of the famous Damascened sword blades in the eponymous city.

Though the Bedouin were feared and detested, the other Muslim Arabs were widely praised for their cleanliness, their respect for the laws and their regularity in prayer. An anonymous fourteenth-century English pilgrim declared that 'they refrain themselves from all the dangerous desires of the world . . . If only they believed in the true god they would be saved'. Nevertheless, the fifteenth-century Milanese clergyman, Pietro Casola was vehement against them: 'And I declare that they may be as great and learned as you like, but in their ways they are like dogs.'

The fifteenth-century Flemish merchant Anselm Adorno prefaced the account of his pilgrimage with an attack on those who were foolish enough to think there was no country except their own and that everybody else lived in dark shadows as savages. Those who had read widely or travelled out east knew better. From such sources one may get a sense for the texture of life and the conflicting faiths and passions of those times, and one may dream of how it was to have lived in the Mamluk Sultanate. Even so, readers should be warned that not all medieval travel narratives are so very informative and some are very dull. For example, Margery Kempe's lachrymose account of her journey to Jerusalem is virtually useless, since she was careful to avoid the sin of *curiositas*. Citizens of Kings Lynne had actively encouraged her to go on pilgrimage, since the locals were so keen to get rid of her.

# INVISIBLE THESSALONIKI

*Boyd Tonkin*

*I*

You can eat better in Thessaloniki than anywhere else in modern Greece. On my first visit, after I'd enjoyed the bracingly spiced peppers, the cumin-filled lamb sausages, the deep-textured fruit-and-meat stews, the creamy pastries, one of my guides began to explain why. 'It's very *political* food,' he said as we drove through the – fairly humdrum – suburbs of a largely modern city that seldom discloses the many layers of its past to the casual eye. His English was well-nigh perfect, but this little, inadvertent Hellenicism told a story in itself.

To Greeks everywhere, for centuries, the magnetic metropolis of Constantinople was simply 'the city', *I póli*. So exalted was its position that it hardly needed another name. Indeed, when Atatürk brought its official moniker in line with the linguistic norms of his new Turkish republic in 1930, it didn't get one. 'Istanbul' is merely a vernacular truncation of the Greek phrase for 'to the city'. Remade in the early twentieth century by waves of forced migration from 'the city' and other places in Asia Minor and European Turkey, Thessaloniki in its daily life – from tongue to table – carries memories of lost homelands and displaced communities. So, yes, that well-spiced, Eastern-tinged cuisine is 'political' in several senses – although Smyrna, another origin of its modern citizenry, flavours the local dishes as deeply as Constantinople/Istanbul.

In Thessaloniki, you can easily taste at least some of the sedimented past. You can hear it too in the 'oriental' strains of *rebetiko*, which flourished here among exiled musicians who had fled Smyrna or Istanbul. But you need to make more of an effort to see it. All around the Mediterranean basin, and far beyond, urban centres with a history of hosting people of different faiths, cultures and languages have learned how to put their hybrid pasts on display for tourists, for investors, for the international image-makers who can boost, or dampen, a city's prospects. Ancient ports in Morocco will celebrate (and restore) their synagogues; even some towns in Poland now cherish historic mosques. The commemoration of the multi-faith *convivencia* of medieval Spain helped quicken the modern revival of Andalusia and added to the new lustre of Granada, Cordoba and Sevilla. Sites in Israel and Egypt, in Turkey, Tunisia or Sicily, blithely invite visitors to ignore the embarrassment of contemporary politics and enjoy the curated traces of a time when – so the tale runs – clearly-defined 'communities' lived in an Edenic state of 'harmony', undisturbed by ethnic or confessional strife. Should, in the near future, Syria wake from its long nightmare into something like peace, the rhetoric of its reconstruction will no doubt draw on these well-worn tropes. And these invocations of paradise lost are far from accidental. Behind them lies the dream, or hope, of a friction-free comity of peoples that may unite the three Abrahamic faiths of Judaism, Christianity and Islam. After all, all agree (more or less) on Eden – and the Fall.

That familiar idyll, or fairy-tale, has yet to become the default story in Thessaloniki. The city that looks out towards Mount Olympus over the Thermaic Gulf – Salonica in its pre-Greek incarnations, Selanik in Turkish – came to fascinate me in part because it defied this pan-Med fusion narrative. Here was a fabled port, blessedly sited between fertile farmlands in the shadow of the Balkans and the sea-lanes that connected East and West, that for centuries really did approach the ideal of a hybrid meeting-place. It offered a common home for people of varied backgrounds to live, work and trade alongside one another in imperfect, but robust, harmony. The Ottoman conquest of 1430 had brought not a sharp rupture with the Greek and Slavic past but a pattern of light-touch stewardship. Ruling *pashas* and *beys* (often Muslim converts of local origin themselves) supported Christian institutions under the *millet* system of devolved control. And, after the expulsion of the Jews from Spain in 1492, Salonica fast became what one Marrano poet called 'a mother city of Judaism'.

The Jewish population, incomers from Iberia and elsewhere around the Mediterranean, grew to be not a minority but a majority in the port area. There were no ghettoes: communities lived and worked in the same, shared spaces. Injustices and imbalances did persist. The *dhimmi* status of Jews and Christians traditionally carried fiscal and legal burdens, as everywhere in the Sultan's lands. But the Gülhane Decree of 1839 had paved the way for formal equality between the communities of the Empire. If, as a British ambassador reported in 1864, the Ottoman government ranked as 'about the most tolerant in Europe', then Salonica was its smart shop-window. Around the same time, an observer lauded its atmosphere as 'a sort of fusion between the different peoples who inhabit the place and a happy rapprochement between the races which the nature of their beliefs and the diversity of their origins tends to separate'.

## *II*

Yet, at first glance, the city I roamed showed little interest in the impacted cultural strata that lay just below the clamorously Greek surface of its present-day routines. Grand mosques, domed markets or splendid *hamams* – lonely, stranded survivors of the great Levantine entrepôt – sat neglected on traffic-clogged boulevards named for Greek worthies who would never have imagined Salonica as part of their state. Much of the Ottoman past remains, literally, unexcavated – unlike the extensive Roman forum now exposed to view between two of the east-west arteries that slice brutally across the city's ancient, buried labyrinth. After the post-1912 Greek government demolished them, a sole minaret endures, next to the Rotunda – one of those emblematic monuments whose stones let you read the entire history of a city, or a continent. Built as a mausoleum for the Roman emperor Galerius around 306AD, it became a church for a millennium, then in 1590 the mosque of Suleyman Hortaji Effendi; in 1912, it mutated into the church of Aghios Giorgios again.

Taken in 1913, the first modern census of the core city found that it contained almost 40,000 Greeks, 45,867 'Ottomans' (in other words, Muslims) and – for centuries, the largest community in its urban heart – 61,439 Jews. In November 1912, Greek forces had seized Salonica from the tottering Ottoman Empire during the First Balkan War. They only just beat the Bulgarians in grabbing the prize. By this point, a Muslim exodus had already begun from the province of Macedonia, and would soon accelerate: 140,000 had fled by 1914. A Greek police report in 1925 found that a mere 97 Muslims remained in the city. As for the Jews, the shockingly rapid deportations of 1943 at the hands of the German occupiers meant that 45,000 (20 per cent of the city's people) were murdered in Auschwitz within weeks. In 1923, after the so-called 'exchange of populations' between Greece and Turkey mandated by the Treaty of Lausanne, Christian refugees from Ottoman lands filled the space lately vacated by the city's Muslims. By 1928, they made up a third of the population. Even at the time, though, not everyone applauded this rational, geometrical solution to Europe's perennial problem of 'nationalities'. Archbishop Chrysostomos of Smyrna/Izmir denounced the 'counting and exchange of human beings – incomprehensible, unheard-of… as is done by animal dealers with horses, livestock and cattle'. Alas, those 'animal dealers' would continue to trade around the world throughout the twentieth century, and well into the twenty-first.

Thessaloniki/Salonica, then, endured a century traumatic even by the standards of its age and its region. Add to its communal upheavals the Great Fire of 1917 that obliterated much of the old centre, the overall miseries of Nazi control, the conflict-shaken history of post-war Greece, and the fresh refugee waves that started to break in the 1990s but have swollen since the mid-2010s, and the city has had scant chance or inclination to reflect serenely on its mingled legacies. True, monocultural Hellenic nationalism has played a part in forgetting or simplifying this past, with the vast arc of the Sultans' rule – 1430 to 1912 – reduced to a crude 'Turkocracy' of oppression and enslavement. The White Tower may dominate the east end of the city's seafront promenade, but – like so much of the town that surrounds it – it has somehow lost touch with its Ottoman foundations. And the fragile status of the Greek city as a latecomer on shared ground means that Hellenic chauvinism – always a hair-trigger response – always stands ready to bristle into angry life. I once sat at a seaside café while followers of the neo-Fascist Golden Dawn movement assembled by the modernistic statue of Alexander the Great (whose step-sister gave her name to today's city) and marched noisily past the tables of evening drinkers. Who, pretty much without exception, kept on chatting and ignored them.

Yes, nationalistic ideology has abetted the indifference or ignorance that still marks the public memory (or lack of it) of pre-Greek Salonica. But, in my experience, the life-shaking disruptions of the past century have done most to seed forgetfulness. No sustained period of calm has intervened to give citizens time to survey the tangled past and make their peace with it. Soon after the Greek economic crisis began in 2009, I visited and found that – in a place poleaxed by job losses and the sudden precariousness of daily life – the effort to keep a semblance of normality used up much of the city's human bandwidth. You could, at any rate, linger at one of the seafront cafés over a coffee, priced at €1 to lend a business-as-usual veneer to a penurious community. A few years later, the economic crisis had partially abated, but Thessaloniki's biennial art show was now packed with works that tried to visualise the Mediterranean migration emergency. That convulsion not only left tens of thousands of refugees to languish on the islands, but sent many into camps on the Greek mainland. The closest reception centre, at Diavata on the industrial outskirts of Thessaloniki, at its height hosted around 2500 people from the Middle East and parts of Africa. Many of its 'graduates' have settled, officially or otherwise, in and near the city, where they work in the informal economy – as market stall-holders, for instance – and negotiate the labyrinth of obstacles that face asylum-seekers. They may encounter suspicion, but also a welcome with deep (if unacknowledged) roots. 'We have many things in common with the Syrians,' one local market trader told investigators. That includes, of course, a centuries-long history as integral provinces of the empire ruled from Istanbul.

History – too much history, arguably – has rained down on this city like the winter storms that descend from the Balkans. Its regular deluges mean that collective memory here seldom takes on a coherent shape and outline. Mark Mazower, the English-language historian who has done most to assemble the shattered facets of the city's history, believes the 'sharp discontinuities' of this past deter attempts to grasp its movement as a whole. Jewish and Greek histories 'did not so much complement one another as pass each other by,' he writes. The Muslim heritage shrank to a caricature of 'Turkish' domination. These rival narratives configure the past as a 'zero-sum game' in which 'opportunities for some came through the sufferings of others'. Mazower subtitled his definitive book about Salonica from 1430 to 1950 'City of Ghosts'. The ghosts, however, tend to remain invisible until you look. And, if you do notice them, they often seem to be floating in opposite directions.

*III*

All the same, I found this unquiet past – full of jagged edges and rough outcrops – more compelling than the smooth sheen of touristic diversity on show in places that market a cleaned-up version of their stories. When I first went, I wandered freely through the decorated rooms of the great Bey Hamam, built by the conquering Sultan Murad II in the 1440s. Much of its charm – at least at that time – came from the sense that no one much cared about this domed palace of hygiene. The so-called 'Baths of Paradise', indeed, stayed in everyday use until the 1960s; only then did the national archaeological service take them over. Although restored, the Alaca Imaret and Hamza Bey mosques nestle quietly among nondescript apartment blocks. The fifteenth century Bezesteni clothes-market building, with its six domes, still performs its original function, not a theme-park revival but part of the living fabric of the city. For an even stronger taste of Ottoman Salonica, climb up towards the Byzantine city walls. There, in the Ana Poli, time-battered mansions survive with their wooden windows overhanging narrow, winding streets. In the 1920s, this 'Turkish quarter' was occupied by Christian refugees from Asia Minor after its Muslim residents departed. Now gentrification has spruced up (some of) its alleyways.

Meanwhile, efforts to brand Thessaloniki according to the bland norms of European multiculturalism fall foul of local protests. In 1995, a campaign by the Orthodox church to return the Rotunda to regular use as a place of worship – rather than a museum where services could be held a few times every year – became a fierce national controversy. All it took was a pianist practising for a concert in the building and a firebrand priest, backed by a crowd of enraged believers, to thunder that 'It's almost like Tehran' in Thessaloniki. Hellenic militancy does have a comic, as much as a menacing, side. But this volatility reveals that the history buried under the straight shopping streets and nondescript blocks of the post-1917 city is, in fact, very close to the surface. It lies ready to be uncovered and exposed to good, or bad, effect.

Greece's past decade of turbulence, meanwhile, has coincided with a fresh curiosity about the centuries of mingled history that only really ended with the Holocaust. From 2011 to 2019, the mayor of Thessaloniki was Yiannis Boutaris, member of a wine-making dynasty descended from the Slavic Vlachs – another key piece in Macedonia's, and Salonica's, intricate jigsaw of a population. Mayor Boutaris promoted plans for a new, as yet unfinished, Holocaust Museum of Greece. He encouraged the revival of Muslim worship in the city, and spoke warmly of Turkey and Turks. With his Balkan ancestry, he tried to mediate in the opaque, theological disputes over the formal title of the ex-Yugoslav republic now known as North Macedonia. Unsurprisingly, he managed to antagonise the Orthodox-nationalist right and, in 2018, was beaten up by its thugs. For them, the agenda of religious populism pushed by President Erdogan in Turkey has proved to be the gift that goes on giving. Demonstrators filled the city's streets in summer 2020 after Hagia Sophia in Istanbul, a non-denominational museum since 1934, became a mosque again.

Still, the unfinished business that seethes just under the pavements here may breed hope rather than resentment. Local NGOs and volunteer groups have supported the newest migrants even as the national state has impeded or overlooked them – while the EU has paid to turn its back on the issue. Under Boutaris, the municipality proved an active partner in refugee research and welfare. Gestures to reclaim and honour a hybrid past continue. Muslim worship did return, briefly, to the 1902 Yeni Djami (New Mosque) – otherwise an annexe of the archaeological museum – for symbolic prayers in 2013. In July 2020 a new Jewish cultural centre opened, with Spanish official funding, to preserve and teach the heritage of Ladino: the Judaeo-Spanish spoken by the city's Jews, and the lyrical language of their songs and poetry.

Many ghosts, however, remain hard to spot. The grandiose modern blocks of the city's Aristotle University squat on the site of the mighty Jewish cemetery that once held 400,000 graves until vandalised and flattened in 1942. Several Muslim cemeteries have also vanished, although stray tombs do survive – for instance near the Rotunda. The largest visible congregation of the Muslim dead probably lies not in the old town but within the post-First World War Indian Cemetery – one of the traces left by the multi-national Allied forces of the 'Army of the Orient' which occupied the city and its environs after 1915.

Nothing remains of the lodges of the Sufi orders (Mevlevis, Bektashis and others) that exerted a unifying, connective influence on Salonican society for centuries. They worked, studied and argued together with their Orthodox counterparts; their own syncretic rituals often had a Christian flavour. During the worst atrocity of the Ottoman period – a massacre of Christians authorised by the rogue *pasha* Yusuf Bey after the Greek revolt of 1821 – the monastery *tekkes* gave shelter to their Nazarene brethren. But one monument built in the Ottoman twilight does still stand as testimony to the mind-bending plurality of identity and affiliation found in these parts. Constructed in 1902 in an ornate Italianate style, the Yeni Djami served the mysterious Ma'mim or Dönmeh community. They were descendants of the Jews who had followed the false Messiah, Sabbatai Zevi. He settled and recruited in the city in the 1650s during his empire-wide millenarian cult. When Sultan Mehmed IV told Sabbatai to convert or die, the wannabe saviour chose the prudent course. His many adherents clustered in Salonica did the same. Yet they retained a distinctive sense of community: Jewish Muslims distrusted by the orthodox in both camps, but able nonetheless to flourish, and to play leading roles in the city's commerce, culture and education. Embodied in this discreetly flamboyant mosque, the progressive Salonica of the decades up to the First World War owed much to this unique fusion of Islamic and Judaic belief and practice.

There's a stubborn legend, unsupported by any evidence I know, that the most celebrated child of late-Ottoman Selanik had Ma'mim ancestry. Mustafa Kemal, who would become Atatürk, was born in 1881 to a family of officials on what is now Apostolou Pavlou Street. The future founder of the Turkish Republic spent his schooldays in the city and, after he left for military academy in Istanbul, would return to his relatives in their three-storey home. Now a museum-shrine where the life and work of the nation-builder is reverently chronicled, the house has been under Turkish management since the 1930s, when the Greek municipality decided to buy it for the Turkish Consulate. It opened as a public museum in 1953 but, two years later, became the trigger for a notorious 'false flag' operation. Turkish nationalist agents planted a bomb here in order to blame Greece.

As they had planned, anti-Greek riots swept Istanbul, hastening the exodus of the city's Greek – and other non-Turkish – communities. Ethnic cleansing has diminished the original 'polis' as much as its Balkan sister.

## *IV*

Bristling with armed security and curated into a hagiographic shrine, the Atatürk House scarcely invites fond thoughts of old, multi-faith Salonica. Neither, for all their gastronomic charms, do the tourist-trap restaurants of Ladhadika, the sole small patch of the port district to have come through the twentieth century more or less unscathed. More than in the other great cities of the Ottoman Empire, the historical imagination has to work hard to summon up Salonica in its pre-Hellenic heyday. Spiced with the past, the good food helps. So does the music – such as the *rebetiko* songs of Roza Eskenazi, the great Istanbul-born (and Jewish) diva who grew up in the Salonica of the 1910s and perfected her art in its cafés. And literature too – although here too, a recent history of division has fragmented the record. Turkey's best-loved modern poet, Nazim Hikmet, was born here in 1902, into an elite Ottoman family with typically multinational origins that stretched from Poland to Georgia. He left early, though, and never returned. His poetry speaks of exile and loss but his own birthplace hardly figures in it. 'Some people know all about plants some about fish,' laments his poem 'Autobiography': 'I know separation.' By contrast, Nikos Gabriel Pentzikis, born in the same city in 1908, dwells intently on its past in the Modernist fiction he began to publish in the 1930s. Pentzikis, however, looked back beyond the Ottoman epoch towards an imaginary Byzantium that fired his mystical, inclusive version of Orthodox Christianity. His visionary memoir *Mother Thessaloniki* fuses author and city so completely that his own body-parts come to represent its different neighbourhoods.

As a Greek, Pentzikis never had to quit his adored maternal home. The émigrés, willing or forced, whose departure bleached the city of cultural complexity in the twentieth century also created a city of the mind and heart. In their exile, nostalgia for a ruined urban paradise began to bloom. Nowhere do you find it voiced with more bittersweet fervour than in Leon Sciaky's memoir *Farewell to Salonica*. Born in 1893, the son of a grain-merchant, Sciaky grew up in the Ladino-speaking Jewish hub of the old city, cosily nestled among co-religionists but in amicable daily contact with Muslims, Orthodox Greeks and Bulgarians. In gorgeously wistful prose, he evokes the muezzins' calls at sunset, the scent-filled streets crammed with the crafts of pastrycooks, coppersmiths, woodcarvers and weavers of various nationalities and faiths, the romantic Spanish ballads sung by his *nonas* (grandmothers) and *tias* (aunts), the stout Slavic peasantry of the fertile hinterland who supplied the family business. The railway, that symbolic spearhead of the 'powerful but soulless' *Frenks* (ie Westerners), brings its ironclad foretaste of modernity to this timeless late-Ottoman idyll. Still, 'No consciousness of gathering clouds obscured the sunshine of my garden.' But the real serpent in this Balkan Eden is nationalism itself. The Bulgarian insurgents of the IMRO underground blow up banks to ferment inter-communal suspicion. At first, the Young Turk movement of radical army officers – which seized power in Salonica in 1908 – promises a final 'end to discrimination and injustice' in a reformed Ottoman Empire. Sciaky recalls that 'Mohammedan *hodjas*, *softas* and dervishes walked arm in arm with Orthodox priests and Jewish rabbis' to greet their anti-sectarian revolution.

Within a few years, however, the Young Turk leaders had set out along the path of ethnic exclusivity that, during the First World War, would result in the Armenian genocide. The fissile demagogy of the two Balkan wars that preceded general European conflict not only divided Muslims from Jews and Christians. It even set Greeks and Bulgarians at one another's throats. Outbursts of ethnic fury reduced the mixed Macedonian villages where Leon and his father passed happy summers with Muslim, Greek and Bulgarian friends to smoking, bloodstained ruins. The Sciaky family left for America in 1915, and never went back. Published in 1945, after the Nazi deportations had left a mere few thousand Jews alive in the port whose society and culture they had substantially shaped for half a millennium, *Farewell to Salonica* closes with an anguished exile's plea that humanity free itself from 'the world of narrow nationalisms… of the smug belief in the supremacy of one people over another'.

That 'world of narrow nationalisms' still batters and splinters Thessaloniki. After a spell of deceptive calm, the Mediterranean refugee emergency returned in 2020 as the EU's migrant-control bargain with Turkey began to unravel. Renewed instability gave a fresh impetus to nationalist agitators in and near the city. The policy of shipping asylum-seekers from island camps to the Greek mainland led, in May, to protests intended to prevent a busload of refugees from occupying a hotel in Pella, north of Thessaloniki. History has a way of devising ironies and punchlines no author would dare invent. For Pella – where grand expanses of columns and mosaics hint at the scale of its ancient palaces – was the birthplace, in 356BC, of Alexander the Great. He would conquer not merely Asia Minor but the East as far as today's Pakistan: in other words, the whole span of nations that now send their uprooted people back to the world-devouring warrior's homelands in search of a safer and more hopeful life.

It would, of course, be a blessing if Thessaloniki chose to take more care of its non-Greek past; if not only the Holocaust Museum but an (as-yet unthinkable) Ottoman-era museum rose to remember and celebrate the different peoples who lived here. Yiannis Boutaris's tenure as the city's mayor did see non-trivial progress along the road to historical inclusivity. Yet the deepest honour to old Salonica would be a long-term welcome for the latest communities of homeless arrivals in Greece, given by a city stable and prosperous enough to embrace incomers without fearing that the present, as well as the past, amounts to a 'zero-sum game'. When Leon Sciaky heard the music of the Middle East drifting through the streets of Salonica, the 'nostalgic note' of Turkish songs spoke to him of 'a world in which I was secure and happy'. If his non-Greek successors can hear the same sounds, and feel the same warmth, that civic peace will mean more than any concrete tribute to the faded patchwork of the past.

# STRANDS OF KAZAKH CULTURE

*Natalya Seitakhmetova*
*Zhanara Turganbayeva*
*Marhabbat Nurov*

As we go about our daily routine and listen to the chatter of our internal monologue, we rarely find time to pause to consider why we behave in particular ways. What motivates our thoughts or actions, the way we respond to certain situations or our attitudes to people? Is our way of life and our thoughts shaped by ethnicity or religion? Or perhaps age or education determines our habits and views? As we ponder such notions, we ask ourselves how 130 nationalities traditionally living together in the same territory, which is today's Kazakhstan, can have an identical way of life and thinking? Kazakhstan is perhaps a forgotten part of the Muslim world. Like Turkey or Malaysia it is not on the Muslim tourist maps. Yet, Kazakhstan has an immensely rich Islamic history, while also being a multicultural wonder.

The multicultural processes of our time are formed by different configurations, which are often unpredictable, and culture along with its traditions is in constant flux. The fragility of national cultures, paradoxically, is also a mode of survival. Traditional cultures that preserve the origins of being and ethnic identity transcend dialogue with the Other. They do this by communicating and engaging via different mediums. To understand the Other, one needs to appreciate the history, values and the culture that shaped them. To understand the phenomenon of 'Kazakhstani culture', we need to appreciate the different religious and ethnic strands that have, over centuries, come together, intertwined, and created a mosaic for which there is no unambiguous explanation.

The interweaving of Turkic, nomadic and Islamic traditions in the Kazakh culture has created a unique model, an organic combination of ancient and modern traditions. The inclusion of spiritual and religious traditions of the past, create a uniqueness that gives Kazakh culture its exceptional identity.

The history of Kazakh culture, especially of the Soviet period, has for many years been viewed through a biased lens as the history of Kazakhstan was seen largely in relation to the Soviet era. It denigrated the nomadic culture and suppressed spiritual traditions. This tendency extended to coverage of the Turkic and Islamic periods in the history of Kazakhstan culture. However, a new era of more objective history of the country began with independence. Neglected aspects of our history were brought to the fore, and a more impartial and multi-layered cultural picture of the past, incorporating spiritual and ethnic traditions, began to emerge.

The inclusive history of Kazakh culture begins with a re-examination of the role of the Great Silk Road, along which were transported not only goods but also spiritual artifacts, and which served as a bridge of dialogue between communities. Merchants brought manuscripts, jewellery, knowledge of religions and cultures, and offered alternatives to existing customs and models of life. Today the importance of the Silk Road in global history is beginning to be appreciated, with Iftikhar H Malik's excellent publication *The Silk Road and Beyond* an example. The great Silk Road, so effectively brought alive in Malik's writing, is a dialogical exchange of cultural traditions and an embodied interchange between East and West, West and East. The ancient land of Kazakhstan was not only greeted with the traditions of other cultures, but was itself the fertile soil on which spiritual and religious traditions grew. Buddhism, Manichaeism, Zoroastrianism, Confucianism, Taoism, Judaism, and later – Christianity and Islam illuminated the paths here, sometimes lingering, sometimes dissolving, sometimes absorbing the life-giving juice of another, nomad culture. The diversity of cultural traditions had the potential to alter beyond recognition the nomadic culture, but it remained fundamentally unchanged, thanks to its own culture code.

We owe the very term 'culture' to the Roman orator and lawyer, Cicero, who defined it as 'cultivating' the soil. Cicero used an agricultural metaphor for the refinement of the soul. A notion reflected in *Avesta,* the main collection of religious texts of Zoroastrianism, written in the Avestan language. Later, this idea was developed by the great Persian poet, Firdowsi (940–1020) in his *Shahnameh*. It is here that we read about the one who cultivates the land as being a moral person, 'He who sows bread, he sows righteousness', and learn that the nomadic way of life is led by 'the owners of beautiful herds'. Nomadic civilisation has evolved over millennia, it has a long and distinguished history, which includes the tribal and cultural practices. But modernity looked down on nomadic culture, indeed it did not even recognise it as culture, as cultural progress was associated first with agriculture of settled communities and then with urbanisation. But a reassessment of nomadic culture began in the early twentieth century with studies of the spiritual and material monuments of nomadic culture, and its enormous contribution to the history of human civilisation

In Kazakhstan, the objective assessment of nomadic culture was pioneered by archaeologist and historian, K A Akishev (1924–2003). Akishev published extensively on the history of nomads; and from 1954 onwards led a series of archaeological expeditions which made some astounding discoveries. Akishev excavated Otrar city, located along the Silk Road in Kazakhstan, and described as Central Asia's 'ghost town'. He explored the Saka pyramids in the Bessjhatyr Kurgan region; the Saka were nomads of Iranian origin. And he excavated the fourth and third centuries BC burial mounds in Issyk Kurgan. For Akishev, it was important to study the original historic sources that talk about ancient nomads; and he and his colleagues based their excavations on their reading of Herodotus, the father of Greek history, Diodorus, the famous historian, Strabo, the founder of ancient geography, and ancient Pahlavi and Iranian sources.

Herodotus, for example, informs us of the origins of the Scythians, desert tribes that created a highly spiritual and material culture. The ancestor of the Scythians – Targitay and his three sons: Lipoksay, Arpoksay and Koloksay – became the founders of this civilisation. Herodotus suggests that the Scythians from Asia are Saks tribes, more specifically the Tigrakhaud Saks.

Thus, we see that the history of Kazakhstan began in those distant times when humanity 'cultivated' the world with its material and spiritual practice.

In the burial mounds of Issyk Kurgan, in the northern Tian Shan mountains in eastern Kyrgyzstan, Akishev discovered 'a man in golden clothes', or the 'Golden Man' – 'Altyn Adam' – which opened up opportunities for restoration of a period of intense development in the formation of Saks' culture. Female jewellery made of gold, crafts made of bronze and sheet gold, hats, products with images of animals in the so-called 'beast' (Scythian) style were all found. They provided evidence that back in the 7th, 5th, 4th centuries BC there was a sophisticated culture practiced by the Scythian tribes. Later, in the era of independence, archaeological research would continue and several more of the same artifacts would be found. But Akishev's 1969 discovery was a hugely significant event for contemporary Kazakhstan. In 2001, the government issued a coin with the model of the Altyn Adam and the gold ornaments found at Issyk Kurgan.

Akishev revolutionised the study of nomadic culture. His scientific research, hard work and archaeological finds laid the foundations of nomadology in Kazakhstan. He rescued the history of Ancient Kazakhstan from obscurity and showed how it evolved through the stages of development from Sak's culture to Turkic, Turkic-Islamic, Kazakh and Kazakhstani, organically incorporating other cultures while maintaining its spiritual and ethical source. Thus, it was proved that the nomad culture reached its civilisational peak by the sixth century.

Nomadic civilisation became the foundation on which other cultures flourished, incorporating the spiritual and religious values of Islam. The pluralistic space of Ancient Kazakhstan was tolerant and open. Maverannahr and the whole region of Semirechye, the southern part of south-eastern Kazakhstan, were flourishing centres of arts and learning. Here the sciences, theoretical and applied, were born and thrived, masters of applied art worked, ancient *akyns* (poets) composed poems, people used letters, the language was polished, the ancient Otrar library was a hive of learning, and livestock management was practiced. Russian archaeologist M P Gryaznov has pointed out that researchers had long concluded that the material culture of ancient Kazakh society was formed under the influence of the Mongolian culture. This has now been shown to be false. The types of burial and the production of bronze arrowheads of the Mongols and the ancient Kazakhs are totally different; as are the monuments of the two cultures. The ancient tribes of Kazakhstan did not need the Mongolian experience, since they had long mastered the technique of constructing monuments. The culture of the Karasuk era symbolised an independent material and spiritual practice of the Kazakh tribes of antiquity. The technique of casting bronze and making sleeve tips for arrows, cooks implements and ornaments – all speak of a high stage of material culture.

Kazakh culture is not just a product of its ancient roots; it also has enormous influence from various religious traditions of the regions. Different local traditions created various opportunities for the adoption of a religion, involvement in it, and their relation to the nomads. The history of religious traditions on the land of Kazakhstan shows that Buddhism, Manichaeism, Zoroastrianism, Christianity and others were widely practiced before the advent of Islam. Manichaean preachers widely used the Turkic language to popularise Manichaean teachings, which in the third and fourth centuries was popular in Central Asia. The famous tenth/eleventh century polymath, al-Bruni, notes the influence of Manichaeism on the Eastern Turks. Both he and the tenth century bibliophile, al-Nadim, point out that Manichaeism was in fact persecuted during the period of Islamic dynasties. Buddhist texts existed in the form of 'jataka' – a genre of Buddhist instructive stories related to the reincarnation of bodhisattvas becoming Buddhas, as well as in the form of sutras that explained the basic tenets of Buddhism. They were translated from Sanskrit and Chinese into Sogdian and Uyghur. Buddhism penetrated the territory of ancient, late medieval Kazakhstan but despite permeating the national consciousness, it did not exert a strong influence on existing ideas about spiritual life. Judaism and Christianity were more popular, with some tribes embracing these religious traditions. A few Turkic tribes accepted Christianity – one of the Kazakh tribes, the Kerey tribe, is a noted example. However, Judaism and Christianity did not spread widely largely because they clashed with Tengrism, the prevailing religion of the Central Asia Steppe. Nevertheless, the culture of this region, one way or another, changed under the influence of different religions, which affected the styles of architecture, linguistic borrowings in languages, music, except for one genre – poetic, which remained original and exclusively authentic, consisting of the unity of word and music, that entered the treasury of world poetry labelled 'Kazakh poetry'.

The restored picture of Ancient Kazakhstan has made it clear that the cultural space was surprisingly filled with rich traditions in languages, literature and spiritual creativity. Gradually, Saks' tribes began to play a prominent role in the history of the vast expanses of Central Asia, the whole of Turan, which included Turkestan (East, West, Chinese with the capital Khan-Balyk), Maverannahr, Tokharistan, Badakhshan, Khorezm, Desht-i-Kypcha – all the lands that came to be called the lands of the Turks. After the fall of the Sassanian dynasty, Turkic nomads founded the Turkic Kaganate, which was important for the development of the economy, politics and culture not only locally, but also globally. The Great Silk Road passed through it, and the Turks occupied a leading place in the trade, economic and cultural exchange of East and West. When the Muslim armies moved towards Iran in 651, the Arabs tried to conquer the lands of the East Turkic and West Turkic Kaganates, and later the Turgesh Kaganate but faced fierce Turkic resistance. Arab historians referred to part of these lands by the Arabic term 'Maverannahr', captured from 651-671. Located beyond the river, north of the Amu-Darya, Maverannahr was a military-administrative enclave but not politically important.

The year 751 was a turning point in the history of the Turgesh Kaganate. During the battle of the Talas Valley, in the area of the modern city of Taraz, Arab armies defeated the Chinese invaders with the support of the Karluks. In 756, Karluk Kaganate was formed as a reward for Karluk support in the fight against the forces of the Emperor of China and the Turks became part of the Arab Caliphate. But to suggest that the Islamisation of Turkic culture took place immediately would be wrong. Indeed, the Islamisation of Turkic culture is a slow process that has never been completed. The cultural construction of the Turks has taken the form of two traditions: Turkic and Islamic. It could not be otherwise, given the highly developed cultural and traditional space of nomads which Islam encountered.

Maverannahr and historically adjoining territories belonging to the Turks, witnessed the interaction of various ethnic groups of people and languages. As a result, the Sogdian language was gradually supplanted by the Turkic language. The eleventh century Turkic linguist and scholar from Kashgara, Mahmud al-Kashgari, who wrote a 'Dictionary of Turkic dialects' – Divan *Lugat at-Turk* – noted that Sogdians who lived in Semirechye accepted the clothes and customs of the Turks and residents of Balasagun in Semirechye spoke Turkic, while the language of the population from Balasagun to the modern Shymkent city of Ispidzhab, was mixed, Turkic and Arabic. But by the beginning of the twelfth century the dominant language of this region was Turkic; Arabic played an important role in the scientific and business world. However, by virtue of linguistic exchange, Parsisms, Arabisms and various Turkic-Iranian dialects appeared in the languages of Maverannahr.

The advent of Arabic writing helped with the spread of Islam. But there are also other reasons why the region embraced Islam. Pre-Islamic religions of the region – Manichaeism, Zoroastrianism, Buddhism, Judaism, and Christianity – were dominated by privilege and class in the form of priests, castes, clans, and so forth. In contrast, the Turkic society was, comparatively, a society with less hierarchy, where freedom and justice were considered the main principles of life. Islam appeared to be more closely aligned to their pre-existing values. But Islam was adopted with some changes. Arabic writing was modelled in accordance with the sound characteristics of the Turkic language, and sometimes even additions were introduced. Turkic spiritual traditions were maintained; as were the folk traditions, values, principles, and even the routine of everyday life.

Turkic nomads and Arab Bedouins were mainly engaged in cattle breeding and military affairs, which were at the highest level of development. In both nomadic and Bedouin societies, codes of honour based on the Turkic or Arab ethical tradition were developed. Like the Turks, the Arabs were proud and independent, both considering it important to have status and to be ranked as a tribe. The cultural space of medieval Kazakhstan developed in the crucible of this economic and political time. It was the most difficult period of the first state formations, such as the First and Second Turkic Kaganate, the Turgesh and the Karluk Kaganates, Kypchak Khanate, and Karakitays and Oguzes. In 960, the Karakhanid government carried out religious reform and established Islam as a state religion.

Today's Kazakhstan is a state with a history of many thousands of years, with ancient cultural traditions, and we, the modern generation, are not just heirs to a great culture, but, as the Japanese say, we own it. In the cultural palette of traditions, Islamic tradition is paramount, and Islamic culture, formed and developed on the territory of Kazakhstan throughout history, plays a vital role in the formation of the spiritual world of modern Kazakhstan. The majority of the population following the Hanafi madhab, a moderate traditional Sunni school of thought. Kazakh society is liberal, and tolerant of religious and cultural differences; the emphasis is on promoting dialogue. Islamic traits in modern Kazakhstan's culture are to be found in art, poetry, architecture and music. The development of cultural trends is associated with Turkic, Kazakh and Islamic traditions.

The vast intellectual heritage of Kazakhstan goes back to the ninth century and Abu Nasr al-Farabi, the great philosopher considered second only to Aristotle, whose famous works are the basis for the development of humanitarian areas and the complementarity of the cultures of the Islamic World and the West. Brilliantly combining the advanced ideas of ancient philosophy, ancient science and Islamic tradition in his work, al-Farabi opened the prospect of a new hermeneutics of intellectual and religious texts with critical thinking. In September 2020, the 1,150th anniversary of Al-Farabi was celebrated with seminars, symposiums and cultural events throughout the universities, scientific centres and cultural organisations in Kazakhstan – particularly in the university named after him, the Al-Farabi Kazakh National University, based in the capital Almaty.

Chingiz Aitmatov (1928–2008), the prolific novelist and leading literary figure of Kyrgzstan, coined the concept of *mankurt* – the image of a person who has forgotten his cultural origins and has erased his cultural memory. The people of Kazakhstan have not become *mankurt* for we have preserved our diverse cultural and religious heritage and memory, including the ancient legacy and uniqueness of nomadic traditions. Contemporary is a secular state, but the presence of many religious and cultural traditions is Kazakhstani historical reality. They are the source of our spiritual strength. With such a long history, Kazakhstani culture strives for innovation, cultural adaptation of its values, and, at the same time, seeks to maintain its own national identity.

# INNER JOURNEYS

*Saimma Dyer*

I was very young when we were gathered at my uncle's home to mourn the sudden passing of his wife in childbirth. The small apartment was packed, in the manner of South Asian custom, with every family member who had travelled across the country to be there, and the noisy prayers were difficult to follow with so many people crying. My mum was busy in the kitchen and I was left feeling lost and confused. I hadn't even cried for my aunt of whom I had vague memories – a beautiful, glamorous woman who was kind to me the few times we'd met. But prayer seemed appropriate and I searched for a way to do that, to let my aunt know that I was thinking of her. I found escape from the noise in the garden and picked a buttercup, its bright yellow warmth perhaps reminding me of my aunt's radiant smile. I said a prayer to God to look after my aunt's soul and not let her be too sad that she had left her children behind, and I placed the flower in a niche in the stone wall. I told myself that my prayer would be accepted if God took my flower.

A few hours later I dashed back to garden, full of trepidation. The flower was gone. I felt a sense of gladness, and I thanked God for accepting my prayer, believing that my flower had flown up to heaven and joined my aunt. I felt like I had truly spoken to God – and I had been heard. That was my earliest memory of connecting to God.

As the years passed, my connection to God diminished as I was exposed to a dogmatic, rigid and fear-inducing Islam. At my daily madrasa lessons I learned how to read and recite Arabic, but not to understand it, a peculiarity of South Asian culture I was to learn later in life. The imam warned us about the dangers of hellfire and how almost everything in life seemed directed to lead us into that hellfire. I was taught how I must be a good Muslim, with all the rules that entailed. And yet, the examples of the adult Muslims in my life were at stark odds with what I was being taught.

My environment was steeped in toxic patriarchy and this became my Islam, where men could physically and mentally abuse the powerless in one moment and in the next breath be extolling the virtues of the Prophet Muhammad as the perfect man and how we must all love him unconditionally. I questioned how perfect this prophet could be if he allowed this type of behaviour. How could he be a messenger of God – unless God also allowed this behaviour? In which case, why would I follow this religion when all it seemed to bring was fear and heartache? And how did I know I was even following the right religion?

In my early teens, I tried to confront this internal confusion. Sitting in my room late one night, I braced myself and whispered... 'I don't believe in God – and I don't love Muhammad!' I sat, breathless with fear, and waited for lightning to strike me down for my blasphemy. Nothing came for some time. And then extremely slowly, a gentle feeling came through my heart with such certainty: *God exists, nothing else matters.* I felt reassurance and the truth of a divine intelligence, beyond religion and prophets. And I decided to stop worrying about the details and just get through life.

But I still performed outwardly as a Muslim – necessary in my family, and sometimes also a comfort to be part of the ritual. Even when I left home I still did my *salah*, turning to it when I felt hopelessness and despair, finding comfort in trying to connect with that voice in my heart that told me God did exist. And I still fasted during Ramadan – not doing so would have upset my mum. And since *salah* and Ramadan are such key pillars of Islam, I accepted myself as nominally Muslim, *culturally* Muslim: Muslim enough for my family. And while I survived, just about, through university and my early working life with this minimal connection, things started to unravel in my mid-twenties. I only did my *salah* during Ramadan, and even then I missed many fasts. My heart felt hardened and completely disconnected from anything beyond that which I needed to survive from day to day. So when love came knocking, hand-in-hand with God, I had a hard time accepting it.

My husband's journey to Islam came through the thirteenth century poet and mystic, Muhammad Jalaluddin Rumi, whose message of love, beauty, and ecstasy in God sounded a far cry from the Islam I thought I knew. Despite myself, I became curious about this Sufism that Rumi spoke about.

I was highly critical at first, even attending my initial Sufi gatherings with a mind to save everyone from these so-called shaikhs who attempted to place themselves between God and the individual. The irony was not lost on me that I was a hypocrite – if I didn't really see myself as a *proper* Muslim, what did it matter whether Sufism was Islam or not? But it seemed I really was a *cultural* Muslim and very self-righteous about my inherited religion. And there was surely hidden mercy in that as I went in with such arrogance and was tricked, *tricked I say*, by the beauty, love, and honesty that I was faced with. This was not the Islam I had grown up with, this was not the Islam I knew. And then I realised – I had not known Islam.

The people I met were kind, compassionate, and honestly talked about the difficulties they found in the Qu'ran and the hadith – they questioned and explored everything! No issue was taboo and my eyes were opened up to the essence of this religion that I had struggled with for so long. I learned about the many tools of awakening and so began my journey to opening my heart and mind.

It started with an Awakening to Presence. Kabir Helminski describes presence in his book, *Living Presence*, as the state of being consciously aware, in alignment with our deepest and highest capacities:

> The practice of presence invites us to a conscious relationship with God. Faith, righteous action, ethics, and social justice are all founded upon a state in which the human being remembers God. Yet, the capacity to remember God is related to the ability to be awake, to be here. To act with intention (*niyah*), with reflection (*tafakkur*), with self-vigilance (*taqwa*), and with beneficence (*ihsan*) presumes a state of conscious presence…
>
> Presence signifies the quality of consciously being here. It is the activation of a higher level of awareness that allows all our other human functions – such as thought, feeling, and action – to be known, developed, and harmonised. Presence is the way in which we occupy space, as well as how we flow and move. It shapes our self-image and emotional tone. It determines the degree of our alertness, openness, and warmth. Presence decides whether we leak and scatter our energy or embody and direct it.

This was an extremely difficult concept for me to get my head around at the start of my spiritual journey. This 'presence' seemed simple and yet at the same time so profoundly beyond my conception that I felt like I would never understand it, let alone be able to achieve it. The more I tried to intellectually comprehend this state, the more elusive it became. It was only when I stopped using my mind that was I able to see how it could manifest in my life. I focussed on my *niyah* (intentions) and started to be more conscious when I made them. First with the ritual ablution: something I had always done quickly, never paying any attention to the action but seeing it merely as a requirement of prayer. Conscious ablution became a beautiful way to connect with God, thinking about each movement and the purity of the water brought such gratitude. Camille Helminski writes that ablution 'is washing for the purpose of worship and purity, to be in a state of receptivity and clear openness to the Divine Presence'. In her explanation on how to perform the ritual ablution, she offers ways of understanding each cleansing movement through prayer and gratitude: for hands that 'might be used for the Good, for healing, for the sharing of Grace, that they might touch with compassion'; to consider 'what enters and goes out from one's mouth – how do we eat, and how do we speak'; to consider how we can breathe 'with gratitude for the air that brings us continued life, that purifies our cells, for the capacity to perceive fragrance'; how the face is 'the place of manifestation of individual being...might shine with awareness of the Life-Giver; as our hands pass over our eyes, we consider what we perceive with these eyes, where do we let our glance rest?'; how we move and embrace with our arms and 'pray that our movement might be for the Good, in alignment with the best of our being, the truest capacities of our God given nature'; when wiping our head and 'our hands pass over the crown, we honour also this portal of light, that last place to close over with bone when we arrive in this world, still resonant with subtle energy, and we give thanks for all our capacities and receptivity of mind and the structure that protects it, for the sensitivity of hair and its warming and cooling protection'; cleaning our ears 'we offer prayer for better hearing of the messages of the Divine through all the sounds of this creation, of the resonances of Revelation, paying attention to what it is to which we listen'; wiping our necks and 'bringing one's awareness to this sensitive area that contains nerves of conveyance between head and torso and extremities, relaxing any tense energy that may have accumulated there, easing constriction, opening, and giving thanks for all the communication between systems of this body'; and finally as we wash our feet 'we consider where it is they have been walking, where we might best be called to walk, and where we are walking now, to prayer. With awareness and intention, we might bring the traversal of these feet always within a place of prayer, carrying that state of prayer with us everywhere.

When I started completing my ablution in this way, I arrived in a state of presence without effort, and as I moved into my ritual prayer, my mind was calm and clear. And I became full of awe at this tradition that connected the mind, body, and heart in such a simple yet profound way. My awareness of my body, heightened during ablution, extended into my *salah*. Stepping onto my prayer mat became intentional. Sometimes, if I had lost awareness, I would step off and step back on with presence. It became an act of permission – requesting an audience with my *Rabb*. I didn't take it for granted that God would listen if I wasn't making an effort on my part.

And my attention during *salah* changed. I had never been taught about this concept of presence at my childhood madrasa, where *salah* was completed as quickly as possible. I remember those who lagged behind were mocked for their slowness, and those who were deemed most proficient would hit the floor in *sujood* with a thud, the positions done in a quick mechanical manner. I had always been somewhere between the two, and my mind had certainly always been on something other than remembrance of God. So while in my childhood I had learned the *outer* form of how to pray, I was now learning, in my late twenties, the *inner* form of how to pray.

Maintaining presence during *salah* was still a tricky journey, and, at one particularly difficult point in my life when I felt like I was going backwards, one of my teachers suggested I try concentrating on performing just one *rakat* with no recitation and just mindfulness of my breath. It sounded like such a radical idea but it worked. By breaking my habitual recitation, where my tongue spoke the words by rote but my mind was planning dinner, I was able to connect again to my body and my heart with a calm mind. Every so often, I still do this practice when I start to feel my monkey-mind chattering when it should be still, and bring myself back to awareness of my breath and movements and connection to Allah. As Rumi tell us in the *Mathnawi*:

Since consciousness is the inmost nature and essence of the soul,
the more aware you are the more spiritual you are.
Awareness is the effect of the spirit:
anyone who has this in abundance
is a man or woman of God.

In time I would learn Awakening with Zhikr. In my childhood, not a month would go by without somebody holding a *khatam*, a gathering of remembrance where Arabic phrases were repeated using dried date stones to count the quantity recited. These were held to commemorate a variety of events – births, deaths, returning pilgrims from hajj, the Prophet Muhammad's *mawlid* (birthday). There was little to no presence in these gatherings as everyone gossiped while reciting, date stones clicking into a bowl at a speed I marvelled at. I was woefully slow, worried that any miscounts on my side would nullify the prayers for whomever we were holding the *khatam* for – and I was irritated by the noise and distraction. Whenever possible, I used homework as an excuse to get out of attending these gatherings, preferring to recite a set amount at home and let my mum add it to the tally at the *khatam*.

When I came to learning about the practice of *zhikr*, I didn't immediately connect it to these gatherings from my childhood. The way I experienced it was quite different – and at first, extremely disconcerting. When I attended my first Sufi gathering, the *zhikr* began and the attendees intoned aloud with eyes closed and gentle movement of their heads. I kept peeping through my eyes, not wanting to do it wrong but also not completely comfortable. What if someone was watching me? Why would they watch me? How long was it going to go on for? It was going on too long… I ran out of breath trying to keep up with the recitation. The phrases were familiar, but I had never said them out loud like this…*Astagfirullah*…*La ilaha il Allah*…*Allah*… And then came *Hu*, a long intonation that lasted the length of a breath – and these people had very long breaths. I had to bite my cheek to keep from giggling with nervousness and surprise. I had heard people say *Allah-Hu*, but I had never heard just *Hu* before – I hadn't even known it was a word. It sounded like something was missing.

As time went by I became accustomed to the strangeness and found myself more comfortable with the people. It was a small group that met one evening a week in someone's house. We learned to develop a resonance with our voices, attuning to each other so that the *zhikr* sounded more refined and melodious. We were no choir, but we became a small community, sharing this break in our busy London lives, just a few hours a week of conscious breath and awareness.

The first retreat I attended comprised a group of thirty-five people – and the first time we did *zhikr* I could not close my eyes. The sound of all those voices, male and female, united in calling out *Allah*, was astonishing. My bones vibrated with the intensity and I cried uncontrollably, my sobs muffled by the resonance of the Divine. 'In order to become human', writes Suleyman Hayati Loras,

> we need to always be within the Divine Presence – to be aware of God, to hold God in our hearts. When a human being performs *zhikr*, their spirit – their heart starts to open. Their intelligence becomes more refined and more expansive. Their bodies become healthier. A beautiful condition comes about – similar to the one that is brought about by good music. The whole being opens up like a flower, and the divine secret – the things you couldn't understand or know about before – begin to be revealed to you. This is why it's necessary to make *zhikr*. For human beings, it's a very good thing.

I wanted to experience this state, to open up, to understand myself. Having had a taste of this at the retreat, I started working on developing a daily practice and not just once a week during our small gatherings. A hadith of the Prophet Muhammad states that the best spiritual practice is that which can be sustained. Commitment and dedicated practice is paramount but it was not easy. Apart from doing my prayers at home I found that I could do zhikr in any moment I wished – at lunchtime on a park seat, sitting on the train, or on the rare occasion I made the effort to pray salah in an empty room at work, I would add some moments of zhikr too. And it very quickly became a lifeline. I would find myself drawing upon zhikr when I was feeling overwhelmed or going through difficulties. On a number of occasions when I had to deal with challenging circumstances and needed some extra support from the Divine, I would wrap my prayer beads around my wrist and feel like they were a shield, protecting me. My 'go-to' zhikr became (and still remains) the declaration of faith: La ilaha il Allah. I learned how to recite La ilaha on the out breath, emptying myself of any negative thoughts, and breathing in il Allah, filling myself with God. The Mevlevi Wird, the daily litany of prayers that students in the lineage of Rumi recite, includes a list of short prayers and invocations, including La ilaha il Allah for 'facing all fears, "There is no God but God."' I had never seen the shahada used in this way but the more I did the zhikr, the more I saw how it really did work in the face of fear. Zhikr starts with bringing your awareness to your breath, and with this zhikr that followed the flow of breath in and out of the body it very quickly calmed the mind and brought my thoughts under control. I felt the truth of Loras' words that my 'intelligence [became] more refined and more expansive'.

But there was still some distance to travel before I could reach my destination: the struggle with my Self or ego. Different Sufi traditions have different ways of observing meditation – *muraqaba*, defined as the practice of watching over the heart with meditation to acquire knowledge about it, its surroundings, and its creator. An associated notion is *muhasaba*, the practice of self-reckoning, analysing your deeds and thoughts in the hope of refining them to bring one closer to God. Jeremy Henzell-Thomas notes that 'self-reckoning is to take on board that sense of personal accountability and responsibility which is absolutely integral to the *jihad al-akbar,* the struggle with the lower self, the false self or ego.' Developing a state of witnessing one's behaviour and being able to objectively analyse it without being overly critical and harsh about oneself is a process that requires compassion and truth. So *muhasabah, as* Henzell-Thomas explains, is not simply about 'annihilating or supressing the apparently disabling aspects of one's personality, but of finding the essential virtues underlying them'.

The Islamic understanding of the *nafs* is about bringing it under control, not of annihilating or supressing it. This is a more coherent viewpoint than the concept that we should destroy the ego – how can we be sovereign beings without a healthy sense of self? And getting to a healthy state requires witnessing those aspects that are out of balance within ourselves – 'disabling' us from achieving our full potential. This process was not pretty: being willing to look at all the ugly aspects of myself, really accept that it was me and not being able to blame these parts on others, was challenging and I had to take it slow. It felt like every time I peeled an onion layer off my personality I discovered more of my unhealthy *nafs* that kicked and screamed at the exposure to light and awareness.

I sometimes compare the spiritual path to the sci-fi movie, *The Matrix* – if I knew how hard it was going to be, would I have instead taken the blue pill and remained asleep? Once you start on the journey, it is difficult to ignore what you have seen of yourself. But these practices are not done in isolation, everything supports them to create a coherent system of knowing yourself. My practice of *muhasaba* deepened through *zhikr* and learning to still my mind in meditation.

However, out of all my spiritual practices, meditation is the hardest for me. I am not particularly good at doing 'nothing'. *Salah* is movement with presence, *zhikr* is reciting with presence, *muhasaba* is reflecting with presence. But *muraqaba*, the ability to watch over the state of my heart without distraction – no movement, no reciting, no thinking – remains a struggle. One of my teachers once explained *zhikr* as calling to God, and *muraqaba* as listening to God. This helped to give it context and allowed me to stop forcing something to happen – after all, if I was too busy trying too much, how could I hear?

But hearing God is not like hearing a voice in my head, and again I had to work on my projections of what I was expecting during meditation. The twentieth century scholar Abdülbaki Golpinarli described *muraqabah* as 'seeing and being seen by Allah'. *Muraqaba* contains the Divine Name of *ar-Raqib*, the Watchful, and this watchfulness is full of presence.

Another twentieth century scholar, Huseyin Azmi Dede, in his *Selections from Adab* (*Nuhbetü'l-Âdâb*), points out that the practice of *muraqaba* is rooted in the Prophet's practice, which he performed with his congregation after *salah*. This helped me to connect to it beyond my understanding of it being primarily a Buddhist practice, where they calmed the mind but there was no connection to God. Shams of Tabriz brings all these practices together when he says:

> Remain watchful. Struggle with alien thoughts. Keep your attention on what you are doing, whether outwardly or inwardly. Observe what captures your attention and why. Be constantly aware of the Divine Presence. Accustom yourself to recognise the quality of the divine presence in your heart. The "loss of self" allows us to participate in a greater Being.

It wasn't long before I was Awakening to the Feminine. I had always struggled with reading translations of the Qur'an – I had tried in my teenage years when I was struggling with my faith, thinking that reading the meaning for myself would surely be different than hearing it from the men at the mosque. I did not get far. My local library had one translation in English (and I never thought there could be more) and it reinforced what I had heard at the madrasa – Abraham's God was a harsh patriarch and we were destined for the hell-fire, particularly the women. There were many footnotes that referenced hadiths that spoke to the failings of women, and why they would make up the majority of those in the hellfire.

I only came back to the Qur'an after my first retreat, when I heard Camille Helminski reciting and translating verses from the Qur'an – and instead of using the usual masculine gender noun of 'He', she described God as 'He/She'. It was mind-blowing. And confusing – part of me felt it was wrong and blasphemous but I couldn't understand why. My inner turmoil left me unable to approach Camille and speak to her directly, but I noted that the book that she was reading from was available in the retreat bookstore and I grabbed one of the few copies to dissect when I returned home – *The Mevlevi Wird*. Compiled by Camille Helminski, the current publication has English translation and transliteration of the Arabic so you can read it in either language.

I was amazed to find verses translated in new and unexpectedly beautiful ways. The Throne verse is one I had recited regularly in Arabic. I thought I had a cursory understanding of the English meaning but the *Wird* gave new depths to the familiar words. And the jarring quality of seeing 'He/She' instead of the traditional 'He' shook me. Intellectually I knew God was beyond gender, and yet a whole lifetime (and centuries before me) had shaped God into a male, patriarchal, stern father figure – not quite the old man in the cloud and yet not far off that image either. To see the gender-inclusive language was a physically shocking experience and reading God as 'She' opened me in new ways to the compassion and mercy that is promised at the start of nearly every surah of the Qur'an. The first time I recited the Throne verse in English, aloud after my prayers, using the feminine pronoun, left me sobbing for some time into my prayer rug. And so I finally met the Qur'an.

> In the name of God, the Infinitely Compassionate, the Infinitely Merciful.
> God – there is no deity but Hu,
> the Ever-Living, the Self-Subsisting Source of All Being.
> No slumber can seize Her nor sleep.
> All things in heaven and on earth belong to Her.
> Who could intercede in Her presence without Her permission?
> She knows all that lies open before human beings and all that is hidden from them,
> nor can they encompass any knowledge of Her except what She wills.
> Her throne extends over the heavens and the earth,
> and She feels no fatigue in guarding and preserving them,
> for She is the Highest and Most Exalted.
> [2:255]

My study of the Qur'an grew through reading Camille's translations in *The Light of Dawn: A Daybook of Verses from the Holy Qur'an*. This volume collects some of the most essential verses from the Qur'an and continues to shake preconceived understandings with its gender-inclusive language that forces a fresh evaluation of the holy message. Mevlana Rumi has observed that:

> The Qur'an is like a bride. Although you pull aside her veil, she will not show you her face. The reason you have no pleasure or discovery in all your study of it is that it rejects your attempt to pull off its veil.

I realised how important the 'unveiler' is in understanding the Qur'an. If the majority of translations have been done by men, *pulling* and *ripping* meanings, then how can it really speak to all of humanity? And if God is truly beyond gender, why do some many of us have such problems calling Allah 'She' or 'It' as well as 'He'? How is it that the toxic patriarchy that controls the world is so insidious that people get angry at Allah being referred to as 'She' while accepting Allah is not 'He'? What has centuries of this mindset done to us that we cannot fathom a truly genderless deity?

I feel it is imperative that we redress the balance and be allowed to call Allah 'She' – only until both genders have been honoured in God can we move beyond to a truly integrated *tawheedic* paradigm. And embracing the feminine has been my greatest awakening in Islam. Not only seeing the feminine attributes of Allah through understanding the 99 Names, but through the exploration of the female saints and companions of the prophets: the mothers, sisters, wives, and community members who walked, talked and lived the message, whose records have not been kept in as meticulous a manner as the men, but nevertheless are guiding lights of wisdom for humanity. It is through their struggles and elucidation of the spiritual path that I have connected most deeply to my essence, my *sirr* – the secret dimensionless part of my heart that holds my *Rabb*, She who is compassionate, loving, tender, powerful, embracing, protective, nurturing, and the Ultimate Truth. It is She that I turn to when I am happy and when I am sad, She that I see in the world around me, in my mother's eyes and my husband's embrace, in the breeze through the trees and the buttercups shining their radiant yellow smiles up to heaven. As the famous eighth century Sufi Rabia al-Adawiyya declared:

> O God, whenever I listen to the voice
> of anything You have made –
> the rustling of the trees
> the trickling of water
> the cries of birds
> the flickering of shadow
> the roar of the wind
> the song of the thunder, I hear it saying:
> "God is One!
> Nothing can be compared with God!"

# CANADA'S MUSLIMS

*Eric Walberg*

I set about my weekly Food Bank ritual (a special 'once a week' in honour of Covid-19) on Wednesday. Rituals are comforting even in thirty degree heat. A leisurely twenty minute bike ride across town, leisurely thanks to the virus, no one in sight, the barred gate ominously closed. No sign. Approaching Armageddon? It wasn't till I got home that I realised it was 1 July – Canada Day! Then it struck me, our national holiday has been so completely trivialised that it is erased from my consciousness. Yes, post-colonial multicultural Canada really has nothing much to celebrate. Much like its twin, July 4, it does little other than eulogise rampant colonialism, Great Game scheming. I am reminded how urgently all this is in need of a major overhaul.

Canada Day celebrates the British North America Act of 1867, uniting Upper and Lower Canada, Nova Scotia and New Brunswick, with Manitoba and the Northwest Territories hastily added in 1870, and British Columbia in 1871. This was a desperate attempt to forestall the now independent settler-colony US from gobbling up the last of British America. A precarious federation was patched together and looking back a century and a half later, it is hard to believe Canada survived. The US was already rapidly taking over the entire continent, including the purchase of Alaska from Russia just months after Confederation in 1867. We can only be grateful the US was too busy expanding west and south, leaving the cold wasteland to the north till it was too late.

The intent from the start for Alaska was to build a tunnel and unite the world by rail. William Gilpin, first governor of the Colorado Territory, envisioned a vast Cosmopolitan Railway in 1890 linking the entire world through a series of railways. Tsar Nicholas II approved a tunnel in 1905. Imagine if the US had managed to swallow up Canada and unite with Russia. To any Canadian, that thought is chilling these days. Yes, Canada is as artificial as countries come - the land cleared of natives, poor British, Irish and later Germans, and then just about anyone who looked white, hence the Lebanese, Albanians and Jews slipping in - now faithfully parroting whatever the US says. It is hard to get emotional about being Canadian after 70 years of wholesale multiculturalism. The only glue, Hollywood movies and Chinese toys, leave Canadians in a situation at least as precarious as in 1867.

Canada is one of many of course. Across the globe humanity has been on the move since we descended from the trees, stood up and started heading for the horizon. We have always been at war with each other too, and as we developed more advanced technology, our wars become more surgical and more lethal. Enter imperialism. US-Canada were settler colonies, unlike the Asian subcontinent, which was merely raped and pillaged, with no real intent for Britons to settle and replace the natives. While colonial Muslims began appearing in the 'mother' country as sailors, servants, students, soldiers as early as the seventeenth century, there were few Muslims crossing the Atlantic.

It was not until the nineteenth century that a few brave souls popped up in Canada, the legendary wandering aforementioned Lebanese, who spread out across both North and South America, and Albanian revolutionaries, incidentally Toronto's oldest Muslim community. Once the native Canadians were pushed aside, 'Canadians' were de facto, mostly British and Irish white immigrants. The flow of Muslim immigrants into Canada was almost non-existent until after WWII. The arrival of Muslims, arose directly from the shambles left behind by the British, French and Dutch. After the end of WWII, the US made them natural allies of Canadian natives, who suffered even more than Indians at Plassey or in 1857, if that is even possible. The logic to Muslim immigration was formed there: a colonial consequence, though a very different one from mother Britain. Suddenly the ummah, the coherent Muslim civilisation at least in theory centred on family and worship, took on a prominent role among immigrants and their second and third generations. Other immigrant groups focused on ethnicity but Muslims gained an outsize presence in the media, via their dress, through their celebrations of Ramadan. Muslim organisations took on French and English in their stride. The ummah spoke one language.

Imperialism just keeps on giving. Just as communism is the logical end of capitalism, multiculturalism is the logical end of imperialism. Reducing the world to warring nations whose essence is profit-loss with 1% owning 99% leads to demands for the radical solution of peace, equality and world citizenship. Of course the struggle against imperialism does not have to aim for that equally extreme, communist society or for a corporate-dominated internationalism. The point is to recognise the logic at work and go from there.

Muslim emigres were traditionally merchants or sufi teachers. In pre-capitalist times, there never was any large-scale movement to Christian-dominant countries. The Muslim world was highly advanced as a civilisation, richer than the West, which viewed the Muslim world with some hostility. But that changed as the Muslim world was occupied and despoiled, blurring the difference between *dar al-salam* and *dar al-harb*, pushing the new casualties to seek a better life somewhere, anywhere that was less raped and pillaged. Now there are large muslim 'colonies' in the centres of world capitalism, including all British settler colonies, France and Germany. Muslim nations themselves are captive to world capitalism in our post-colonial global soup. Can Islam survive in this global dar al-harb?

Islam is the only visible force with a clear civilisational platform, which, in *Desperately Seeking Paradise* (2005), Ziauddin Sardar describes as 'liberal humanism', reaching back to the Abbasids, Mutazilites, and twelfth century Ibn Rushd as the most articulate exponent. Muslims should be the natural allies of the oppressed, be they slaves or just natives pushed aside in the rush to conquer and exploit the world as fast as possible before others get there first. 'No force in religion' is the clarion call of the Qur'an, but also 'Islam as a powerful force for social justice'. This is a threat to those despising the moral call of all religions, and those intent on exploitation as their way of life in the *dunya*. It comes as no surprise, therefore, that as Muslims continue to arrive, grateful for Canada's still open doors, Islamophobia accelerates.

As the 2020 Covid-19 pandemic begins to wind down, places of worship have begun to open. I attended Toronto's oldest functioning mosque, Jami Mosque, on a sultry high summer day in July. Built in 1910 as a Presbyterian church, the building was purchased in 1969 by Toronto's small, still predominantly Balkan, Muslim community and converted into the city's first Islamic worship centre. Jami originally had a large cohort of Tablighi Jamaat followers, though the numbers declined after an influx of Gujarati Muslims settled in Scarborough, east Toronto, converting the 'Second Church of Christ, Scientist' church into the Madina Mosque. Jami was saved with the help of the fledgling Muslim Students Association.

As I rode my bike along the quiet, shady Boustead St looking for a church-mosque, I noticed a short, stocky bearded fellow who looked equally lost. Ahmed, a recent political refugee from Egypt, was standing in front of the mosque, with no one else in sight, as Friday prayer time approached. Ahmed is Nubian and explained how he had been thrown into a Cairo jail for campaigning for Nubian rights. Those Nubians who can escape, have fled Egypt, he tells me, for Canada, their 'promised land'. We were clearly not-in-the-know, but finally found a small notice among the postings, instructing us to use the rear entrance, which required a long detour round the block. Neither of us had registered online, as is now required at all mosques, in case of Covid-19 problems requiring later contact. The first congregational prayer session was already underway. There were just four spots left for the second service and the organisers registered us on their mobile phones. We were reminded: didn't you hear about Dallas? thirty-eight infected at one go, and all mosques shut down again! We must have everyone's email and cell phone number. Woe betide anyone trying to stay out of the internet age.

Both services were 'packed', with fifty men and ten women, thirty per cent capacity. Our khutbah was about a sandpiper laying her eggs in the road at a provincial park the Imam was visiting. A nice parable about how we must respect and celebrate Allah's miracles of life and family. After offering our prayers, Ahmed shared his nightmare experiences in Egypt. 'The Aswan dam destroyed our livelihood, our culture. We are despised as "black" in Egypt. All we can do is try to stay alive.' An accountant who had worked in Saudi Arabia, Ahmed recounted how he managed to enter the US as a tourist, and immediately headed for the border at Niagara Falls. His English is still poor after a year in Canada, so I marvelled at his courage to gamble everything on a wing and a prayer, and throw himself at some border guard's mercy. His gratitude to Canada makes him the idealised Canadian today, a hardworking, devout citizen who will bring his wife to build a solid family for the future. Worshipping with Ahmed was a fitting celebration of this extraordinary Canada Day. Proof to me that Muslims can form part of the sturdy glue holding precarious Canada together.

I live in Kensington Market, about the only really nineteenth century style community left in downtown Toronto. It traditionally has been home to new immigrants – Jews, Italians, Portuguese, Chinese, now West Indians. Good Jamaican restaurants. I love the feel in that bit of the market. You're not so much a client, customer, but a friend dropping by. Two synagogues from the early 1900s when Jewish immigrants arrived from Russia, but now almost unused. Just 'heritage'. Canada's history writ large. Or rather small, as Kensington is that rare phenomenon in the age of suburbia and the car, a genuine urban community where cars and trucks are barely tolerated.

No mosque, but the University of Toronto nearby, and like all universities, with a healthy Muslim community and prayer spaces. When I studied Qur'an recitation with a group of students and paused for prayers, I noticed that we were the only people in the university praying. For me, that was a 'wow!' moment. I don't think the students had thought of that.

There are 1.2 million Muslims in Canada (3.2% of the population) making them the second largest religion after Christianity. In greater Toronto, 7.7% are Muslim, and in greater Montreal, 6%. Toronto has the most Muslims in Canada, but still no central mosque. As most Muslims live in communities in distant suburbs, worship there means owning a car, and the mosques are more like box stores with the *de rigueur* massive parking lot. But many Muslims work in the financial centre, and in 2002, Masjid Toronto, became the only downtown mosque, taking over a branch of the Royal Bank of Canada near the central bus station. It is small and always full.

Pre-Covid-19 times, I frequented the Multifaith Centre at the University of Toronto for Friday prayers, as it is a stone's throw from my apartment. Prayers are always packed during the school session. The assembled are mostly science grad students, toying with extending their visa and abandoning the thought of returning to a nightmare, be it in Egypt, Syria, Iraq, Pakistan, Afghanistan. Though they become part of the (imperial) brain drain, I can hardly blame them. Already, second generation Muslim Canadian undergrads make up the majority, with the occasional convert, both white and native.

Just as Britain and Ireland have a vibrant Federation of Students Islamic Society (FOSIS), Canada and the US have their student associations. The MSA was founded at the University of Toronto in 1965, and later given funding by King Faisal. The MSAs in the US were started in 1963, with other branches now in all Canadian universities, and the umbrella Islamic Society of North America (ISNA) set up in 1977. These organisations underwent a series of toxic shocks and challenges. ISNA eventually suffered a nightmare of legal cases starting in 2003, accused of terrorism. The 2007 case focused on support for the Muslim Brotherhood and Hamas. Though no smoking (terrorist) guns were found, the cases highlight the close watch on all things Muslim. The draw of ISIS to some frustrated young Muslims, forty-seven of whom have been abandoned by their Canadian government, now languishing in prisons in Syria, has exacerbated this trend.

It was, however, in 2001, that Islamophobia jumped; notoriously, a feminist militant attacking a hijab-wearer in a university washroom, rotten eggs on Women's Day, pushing the MSA to initiate Islam Awareness Week, and to found the journal *The Muslim Voice*. In 2009, the first female president Asma Maryam Ali was elected and a strong Shia participation emerged, illustrating the efforts to inclusivity. The Chaplaincy started in the 1990s and became a full-time position in 2012. The current chaplain is Imam Yasin Dwyer, a Jamaican convert who was previously chaplain to Canada's federal prisons. Over time, more women became involved, the eponymous Koffler Multifaith Centre opened in 2005, funded by the Jewish 'Shoppers Drug Mart' magnate, for prayers, iftars and meetings.

I attended the 2019 Reviving the Islam Spirit conferences, which have been organised each year by Toronto MSA activists since the 1990s. Held in the last week of December, I was struck by the intense and thoughtful spirituality, unlike the commercial Christmastime spirit I felt on the streets. It resembled a mini-UN, a productive period of outreach and networking. I was surrounded by American Muslims, probably half of them converts, even a (very odd) retired US marine, Mark, who staunchly defended his time in Iraq, swearing that troops were only there to help. He had just converted, abandoning an Episcopal theology degree. While there were surely informers at RIS, Mark was just too strange.

The political activism of the late Kalim Siddiqui (1931-1996), one of the founders of the 'Muslim Parliament of Great Britain', is evident at The Islamic Society of York Region, co-sponsoring Al-Quds Day and other Palestinian solidarity actions. There is the Muslim Association of Canada centred in Edmonton, which is more Deobandi. The Muslim Association of Canada is the main Sunni organisation which provides religious and educational services for the Muslim community of Canada, including Masjid Toronto's two locations and seven Islamic schools in the Toronto area. There are seventy mosques across Toronto, financed independently. There is also a large Ahmadiyya community in Toronto, as well as Bahai. And then there is Salaam Canada, centred in Toronto with groups across Canada, which 'supports queer/trans people who identify with Islam ritually, culturally, spiritually, or religiously.' A cacophony of inclusive voices.

Activism generally avoids touchy political issues, though in 1984 the MSA held demos against Israel's occupation of east Jerusalem. Yusuf Islam, formerly known as Cat Stevens, was invited to give lectures on Islam in 1983–4 and even Salman Rushdie became a focus for education in 1988. H. Rap Brown came in 1995 to talk on Islam and black civil rights and Sarajevo Mayor Tarik Kupusovic in 1995. Muslim Awareness Week is the main university activism, but not involving politics, an unspoken rule. The only political campaign recently was passing out a postcard to send to your MP, supporting Egyptian Canadian Yasser Ahmed Albaz, who ran an engineering firm in Oakville, Ontario. He was about to board a plane in Cairo on his way back to Canada in February 2019 when he was 'flagged', arrested and transported to Tora prison, described by Human Rights Watch as 'the central site for those deemed enemies of the state'. Albaz's daughter Amal Ahmed Albaz said, 'My father has no political affiliations', but the strong antipathy to el-Sisi in Canada is surely being noted in Cairo. The likely scenario is that someone informed the Mukhabarat that Albaz was speaking out too loudly about Egyptian 'justice'. His arrest sent a chill through the Egyptian Canadian community.

Canada has 67,000 Egyptians, many of them having fled in fear of persecution. It's safe to say that no one approves of the country's regime after the coup. Former Muslim Brotherhood adviser Wael Haddara, professor of medicine at Western University, London, Ontario, said

Morsi's death was not a surprise. 'We had been expecting the worst for some time. … There were many failures during the year Morsi was in office, but also many successes. The former have been amplified by many, the latter muted.' But while anti-Morsi/MB sentiment is fine, pro-MB sentiment among the Egyptian Canadian community is targeted by both Canadian and Egyptian security forces.

It is the National Council of Canadian Muslims that deals with contentious and politically sensitive issues such as Quebec's anti-hijab law, which is now being appealed in the courts. Whether Islamophobia is increasing or not I find hard to tell. The murder of six worshippers in Quebec City in January 2017 has left an indelible mark. Defacing of mosques occurs. The number of police-reported hate crimes targeting Muslims in Canada more than tripled between 2012 and 2015, though the overall number of convictions over the same period fell.

Yet, arriving as a refugee from Egypt only last year, Ahmed can't thank Canada enough for being open to him. After Trudeau welcomed more than 25,000 Syrian refugees in 2016, that sense of gratitude became effusive within the Muslim community. Generally perceived as the 'good' immigrants for the quietism they display, particularly when it comes to politics is hard to ignore. Despite Quebec's anti-hijab law, Muslims in Canada keep their heads covered as a collective, out-of-sight.

Islam is finding more presence in popular culture in Canada. In contrast to the Hollywood stereotypical Muslim as terrorist, an unlikely tv sitcom, Little Mosque on the Prairie, created by Pakistani-born Zarqa Nawaz, captured the attention of Canadians, first broadcast from 2007 to 2012 on CBC, and since then a hit around the world. Muslim stand-up comics, male and female, from India, Egypt, the US are fashionable in Canada. Nour Hadidi hosted 'Being Muslim in Canada: A Comedy Show', part of the inaugural Comedy is Art festival in Toronto in 2019.

As with Jewish immigrants in the late nineteenth century, Canadian Muslims generally look south for inspiration rather than to Britain. Colonial ties are too weak. US native Muslims, both immigrant and Afro-American, and converts such as Hamza Yusuf and Yahya Rhodus are popular speakers at the Reviving the Islamic Spirit conference. The energy unleashed following the killing of George Floyd in May 2020 will give Canadian Muslims the opportunity to help Americans (and Canadians) build the case for Islam arising out of the US legacy of slavery. Malcolm X, who was both Muslim and Black, advised shortly before his 1965 assassination: 'America needs to understand Islam, because this is the one religion that erases from its society the race problem.'

The situation in Canada became tense after the mass shooting in 2017 in Quebec City and the anti-hijab law now in Quebec. On the other hand, Ottawa, Toronto, Hamilton, London, Edmonton, Calgary, Vancouver and others allowed mosques to call the *Azan* during Ramadan for the first time. Muslims enrich the meaning of being Canadian when we confirm the bond that Islam offers, a reliable glue to bind us to our so-called 'host' countries.

# CUBA IN THE TIME OF COVID-19

*Tamanna Rahman*

The last of the great escapes. I knew in the back of my mind that going to Cuba in the first weeks of the Covid crisis was risky. The world watched in horror as news came out of Italy that hundreds were dying daily. All the reports suggested that the UK was two weeks behind and would follow the same trajectory. In the back of my mind, I was worried that Cuba had not had a single case of Covid, and that we might be responsible for transporting it.

But when adventure calls with two other friends, it's hard to be the sensible one and let them down. I made noises suggesting that the virus wasn't going away, was likely to get worse and maybe we should cancel, but they were optimists. My half hearted objections were pooh poohed and I felt I had no choice. Being a loyal friend meant going. Boris Johnson's government was saying it was still ok – all we had to do was wash our hands. But I'm no idiot. I knew what was coming down the line. It was irresponsible to go. There I admit it. In hindsight I wouldn't have gone. But I did.

Cuba has always been a land of mystery to me, shrouded in romance and revolution. Cigars and sanctions. Salsa and espionage. Blockades and Buicks. Che Guevara, Fidel Castro, the Bay of Pigs invasion. In reality these words meant little, and as we flew the four thousand odd miles to the Caribbean I reflected on my idealised view of this small country that had stood up to America. That it was paying the price for its socialist ideals and welfare state. And that it had good doctors and teachers. What we found, of course, was a far more complex reality.

Leaving the steps of the plane as the sun went down, we could see the change from London. All the airport staff were wearing masks. It's a common sight now, but back then, in the early part of March 2020, it felt like a serious statement. The reason soon became clear as word went around the hot, humid airport that the island had had its first cases of Covid-19 confirmed the day before. Three Italians and a Cuban had brought over the disease. They were now in isolation. Phew. At least it wasn't going to be our fault for introducing the illness. We just needed to keep washing our hands and not dance with strangers.

As soon as we emerged from the double doors and into the beautiful red 1950s Chevrolet taxi our host had sent for us, Covid was out of our mind. This was the Cuba of postcards. Classic cars and a wide highway. Music blaring from the radio, we chatted excitedly at having made it to a country that none of us really knew anything about. We were seasoned backpackers, used to landing in places with barely anything planned bar the first couple of nights, and making things up as we went along. We were millennials – the internet would provide. We would meet other travellers and tag along with them. The night would lead the way to exciting experiences that we'd happily recount when we returned home. Unfortunately, we were stymied on pretty much every single one of these points, and our Cuba adventure became increasingly frenetic.

As we turned off the highway and into the narrow streets of Habana Vieja, it was clear that something was amiss. It was 10pm on a Thursday night in the centre of the tourist trap, but the music that should have been pumping and the roads that should have been thronging with crowds were silent and mostly empty.

We had booked to stay our first three nights in a *casa particular*. Up two flights of stairs of a colonial terrace, we entered *Casa Amistad,* with high ceilings and enormous windows flung open to the breezy night air. We had two bedrooms, and the living room, while our hosts Lazaro and his wife and child lived in a small, dark room towards the back of the house. We might not have agreed to stay there, had we known we were consigning them to the corners of their home.

But in a country where capitalism has been apparently rejected, and private entrepreneurship is frowned upon, renting out your home to tourists is one of the main sources of income for those lucky enough to afford their own place. Tourism makes up around ten per cent of the country's GDP, and employs a significant proportion of the population. The Cuban Convertible Peso, tied to the dollar and which tourists are forced to use, is ten times more valuable than the currency used by the locals. So the homestays, legal only since the late 90s, offer an opportunity for Cubans to make a decent income. It's also more affordable for those on a backpacker's budget to explore the country and learn about its people.

Sadly neither I nor my travelling partners spoke Spanish well, and Lazaro's English was only slightly better, so our cultural exchange was brief. Ordinarily, I'd have whipped out the phone and got Google translate to help us, but this is where we faced our first hurdle. When I had read going to Cuba was stepping back in time, I thought it meant in terms of cars and commerce. I didn't realise it meant the internet. The internet for goodness sake – a universal human right!

Here's an experiment for you to try at home. Go and do a street view of Old Havana on Google Maps. It's impossible. Cuba has managed to keep Google out of its streets, and while that's a victory for common privacy and should be celebrated, it's not half inconvenient when you're used to being directed with a nice blue line and an ETA to the nearest refreshing drink.

In Cuba, most tourists buy internet scratch cards, in increments of one or five hours, and use either one of the limited number of free wifi parks, or a hotel lobby to log in to the world wide web. Ordinarily I'd throw my hands in the air, and embrace the uncertainty of a country I knew nothing about. Get lost in new experiences, safe in the knowledge that it's much more joyous to look up instead of down into your hands. I'm not addicted to the internet, no matter how much my friends insisted I was. But in the midst of the looming Covid crisis, with minimal Spanish speaking skills, the small snippets that I managed to read in the rationed minutes we had only served to increase the gnawing feeling at the bottom of my stomach about what was waiting for us on the other end. Borders closing, tourists being booted out, airports shut.

Not that my companions seemed to be bothered by this of course. They used their internet minutes to speak to friends and family rather than slavishly checking Twitter as I did. They breezed from location to location in Havana, eating churros and helados from the street stalls, and contentedly sipping on piña coladas. Speaking with privilege that no brown person should ever assume, they told me: 'relax, we're British, we'll get home fine. The Foreign Office won't abandon us.'

During the day time, crowds of tourists still milled around the city. It was quieter than usual, said the locals, but not enough to worry them at that moment. They were confident their government had an excellent track and trace policy in place that would protect them. Everywhere in Cuba seemed pretty chilled out.

We benefited from the thinned crowds. The architecture in Havana is stunning. Town halls, hotels, squares, and the walk along the sea wall at sunset. Everywhere you look, you see the mirage of a 1950s movie scene, as classic cars sweep along the Malecon. There are few high rise buildings. There's no advertising assaulting your eyes at every turn, and there are people of every colour and creed, meaning that as long as we didn't wear our sunhats too conspicuously or didn't open our mouths too loudly, no one batted an eyelid. Once a passerby heard us speaking English and grabbed a hand, encouraging us to dance a little salsa with him in the street, with nothing but the music of the waves accompanying us. On a visit to the grand Hotel Nacional de Cuba, an older, wealthier gentleman asked if we'd like to have drinks with him and his friends. I regret saying no. I had a feeling he might have got there by helicopter.

No helicopter, but we did manage to hitch a ride with one of Havana's grandmother taxi drivers to the Plaza de la Revolución. Seventy odd years old, she had perfectly manicured nails, coiffured blond hair, and the pinkest lipstick you ever saw. Apparently she was one of only five in the city – and rare for being good value in a city where many drivers see unsuspecting tourists as personal cash cows.

From Revolution Square in Vedado we walked back home via Centro Habana, stopping off to eat dinner at the home/restaurant of Tommy Reyes, a former ballet dancer whose walls were filled with china plates and photos of his youth and whose floor was a mass of tiny dogs. Despite these eccentricities, the food was the best we had in Cuba.

We passed doorways and gardens of great beauty, balconies and pillars of grandeur. Many lay like dusty, empty shells, evoking a sense of colonial nostalgia and also sadness. A sense of what Cuba once was and the riches that this land was once able to provide for its inhabitants. Some of its inhabitants anyway. The French style buildings were built by slave labour and its economy, based on the export of sugar, tobacco and minerals no less so. Now there are no slaves, and the wealth inequality lies with the tourists who come to spend their dollars.

At night, we were encouraged to go to the Bueno Vista Social Club, which according to every Cuban we spoke to on the street, was doing a special salsa weekend – this week only. We coughed up the best part of thirty dollars each for what turned out to be a cavernous dining room filled mostly with cruise ship pensioners, and a live band that performed every week – not just that week. We slipped out early and got chased by the waiter for forgetting to tip.

But everywhere was slowly but surely emptying. Each day, the space grew wider and wider, and we had more of the city to ourselves. In the thinning of tourists, we saw queues of locals lining up outside shops and wondered what the buzz was. Only later did we discovered that it was rations for specific items, and Cubans queued regularly for some of the most basic of food items. There were signs on some of the buildings saying 'no running water'. In our own casa, there was no running water for showers or flushing the toilet before 9.00am. On the last day, there was no running water at all but we were generously moved to a different location.

The background note of Covid became a little louder. Every morning, we'd see a team of officials while peering down from our second floor balcony, walking in the narrow streets, going from casa to casa, asking the owners if they had tourists in their homes, whether there were any symptoms, when they were leaving. On the day we left Havana they came in, dressed like the ghostbusters, and fumigated the whole place.

But it was as we arrived in Trinidad, that we really felt the weight of travelling in a time of Covid. Trinidad is truly the Caribbean heart of Cuba. Where you could imagine Mr Rochester meeting Bertha and being intoxicated into a foolhardy marriage. Where music and raw animal magnetism might sway you into carefree abandon. Where you could sit and watch for hours and be entertained by the characters in front of you, sipping cocktails or puffing on a fake cigar.

The steps just off the Plaza Mayor would normally be filled with people enjoying the spring breeze of the gentle Caribbean winds. As the days slowly turn into a lazy, easy going night, the square would, in more joyful times, fill up further. Thousands of tourists waiting for the music and dancing. Cowboys accosting passersby asking if they wanted a good deal on a horse riding tour. Old *abuelas* bent double selling jewellery. Locals using the government wifi spot to check the internet on their phone.

Not for us, that first evening. The main square in the centre of Trinidad was woefully sparse of company. In fact, the numbers of tourists sitting on the steps fell significantly as each day passed. By the third night it was a trickle and the atmosphere was quiet, pensive and maybe a little grim, despite the best intentions of one local who had brought a boom box. There were still some tourists resolutely enjoying their night, but most were on their phones. Like us, they were no doubt worried if they would be able to get home and whether they should bring their flights forward, or wait until their planned departure risking the borders closing, airlines collapsing, or even airports shutting. The news from home had become more serious, and friends and family had been sending increasingly shrill messages to return before a possible lock down on Friday.

It might seem overly dramatic now, but at the time with little to no information online from Boris Johnson, and a lack of help from the British embassy besides 'follow government advice' and check the embassy Twitter feed, it was enormously worrying. In the absence of reliable internet, I asked family to look into bringing our flights forward - Swiss Air said it would cost £4,000 to change or buy a new ticket; and there weren't any flights before Friday anyway. Other cheaper flights were available but only via Spain or Canada – two countries on lockdown and with closed borders. British newspapers were reporting the army might be sent in.

On Wednesday evening, we went to have dinner at our favourite restaurant, *San Jose,* but found it was closed. An American woman had eaten there on Sunday, the day we arrived, and tests confirmed she had the virus. She had also eaten at the place we'd had breakfast and dinner the day before. That was closed too. Looking through their windows, it was undergoing a thorough scrub. Cuba had reported its first death. Every hotel and eating establishment now had staff at the doors, spraying customers with an abrasive alcohol filled solution.

The local economy – heavily reliant on holidaymakers was already suffering enormously before the death was reported. On an excursion to the Guanayara falls in Topes de Collantes, a Russian Rambo truck, with space for more than forty, turned up to take only five visitors to the stunning national park. The guide looked crestfallen at his tips at the end of the day. Walking past the dance rooms in the centre of town, a salsa teacher called out in desperation 'please, lady.' A Stetson-wearing hawker begged we took his horse riding tour for 7CUC$ – barely half the usual price.

But that night, it was a marked shift. Many locals started wearing masks. School children and adults alike recoiled from us as we walked the narrow cobbled pavements. We heard people shouting across the street at each other in Spanish. One word rang clear as we walked past them – 'foreigner'. Almost as if they were spitting the word at us.

As we walked the streets the restaurants were mostly empty. The dance halls had been pumping lonely music for a few days, but now they didn't even bother trying to draw us in. The salsa teachers just looked at us with resigned faces. Even the taxi drivers called out half heartedly, as if they didn't really want us to bring our foreign germs in.

We missed out on dinner since everywhere was closed so we went into a late night bakery, where the staff were all wearing masks too. It was right next to where the locals had shouted 'foreigner'. The baker handed over four rolls and indicated he didn't want money. I thought maybe he was being generous and welcoming. My friend thought perhaps they didn't want our coronavirus infected money.

Trinidad had become a ghost town, and we decided to make a move up north, to Cayo Santa Maria. An all inclusive resort catering for those who didn't want anything from Cuba except the clichés and weather, and yet for us a chance to recuperate from the frenetic pace we'd been moving at, and just chill out. The four-star hotel had everything you could ever want from a beach holiday. Food and drinks on tap, sports, entertainment, music, water activities and white sandy beaches. But again, it was practically empty. On the first night, an auditorium that might seat three hundred had an audience that was only thirty strong. The dancers performed their hearts out – really wonderfully choreographed pieces. We sat on the edge of the hall cheering and whooping loudly – trying to amplify our voices to fill the spaces of the chairs that sat empty. We had no idea that they would come down at the end of the show and wait for us to pass so we could also tip them to fill the spaces of their hats that lay empty.

The next morning we received an email from the airline saying that the second leg of our journey had been cancelled. No flight from Zurich to London city airport. No word on whether the Havana leg might also be cancelled. Switzerland had closed its borders. There were no flights out of Zurich to London for another ten days. Shit just got real. You can't enjoy azure seas and grilled shrimps when you don't know if you're going to get back home any time soon. Also, another reason we couldn't enjoy the grilled shrimps was because the turnover of guests was so low, the masses of food they had cooked ended up being on repeat for several meals.

We decided to head back to the capital early. Some ninety per cent of the remaining tourists had the same idea. We took the penultimate coach back to Havana. The resort was closing its door the following day. The whole place was gutted; built on the promise of the tourist dollar, it was hollowed out in just a few days. The entertainment staff, the waiters, the cleaners, the chefs, the receptionists, the electricians and towel boys lost their jobs with just a few days notice. The beautiful white expanse of the stone resort, perfectly symmetrical with the line of the blue horizon in the distance, as empty and shell like as the colonial homes in Trinidad and Havana. Whether it remains in its pristine form or descends into the cracked and cobwebbed equivalents in the rest of the country remains to be seen.

Havana was a different beast when we got back. It was visibly only filled with locals. We had heard from our new host that the whole country was emptying itself of tourists. Any remaining after Tuesday – the day after our flight – would be forced to stay in government approved quarantine hotels. How much of this was true is debatable – with no internet, no television and no Spanish speaking skills we were lost and reliant on hearsay. The British Embassy in Cuba, no doubt fielding calls from all the Brits in the country, provided no help whatsoever, apart from a hefty phone bill. Mild panic ensued when we heard that Brits were to be stranded in Peru with no help from the Foreign Secretary.

Our host was closing his home too. He told us if we got stuck we were welcome to stay with him and his family. They were the lucky ones and had stores enough for a few weeks. He, his wife and his staff of two were making masks for everyone using a small home sewing machine, copying the pattern from the government approved one that got sent to them. Another woman whose dress we had admired at the Hotel Nacionale had also told us to contact her if we got stuck. A taxi driver we met while trying frantically to get information from the airport authorities stayed with us while we went from terminal to terminal and never once asked to increase his fare. Such is the brotherhood of man when encountering hard times the world over. A traveller can always find good people, especially when desperate, in a good country. The socialism of Cuba may be starting to fray at the edges, but enough exists in the heart of its people that poverty, sickness and isolation are not part of the fabric of its sense of society.

In the end we managed to get on the flight back to Europe – just. For a good two hours it looked as if our cancelled second leg would mean curtains for our return home, but also possibly the beginning of a new adventure in Spanish fluency. Luckily, we had booked a flight from a different airport in Switzerland and officials took a chance that we'd be allowed to move around in country when we landed in Zurich. We boarded the plane with relief. Tempers slightly on edge and blood pressure marginally raised, but our Cuban adventure was at last over.

If you're ever going to go on holiday somewhere, wishing you could experience the culture and scenery and atmosphere free of tourists, then an international pandemic is (not) the time to go.

But here's the thing – how a country welcomes its travellers is one of the best ways to see what that country values in its people and its land. Mass tourism is bad, but some tourism opens up a window into a life just as ordinary and yet spectacular as your own. Fresh eyes reveal the historic might, the latent power and the raw energy of a people, and the spaces they hold dear – the museums, the monuments, the memories. The opportunity to meet people just as excited as you are about learning new things and embracing new experiences - and who open your eyes to new knowledge is part of what makes travelling in Cuba – travelling in any country – truly wonderful and worth it. Happiness is infectious and optimism rose tinted.

Without its tourists, Cuba is stripped bare for all to see. It's still filled with wonderful architecture and beautiful cars and truly beautiful men and women. It's still a 1950s movie set. But it's also poor and broken, and the lives are real. The healthcare is universal, but the medication is not. Everyone is fed, but the food is rationed. The music still plays no doubt, in homes and half empty hotels, but the tourists are not paying the piper anymore. You can't enjoy being a tourist and spending your disposable income in a country when all around you see people struggling to survive.

That's not tourism. That's more like voyeurism. No doubt it's a story repeated the world over, in countries and areas where tourism is an inflated employer. Covid will lay waste to communities and families in more ways than one.

# FIELD WORK

*Chandrika Parmar*

The word destination has a polysemic power which invites thoughts from distant domains. In an ordinary sense it is a place one has to reach. But destination as metaphor packs layers of meaning. Instead of becoming an end point, a terminal, it becomes a symbolic crossroad, a meeting point, a journey. A convergence of different imaginaries. Destination invokes both the idea of travel and pilgrimage. Physically it conveys a sense of reaching a place. Symbolically it becomes a rite of passage where arrival is both transformation and departure. The power of the word allows for interpretation, for metaphor, for unexpected usages. A word generally restricted to pilgrimage or travel, now becomes a pretext to understand field work. The anthropological rite to study a different society.

The idea of field work juxtaposed to destination might seem surprising. But by applying such a term to field work one breaks the current stereotypes of science. Field work is seen as the scientific act of studying the other. In a scientific sense it becomes a catechism of dos and don'ts. It often fetishises rigour and technique, often fossilising the fluidity of conversation into a rigidity of a questionnaire. The idea of field work as destination opens it up to a different set of questions and metaphor. Instead of the scientism of exploration, it becomes the pilgrimage of the self; instead of emphasising objectivity one includes meaning and to the rigor of professionalism one adds a sense of play. Field work then becomes more than a cautionary ritual that an outsider must follow. In fact, inside and outside, neighbourhood and distance become blurred, creating an image of self and other which is both discovery and invention. As a narrative, field work becomes a hybrid entity, a geographical mix of margin and mainstream which helps provide new insight.

One travels not only across space but over imaginary maps and constructs we call classificatory systems. When creativity employs the metaphor of travel one combines the physicality and objectivity of outside as space with the unconscious as the inner continent of exploration. Field work acquires a complexity it has lost in behavioural science textbooks, where it appears like an exercise, a time and motion study of the self, objectivising the other. Consider the word arrival. One equates it with entry but entry is a barren term, it merely denotes access. Arrival is more symbolic: it denotes acceptance, hospitality, understanding, the beginning of homecoming. One senses an encounter with multiple worlds rather than with one space. Space and time acquire a different metaphysics, a liminality when one is at home yet not yet home. This is what makes anthropology a challenge to unravel the pilgrimage of difference it has become.

I work on disasters, crisis-riddled situations which create ambiguity and liminality, an uncertainty beyond the expected and the normal. Ordinary lives get disrupted, categories are discarded, reworked or violated. The insider as inhabitant also feels displaced. As outside and inside gets shuffled one is forced to ask, what is home and what is homecoming? As a narrator moves from banality to crisis, one asks what is it to reach a place? Is arrival home-coming? Can self and other converse in ways one has not yet dealt with? What is destination when there are no markers of stability? Who is insider or outsider in a world without permanence? The metaphysics of field work gets reworked in these moments as one asks the question, is reaching a destination an act of arrival or a discovery of a process which is endless in life and science. A sense of the nomadic haunts the idea of destination. Both pilgrimage and science instead of offering permanence invite you into a world of uncertainty, where the surreal and the everyday mix together.

I look at field work I have carried out over the last few decades, across five themes, to convey a sense of the act and to provide a sense of narrative and reflection. The five themes are: self and the other, time, movement, place, arrival. It is an attempt to cross-pollinate metaphor to arrive at a more reflective and reflexive sense of field work as destination.

One begins with self and the other. The distinction between self and the other is the stuff of anthropology, as Levi Strauss once said that the self is lost without the other. An isolated self becomes an estranged self. The gospel of the self and the other is simple, it is the story of difference and the challenge of difference. Do we assimilate all others into a uniform self? Or do we celebrate difference to enjoy the encounter of self and other? The tragedy is once we invoke the ideology of the nation state or assimilation we lose the plurality called the other. We lose the celebration called diversity. The other is the destination of the self and in discovering the other one reaches into oneself. At that moment one discovers that field work is not an exercise in role playing or social distancing or forced mimicry. It is the self, affirming the other. The other in that sense is the destination of the self. Without the other neither self nor anthropology is possible.

It is interesting to contrast the behavioural sciences and philosophy on field work. The former is desperate to scientise itself in order to reach its destination. But philosophy shows that such an arid costume ball of science is not necessary, when the destination is the discovery of the self. Two noted philosophers have illustrated this magnificently. The first is by the philosopher Martin Buber. In his *I and Thou* he contrasted an objective technical idea of the I-it with the I-thou, which soaks the relationship in the sacred. Field work then becomes an act of reverence rather than an attempt to claim distancing and objectivity. Emmanuel Levinas added to it by showing that the face to face has a sanctity of encounter no other meeting has. What both emphasise is that objectivity as role playing often become objectification. One creates an unreal sense of the other. Role distancing is only permitted as a playful act and in fact a genuine science adds the ritual of play to the sacred to create field work. One does not merely arrive at a destination, one constructs it as an imaginary to reach it.

Time is the second critical category in understanding the movement to destination. Time is not merely the clock time of access, arrival and closure. Time is the lived time of the universe . One internalises the other through the melody of time before one arrives physically at one's destination. It is in this sense that the Spanish Catholic priest, Raimondo Panikkar, called pilgrimage a discovery of self through difference. Field work is a pilgrimage laced with scientific questions. Time also loses its linearity as one realises arrival is movement across different times. A rite of passage that field work is a movement across plural time. Destination as space might be uniform is time. But destination as place is an amalgamation of time. Arrival is a recognition of the quilt patch of time. One realises that different modes of travel from tourism, pilgrimage, exploration, and field work involve different bundles of time. Destination in that sense is not arrival in objective time but a prolonged sense of becoming. In fact, one realises that destination in a physical sense is closure but destination as search or research is a process. One arrives only to move on in the perpetual search for knowledge and meaning. Destination is a symbolic marker rather than a physical milestone.

Narrative is the third marker of any travelogue of research or discovery. A sense of destination cannot do without a story. A storyteller is a map maker who turns travel into a fable. Storytelling in field work is of three kinds. You understand the other as a form of knowledge we call a paradigm. You talk to the other to comprehend the other as a discourse or text. You turn the case study into a myth or fable to understand the other beyond locality. Between map and story a new sense of the other is born.

Finally, one has to talk about place. Place is not empty space. Space is Kantian and homogenous; place is the geography of memory. Place is a weave of myth, fable, and memory. It goes beyond geography as physicality to geography as an imagination. One reaches a space subliminally, one arrives at a destination, but one reclaims the place only through story, memory, and symbol. The traveller visits a place once, the storyteller invents it again and again. Destination becomes the mystery of place in the act of field work.

Field work in an ordinary situation and field work in a crisis area are different not merely in the methodological style involved but in the moral intensity of choices and decisions to be made. One can role play in routine situations, but crisis demands an authenticity and immediacy of response. Storytelling and narratives of suffering become part of the moral responsibility of the field worker as she becomes witness and observer. One confronts issues of vulnerability in a different way.

I remember a woman literally parked on the top of a coconut tree living on salt water. She was seven months pregnant. How does one acknowledge her resilience in the very act of recording her existential situation? More, crisis is full of ambush as one encounters a different range of groups, that one may not meet in ordinary times. One confronts death, pain, suffering, hunger, loss as one fumbles for the memory and language required to describe them. It almost alchemically transforms the writer. The very moral nature of the situation challenges the very idea of scientism and objectivity one brings to the field.

Given the open-ended nature of my studies, I usually used semi-structured but open ended interviews. Although some have cautioned against 'the romantic impulses of identifying experience with authenticity' which can drive the researcher when using 'open-ended interviews', I felt this was necessary for several reasons. First, I was looking for definitions of a situation. Second, as an exploratory exercise, such methods provided a form of preliminary mapping. Third, given the wide differences in ideology and style, I felt that the respondent should be given some feeling of control, some sense that the interviewer is not predefining a situation or imposing his/her categories on the field. It allows the respondents the freedom to construct and define their world. A closed or structured interview is not open or anticipative about a flexible world. A closed interview presupposes preliminary knowledge, defines or lists possible responses, fixed or maps the array of answers possible. Such an approach, with a prearranged list of answers, gives little freedom or flexibility to the respondent.

The semi-structured interview is not an anarchic enterprise. It is open-ended, not based on previously established categories. It possesses the property of emergence and surprise. It allows the serendipity and yet, I feel, its demands on memory, empathy and the act of listening, are enormous. There is a change in power relations. Structured interviews are in the forms of stencils; the direction of the narrative is often anticipated. The informant may not allow for the availability of time an unstructured interview needs and it emphasises the vulnerability of the researcher. Body language becomes a form of communication, even silences become part of the unstructured interview as a mode of communication. Such interviews are not only dyadic encounters. They may be encounters with groups at a station, a wayside *dhaba*, a relief camp. In this sense, such interviews are polyphonic, where the researcher, rather than interviewing, records a multiplicity of perspectives from a multiplicity of respondents.

Let me tell you a few stories, based on my work on the 1999 Odisha cyclone and the 2001 Gujrat earthquake, which illustrate the challenges a researcher faces in field work during immense disasters.

*Story 1*

I visited a coastal island in Odisha. The only access to this island is by crossing the river. On the other side is the sea. And the sea had come in. Almost every home in this village lost family members. In fact, I have not spoken to a single person in this village who had not lost members of their family. The village had only one pukka (cement) house. But it is not the event which stays on in the memory of the people. It is what followed after the cyclone and the tidal wave receded, the village was still marooned. One woman in particular was inconsolable. She wept as she recalled how her children had begged her for food. She painted a graphic picture of how her children had put their head in her lap and said, '"Ma, we are hungry. Please give us food."Their head was in my lap. They were looking at me... begging me. But there was no food' she said weeping inconsolably. In three days she saw her three children die one after another because of starvation.

I continued with my trip of the island village talking to the survivors there. Most of them were women. After a couple of hours, it was time to have lunch. I was told that lunch arrangements had been made for me in the village. A sumptuous six dish meal had been made for me and the persons accompanying me including prawn curry with fresh prawns from the *gheri* (enclosure). I was served food by this same woman. She piled up a huge pile of rice on my plate and served me the various dishes she had prepared. I wondered what it meant in an everyday sense to remember that day when she had no food for her children. Here she was serving me this sumptuous meal and forcing me to have another helping.

*Story 2*

There is another image that has stayed with me. I was visiting a village in Odisha which had been impacted by the floods. I was walking around the village and was directed to a household which had lost younger members of the family. Only the elderly couple had survived. As I was going towards their house, a women shouted out for me. She had heard I was talking to the survivors of the cyclone. She wanted to tell me her story. She was insistent. I told her I would stop on my way back. Two hours later as I made my way back, she spotted me and shouted out for me again. She put out the fire on which she was cooking. 'I want to talk to you about my story' she insisted. She told me her family – her husband, child and in-laws had survived by taking cover in the cyclone shelter. When the tidal wave came she was the only one at home and managed to hold onto pieces of wood and make her way in water which was neck deep to the cyclone shelter. 'I wanted to talk about my story' she kept insisting. As I thanked her, she said, 'Just for this thank you I have been waiting here to tell you my story. I wanted you to listen. I will probably get a beating from my husband as my food will not be ready on time, my children will be back from school and will want food. But, I wanted to talk to you'. Her face has stayed with me. A vivacious face, clad in a coarse handwoven green saree, with a big red dot on her forehead.

Yet, one of the things I learnt from my work on disasters was precisely that vulnerability emphasises openness. It outlines fragility to also record resilience and agency. The field worker in that sense is like the survivor. She realises that her study is both lens and mirror. It is a way of studying a world and it is an opportunity to look at one self. In confronting the Janus face of her work, she celebrates the very nature of the rituals she has engaged in.

## *Story 3*

I recall travelling with a team of Ananda Margis, a social and spiritual movement, which some see as a cult, from Bhubaneshwar to Ersamma, greeting them with all my skepticism. The conversation was easy and open and even carried a lightness of being. The Margis talked of *kuccha* (mud) houses which they felt could still be built. They were concerned that NGOs from outside would replicate a miniature city with their dream of pukka (cemented/ burnt brick) houses which would destroy the local architecture and ecology. They talked of their philosophy of PROUT (Progressive Utilization Theory), of how Prabhat Ranjan Sarkar, their founder, wanted their work to focus on suffering in calamities. They admitted candidly that they were poor, unable to procure large volumes of relief materials. So they did what they could with their hands—just removing dead bodies. We could still smell the stench of carcasses as we proceeded. We reached Ersamma which was the landfall point of the cyclone and found a crowd waiting in the AMURT disaster relief camp.

From here the road narrowed further as we bounced towards Padampur where we caught up with an Ananda Marga carcass–removal party. Dead bodies lay half–burnt on both sides of the road, the bones visible. I saw bodies huddled in the paddy fields, spread like strange images after a storm. The Margis were upset. They complain that many NGOs had left the bodies covered with just a few inches of topsoil. The ground, they say, is not suitable for this and the dogs keep digging up the bodies. Then they point out something we had not quite noticed, that 'the vultures, the jackals, the hyenas, all the natural scavengers are missing.' 'You have to burn the bodies' added another Margi. 'It is the only solution. It is not easy. It takes three hours to burn one. Even the army accepted it as the only solution. But yes, there are religious doubts and observances. But a little science like using limestone during disposal goes a long way.' It ensured there are no breakouts of epidemics.

I saw the Ananda Margis work with their bare hands, handling bodies which were now a couple of weeks old, bloated, flaky and buttery but still preserved because of the salty sea water. I can still remember the stench. However, the Margis got down to the task at hand with no sign of unease or reluctance. Sometimes they waded in water to grab the floating bodies and drag them to the corner before they were burnt with limestone and the materials they were carrying. Disposing of the ones there, we took the boats again across the waters in search of more bodies.

I recall my conversation with one of the volunteer in 2009. His name is Pramod. While travelling in the car he started talking about his experiences as a volunteer. 'I have myself picked up thousands of bodies with my hand … thousands … thousands', he told me quietly. 'There were bodies all over. Some volunteers used gloves. But I used bare hands to lift those bodies and cremate them. You don't know the state of those bodies. Some volunteers had masks to cover their nose and mouth. But I didn't use any. After disposing of many bodies some of the flesh of the decomposed bodies would be on my hands.'

*Story 4*

Boachasanwasi Shri Akshar Purushottam Swaminarayan Sanstha (BAPS) is a major Hindu denomination, with mandirs (temples) all over the world. The BAP a temple in Neasden, London, which opened in 1995, is built entirely using traditional methods and materials. The BAPS approach is expressed in the distribution of food. Food is a tangible object that expresses the values of a culture. The BAPS mandir at Bhuj realised that food would be the immediate necessity. For BAPS, food was a security, a therapy, a provision of dignity which is conceptualised as more than food. It was a ritual of communication and empathy. For BAPS, there was no question of serving cold food in plastic packets. Food had to be fresh, hot and served with dignity. *Khichdi* was prepared for 3,000 people and by midnight on that first day 6,000 people had been served. As they repeatedly point out 'on the first night there were more than 1,200 well-to-do people who had taken refuge at the BAPS mandir in Bhuj'. Night brought a sense of despair. When a fighter plane raced across the sky, people felt that there was another tremor. Every time the survivors rose in panic BAPS served hot tea to 'calm their nerves'. On the first night, tea was served fourteen times.

Food was a ritual of assurance, of community, a return to some semblance of normalcy and everydayness. 'On an average, 37,000-40,000 meals were served every day'. Some survivors were too shy to be seen begging. 'These people had never gone out seeking food. There was shame associated with it. Swamiji silently instructed that tiffin-boxes be filled generously with food. No questions about their name were to be asked. Three to four hundred tiffin boxes were packed and sent daily to various homes or shelters.' Another informant described it: 'In fact, in the early hours, because there was no water, electricity and other facilities, BAPS volunteers like other organisations distributed food packets'. Pramukh Swami intervened quickly observing that food had to be served hot, because it signaled a sense of caring. 'Food packets are fine, but they are cold. If people get hot meals, they will feel better. When a mother serves cold meals three times a day, the family members feel that she has no love for them. Whereas serving only a cup of warm milk makes all the difference'.

### *Story 5*

For Ramakrishna Mission (RKM), a Hindu spiritual movement also known as Vedanta, *seva*, or service and suffering, are key concepts. The ultimate idea is of the Daridra Narayan (God in poor). He embodies a notion of suffering which goes beyond economised categories like poverty or sociologised categories like exploitation or vulnerability. Suffering is an opportunity for service. Suffering is a sign of God in the poor, the miserable, the weak. Suffering becomes a way for the ascetic monk to enter the ordinary world and serve God. Here service seeks the divine in man to serve God.

Service for the RKM is a civilisational challenge to charity. Charity is seen as an arrogance, a self-styled asymmetry of the giver over the receiver. For the RKM, the receiver is superior to the giver, for in that moment of reciprocity, he is God. Such a philosophy alters voluntarism from hegemony of the powerful to a sense of equality. To serve is not to endow but to share. Compassion like charity is the recognition of the divine at a distance. What one has to grasp is the definition of service as *seva* rather than *daya* (compassion).

Another monk I met was Swami P. I had met him earlier at Orissa in 1999. I rang up the Ramakrishna mission. The mission is deeply conscious of time. It is important that you call at certain times. When I arrived, the senior monk was busy. A younger monk offered me *prasad* (sacred food offering) and kept me company as I waited. He appeared quietly. Swami P smiled in recognition. He said 'we met ten years ago, after the cyclone. You came with another gentleman. I gave you both a lot of details.' I told him I needed some documents and he replied, 'yes I will provide it. Come tomorrow, the documents will be ready.' The first encounter was over in twenty minutes. There was something terse, almost cryptic about it. The junior monk sensed my confusion and offered solace and *prasad*.

I went back the next day and Swami P offered me more details. I was supplied all the facts and figures of the work undertaken in Orissa, the dates, the progress reports. He seemed to downplay the mission's goal. 'A lot of people did commendable work then. The Ananda Marg was impressive in the way it handled dead bodies. They carried special chemicals for clean disposal of carcasses and dead bodies. People from Andhra also did good work. I remember it was *saptami* or *ashtami* (seventh or eighth) when the cyclone struck. A hundred houses were immediately demolished. We had setup camp at the campus of the university of Behrampur.' He quietly added 'human beings are living God: *prana pratishtha*' he said. 'Service is both belief and conduct. Mere aid or help is not enough. One has to serve with the right attitude. That is the tradition we have always followed. It goes back to the way Ramakrishna served the poor. Nivedita followed this in the plague. The monks merely relive this tradition. The mutt in Chennai performed the same kind of *seva* after the tsunami. We also did relief then. Subhodananda did remarkable service. Meet G, he will tell you all about.' I blinked till I realised he was speaking about Swami P. Monks have always two names and often they are used interchangeably.

There was something about the matter of fact, the baldness of his narrative that puzzled me. It was a bit like a roll call, bare announcement of name, time, place and event. It was then that I realised each story was a part of a seamless chain of being. Each story was a simple variant of the earlier story. Each was recited in a bland way. There was little digression, almost no detail. It was as if the frugality of narrative itself was a part of the economy of the mission's style. Each monk was an exemplar of service. Each monk did what he was supposed to, each followed an example. Each set an example and each example followed the earlier example in quiet continuity. Each exemplar enacted the original act of service. There was no need for more detail. Each story was immaculate in itself. The chain of exemplars captured the continuity of narrative and the rationale for the maths.

One senses here that suffering as a way of relating is different from the attitudes that accompany poverty or vulnerability. Suffering as a mode of perception possesses empathy. It is not convertible into the social science objectivity of the other two categories. Poverty or vulnerability can be sociologised; one can create a political economy around it, where knowledge and objectivity becomes their own form of distance. Concepts like poverty and vulnerability invite the social science project. Suffering in its demand for directness, for the immediacy of the encounter, hints more at 'I and thou'. Suffering demands, the letter, the diary, or the story. Or more tears, signalling the recognition of the despairing God in man. Yet there is a detachment to the narrative, to the sense, that suffering like any narrative is suspended in time, a sense that the sanity of everydayness will return and when that happens, the monk recognising its signs will move on.

The monks felt there was an intrinsic link between the way they told the story and the way they saw suffering. They argued that suffering had to be felt, seen, touched, and absorbed in a certain way it summons the sensorium. Many of the examples come from the poor but suffering goes beyond poverty. Subsistence has its joys which the asceticism of the monk can understand and empathise with. Suffering seems to imply its own semiotics.

The idea of field work as destination imbues you with a sense of gravitas but also a likeness of being. One realises that it is not predestination and it is not destiny. It is a destination, more secular, more dramatic, more playful and marked with surprises. A destination is open ended, full of adventure and storytelling. In fact, the mixing of concepts and metaphors does much to rework the idea of the field, as juxtaposition of different words becomes a juxtaposition of different worlds.

A destination is no longer a part of an enclosure, it is no longer abstract but becomes a melting pot of anxieties and expectations. A city as destination or even a lonely bus stop now changes persona. A city visualised as such is no longer a dreary point on an abstract map but a variety of expectations. It is no longer terminal or terminus, but open to surprise and joy, a promise of the future. Reaching a destination becomes an act of completion as an act of thanksgiving. It is truly a pilgrim's progress.

# ASSISI

*Ziauddin Sardar*

'Where are all the birds?'

I was rather surprised by Assisi. I expected the home town of St Francis, who was declared the patron saint of ecology by Pope Paul II in November 1979, to be a haven for wildlife. I expected to see birds everywhere — after all, he was famous for quieting noisy swallows and preaching to flocks of unruly marsh harriers and gentle turtledoves. I even expected to see a tame wolf or two, calmly stalking about the narrow streets and squares of the famous Umbrian town. Yet wildlife is conspicuous in Assisi simply by its complete absence.

But in most other aspects, Assisi remains much as St Francis left it some eight hundred years ago. It is situated half way up the slopes of Mount Subasio and reaching it requires a long, circuitous climb. The whole town is one big monastery, its medieval character sometimes blending and sometimes contrasting with its Roman origins, evidenced in the remains of the 'municipium'. The prime focus of the town is the Basilica of St Francis which consists of two churches, one on top of another (the lower one is said to date from 1228 to 1230; and the upper one from 1230 to 1253), and a crypt, dug in 1818, where the body of St Francis is kept.

The full splendour of the Basilica is obvious as one approaches it from the town's coach stop. Walking uphill on Via Father Elia and entering the colonnades of Piazza Inferiore, surrounded on three sides by a portico dating from the fifteenth and sixteenth century, one is suddenly confronted with a magnificent structure that appears to be sitting comfortably on a cliff face. Monks in black habits, some hiding their faces under cowls, rushing here and there, made me think I was inside *The Name of the Rose*. As I stood there looking at the lower church's ornate twin portal, surmounted by three rose windows, and the monks going about their daily chores, I almost expected one of them to come and introduce himself as 'William of Baskerville'. Inside, I discovered the lower church is laid out in the shape of a double 'T' and is encrusted with the words of renowned thirteenth and fourteenth century artists.

I came out of the lower church and climbed the steep stairs that lead to the upper part of the Basilica. Here, I felt as though I was in a completely different church. This one has an undivided nave; its prime focus is an exquisitely carved fifteenth century wooden choir stall. I looked towards the town. The small centre of the world heritage site was full of pilgrims and tourists. I could spot priests, monks, rabbis and imams relatively easily – each revealing their religious identity with their special attire, brightly colourful in the case of Buddhist monks and Hindu gurus. Conspicuously placed banners declared the 25th Anniversary of WWF. It was late September 1986; and the World Wildlife Fund was marking the special occasion with a mega gathering of faiths. 'The Assisi Declarations' were to send 'messages on humanity and nature from Buddhism, Christianity, Hinduism, Islam and Judaism' to all those out there of faith, little faith, and no faith. The meeting was the idea of Prince Philip, Duke of Edinburgh, the patron saint of WWF. And I felt privileged to be there.

I was there in dual capacity. As editor of *Inquiry*, the still much lamented monthly 'magazine of ideas and events'. And as someone who had written 'The Muslim Declaration on Nature'. This latter fact was not universally acknowledged. The Declaration itself was read by my old friend, Abdullah Omar Naseef, who was then the General Secretary of Muslim World League, based in Mecca, Saudi Arabia. But those in the know, knew. And this was enough to secure a special pass, which hung proudly around my neck and allowed me to go anywhere I wanted – even entering what may be called spaces of high privilege.

I entered the Basilica flashing my pass; and discovered that it was virtually empty. A rehearsal for the main event the following day had taken place earlier. Everyone had left and Prince Philip and a few other dignitaries were being treated to a tour of the Basilica. Without drawing attention to myself I joined the small gathering.

The huge walls of the Basilica are adorned by frescoes illustrating the life of St Francis by the Florentine painter Gitto di Bondone – known largely as Gitto. We stood in front of a fresco which showed St Francis with a bird in his left hand and a wolf by his side. Our guide was a certain Father Bernard, a middle-aged man of medium height who wore thick glasses. 'When you consider these paintings are done in water colour and were laid on the wall before the plaster dried, you can begin to grasp the true achievements of the artists,' he explained.

We walked and stood under another painting. It showed St Francis having a vision. 'This vision completely transformed his life,' Father Bernard said. While he obviously held high rank in the Franciscan order and commanded considerable power, his manner never betrayed his position. He smiled frequently, his humility shining through; and sought to communicate when he talked rather than proselytise. 'Until then, St Francis was completely dissatisfied by his life, having enlisted as a knight in the war between Perugia and Assisi in 1202. He then spent a great deal of time in prayer in deserted places and caves around Assisi'. Moving closer to Prince Philip, Father Bernard continued, 'for some time he worked amongst the lepers, much to the distaste of the people around him who were more concerned with material wealth and display of riches. He interpreted the vision to mean that the moral and spiritual life of the Church had to be rebuilt'. Prince Philip listened to him in rapt attention.

The gathering moved in unison to the next painting which showed St Francis' father complaining to the Bishop of Assisi. Father Bernard paused to look at the painting, said nothing, and moved on. The next painting showed Saint Francis asking the Pope to approve his order.

Father Bernard continued. 'St Francis' attempts to rebuild the moral and spiritual foundation of the Church, as well as his efforts to repair old churches, naturally led to a number of conflicts. He had a bitter public quarrel with his father, which led to his being disowned by his family. In 1209 he sought approval of his rule and way of life from Pope Innocent III. After some persuasion, the Pope agreed to recognise the apostolic forms of religious life which Franciscans have followed ever since'. I couldn't help asking: 'Was not his way of life a radical departure from what the Church stood for?' Father Bernard smiled at my question; a little too generously. Behind the glasses, there was a gleam in his eyes. 'St Francis introduced a radically new type of religious life. Apart from preaching love and concern for wildlife and nature, he and his friars spurned the feudal system of privileges and the rat race of newly moneyed middle classes. The Franciscans never owned land; they made a living by working or begging'.

'So how would a Franciscan monastery differ from other monasteries?'

'Our institutions tend to be simple and functional. Even this Basilica is very functional. Quite unlike the opulent monastery described by Umberto Eco in *The Name of the Rose*. In contrast, the Basilica is rather haphazard.'

We walked and stood underneath a painting that showed St Francis with an Arab ruler. 'I take it the Arab is the Ayyubid Caliph, al-Malik al-Kamil. He became a good friend of St Francis.' Father Bernard was surprised by my intervention. 'They became friends when St Francis went to Cairo to mediate between the Christians and the Muslims'.

Father Bernard look at me as to say, ok, carry on. 'There is considerable common ground behind the teachings of St Francis and those of the Sufis. Indeed, some scholars have argued that during his stay in Cairo St Francis became a Sufi. This is one explanation why the Caliph gave him complete freedom to travel in Muslim lands and come and go as he wished. Some people even go as far as to say that the nine months when he is supposed to have disappeared he actually spent in a Sufi *tariqa*'

Father Bernard shook his head vigorously. 'Not true. Not true'.

Our conversation drew Prince Philip's attention. He came and stood by me. 'Is it true', he asked. 'It's a theory', I replied. There is no scholarly consensus. 'What is the Muslim position on nature', he asked. I explained that Muslims regard their role on the planet as a *khalifa*, vice-regent or trustee of God. We are God's stewards and agents on Earth. We are not masters of this Earth; it does not belong to us to do what we wish. It belongs to God and He has entrusted us with its safekeeping. Our function is to safeguard its flora and fauna, and enhance its beauty. Environmental consciousness and conservation of nature, I said, came naturally to Muslims of the classical period. The notion of *khalifa* and *tawheed*, the fundamental principles of Islam, were translated into practical conservation injunctions in the Shariah. Such Shariah institutions as *haram* zones, inviolate areas within which development is prohibited to protect natural resources, and *hima*, reserves established solely for the conservation of wildlife and forests, form the core of the environmental legislation of Islam. The classical Muslim jurist, Izzad-Din ibn Abd as-Salam, used these aspects of the Shariah when he formulated the bill of legal rights of animals in the thirteenth century. Similarly, numerous other jurists and scholars developed legislation to safeguard water resources, prevent over-grazing, conserve forests, limit the growth of cities, protect cultural property and so on. Alas, I said, contemporary Muslims have forgotten all this. I punctuated my deliberation with a few verses from the Qur'an and a couple of hadith. Prince Philip listened attentively and asked probing questions. How different from how I had imagined him, I thought. We were joined by (the late) Rabbi Arthur Hertzberg, Vice-President of the World Jewish Congress, who pointed out that both in Islam and Judaism encounter of man in nature is conceived as a seamless web with man as custodian of the natural world. He emphasised that man and nature are 'one' and went on to talk about what he called 'at-oneness with others'.

Rabbi Hertzberg struck me as an exceptionally learned man but also remarkably humble. I was surprised to note that he shared my views on Israel's policies towards the Palestinians.

The three of us stood in the Basilica talking for quite some time, encircled by protocol officers who were clearly displeased by me. Eventually, two took Prince Philip away – not quite to his pleasure. Father Bernard ushered me and Rabbi Hertzberg towards the exit. At the doors of the Basilica, a man distributing leaflets stuck one in my hand. I began to read: 'Help Assisi Nature Council bring St Francis' songbirds back to Assisi.'

'Bird hunting is a major sport here,' Father Bernard explained. 'For a bird to fly over Assisi is instant death. I think they know that; that's why they keep away.'

The following morning, eagerly looking forward to the ceremony, I woke up early and went straight to the Basilica. It was already crowded and admission was restricted to those with special passes. I sat at the back near the main entrance and passed the time by flicking through the programme booklet; fifty-two pages printed on recycled paper, but not sparing elegance or expense. The ceremony was programmed to start at exactly 10.10am. However, a few minutes before, my attention was drawn by a strange noise.

*'Habbabalu, Habbahalulu. Habbabalu.'*

I had to lean back to see what was happening at the main door. His Royal Highness looked startled, quizzical. He expected the Maori warrior to challenge him; but was he not appearing before his appointed time? According to the published programme, first there were the Assisi trumpeters which cued the procession of world religious leaders he was heading. Then there were the Swiss Alp horns which symbolised the new alliance between religion and conservation. Then there was the muezzin ... The Maori challenge was to come after all this. But he regained his composure, and looked into the Maori's eyes. He was about to make a comment when the Muazzin started the call to prayer. Except he wasn't calling the *Azan* but reading a verse from the Qur'an. The Duke of Edinburgh shook his head, even more perplexed. He was obviously not used to being attacked by such a quadraphonic multi-cultural melange; and the rehearsals yesterday had not prepared him well.

'*Habbabalu. Habbabalulu.*' The warrior danced and waved his lance. There was a commotion and a considerable amount of confusion. Prince Philip mumbled something only he could understand. Someone moved forward and whispered something in his ears. He mumbled something else. Having accepted, on behalf of the world religions, the challenge of conservation and that the major faiths and cultures of the world should take seriously the perspectives and values of indigenous people, the procession moved forward and entered the Basilica di San Francisco.

*'Chan, chan, chanan. Chanananon.'*

Yamini Krishnamurti performed a Hindu dance of creation. Following the psalm of praise of the Franciscan Choir and Father Serrini's brief welcome address to the congregation, witnessing the recreation of Veda was quite a drastic transformation:

'There was at first no Being —
nor blank.
There was no air, nor sky beyond.
What was in it? Where?
In whose protection?
Was water there, deep beyond measure?

There was no death, nor deathless state,
No night, no day.
The One breathed, without breath
By its own power.
There was nothing else; no, nothing else.

Darkness lay wrapped in darkness.
All was water, all, all over.
Love began, at first; desire
Was the seed of mind.

Sages and poets, searching within,
Saw the link of Being and non-Being.
But who really knows? Who can tell —
How it was born, where creation began?
The gods came later: Who then knows?

That from which creation came.
Whether founded well or not.
He who sees from heaven above,
He only knows. Or, He too knows it nor!'

'Booo. Booo. Booo'.

The sounding of the shofar, the Jewish ram's horn, changed all. A host of repentance prayers followed. First the Jewish. Then the Song of the Prayer of Truth, specially written by His Holiness the XIVth Dalai Lama. Followed by an extract from Bhagavad-Gita. A few verses from the Qur'an. A reading from the New Testament.

*'Hustle, hustle, hustle.'*

The congregation stood to greet the procession which included representatives of different groups within the major world faiths and conservation bodies. The procession moved slowly. Many members of the procession looked tired; they had walked on a pilgrimage to Assisi. Many carried banners with drawings of animals — fish, fox, chicken, cow, kingfisher, woodpecker. The procession was led by a group which brings *rakshas* to the centre of the stage. The celebrations begin.

The pregnant silence is only occasionally broken by a stray cough. A young man carrying a World Wildlife Fund (WWF) banner takes a few brisk steps and stands at the centre of the stage. Prince Philip stands and reads a prepared speech. He suggests that where there is no vision, people perish. 'Let us therefore listen, with open and receptive minds, to the teachings of the great religions and to what they have to say about the living world and about the part humanity should be playing in it.'

'*Chant. Chant. Chant.*'

A young girl holding a banner representing the Buddhist faith comes and stands in the middle of the stage. The Buddhist monks chant verses from Shantidev's *Guide to the Budhisattava's Way of Life:*

And no-one desires the slightest suffering
Nor ever has enough of happiness,
There is no difference between myself and others,
So let me make others joyfully happy.

A number of young men and women carrying banners of various faiths come and stand centre stage, each is followed by a leader of that faith who delivers the message on nature and humanity of his religion. The Buddhist declaration on nature is delivered by Venerable Lungrig Namgyal Rinpoch, Abbot of Gyuto Tantric University, originally in Lhasa, Tibet, but now exiled to India. The Christian declaration on nature is conveyed by Father Lanfranco Serrini of the Order of Friars. The Hindu declaration on nature is delivered by Karan Singh (who, as the name suggests is actually a Sikh), then President of Hindu Virat Samaj. The Jewish declaration on nature is presented by Rabbi Hertzberg; and the Muslim declaration is read by Abdullah Naseef. There is a great deal of common ground between the five declarations: all agree that looking after nature is an imperative for humanity. Finally the Heritage Singers of Zambia sing a new arrangement of the famous Canticle of the Creatures by St Francis.

*'Hustle. Hustle. Hustle.'*

Everyone stands up. His Royal Highness leads the procession of religious leaders out of the Basilica to the Piazza Superiore. A group of young volunteers distribute *raksha*s. Members of the congregation are asked to tie a *raksha* to the left arm of the person next to them. From the side tower, five Declarations of Faith on Nature are issued to the pilgrims who are asked to carry their particular message back to the faithful. The congregation looks for the copies of the Declarations on the walls of the Piazza Superiore, where the programme says they are posted, but no one finds anything. The bells of the Basilica start to ring. The new alliance between religion and conservation has begun. A group of young actors start performing a street play. A collection of young devotees start recruiting followers for their guru. A group of Swiss men and women start dancing.

I start wandering. Displaying my *raksha* on my arm, I move amongst the merry-making crowd seeking some opinions. 'What did you think of the ceremony?', I ask an old couple emerging from the Basilica. 'Oh, it was very moving. So moving.' What did they do? 'Oh, we work for the WWF.' I try to solicit the view of another couple; they also turn out to be officials of the WWF. I try again, and again, and again. Everyone works for the WWF. And they all think that the ceremony was 'very moving,'. Finally I am reduced to soliciting the view of a fellow journalist from Denmark.

'Did you think that it was a moving ceremony?', I ask eagerly.

'It was moving,' he says. 'But in which direction, I am not sure. If ideas and beliefs held for centuries could be changed with a single interfaith ceremony we would have created a different world by now. But no doubt it provided a good outing for the bureaucrats of the World Wildlife Fund.'

The WWF officials were certainly having a good time. I joined in the festivities for a few hours and then decided to say farewell to Assisi. I collected my shoulder bag and walked down to the main square. At the bus stop several pilgrims were waiting anxiously to catch a bus to Rome. As I joined the waiting crowd an aristocratic lady, way past her middle ages, supporting a rather large necklace of cultured pearls — I guessed they were cultured — turned around and asked: 'Do you know when the next coach leaves, for Rome, young man?'

'No. But someone here must know. Let me find out.' I asked a number of people; but no one had any idea. Indeed, it transpired that all the buses that were going to Rome had already gone! After waiting around for over an hour, I decided to head back to the Basilica. Around Piazza Inferiore I bumped into Father Bernard.

'Any chance of a lift back to Rome?', I asked, looking a bit helpless. 'Oh! I wish I could take you with me. We could have continued our conversation about St Francis' work in Egypt. But I have an urgent meeting with His Holiness. You know he is coming here next month. Why don't you share a ride with one of the other Rabbis. I am sure he will love your company.' He called a monk and instructed him to find me a seat in the Rabbi's car.

I followed the monk to the Basilica. And walked straight into a rabbinical burst of outrage.

I did not hear everything this particular Rabbi was saying. But the gist of his message was quite evident. The Rabbi was angry. In fact, he was very, very angry. 'Don't you know who I am? Do you?', he kept repeating. I did not. All I knew was that he was part of the Jewish entourage which had quite a few Rabbis. A number of apologetic Franciscan monks ran in different directions. One was busy on the phone. 'He is very agitated. Hurry up.'

'It will be here in fifteen minutes,' he reported back to the Rabbi. 'And my escort. Where is my escort?'

'No problem. You will be escorted by the police. They will be here shortly.'

'Shortly?', the Rabbi thundered. 'I have been waiting for two hours.'

'It's all the fault of the WWF. They are very disorganised,' a monk confided to the Rabbi.

'Huh!', the Rabbi brushed him aside as if to say don't agitate me further.

'You are right,' said the Rabbi's assistant, standing behind him in a suitable posture of embarrassment. He was smartly dressed and in his late thirties. Repeatedly, he tried to calm the Rabbi. 'The WWF has managed the whole affair very badly,' he said.

I wasn't sure it was a good idea to share a long ride with the Rabbi while he was nursing his present mood. I tried to make some friendly overtures but he chose to ignore me. Indeed, he avoided even looking at me. When I looked at his face, I saw much more than anger. I saw pride; and I saw arrogance. Arrogance was dripping from his face as though he had just resurfaced after a deep dive in the ocean. ARROGANCE. It called to mind the façade of Assisi. It brought me back to earth with a bump.

I recalled what the Rabbi was saying, only a few hours ago, during the ceremony. He was reading a Jewish prayer, calling the whole world to repentance for its failure to care for nature. He was denouncing the arrogance of man — an arrogance that had led to the present environmental crisis, extinction of invaluable world-life. He was urging the world to show more tolerance, to promote peace and harmony between man and man and man and nature. And he was using Divine words to convey his message. He had prayed:

> 'Our God and God of our fathers,
> Establish Your glorious rule all over the world,
> Establish Your glorious majesty over all the earth,
> Let all who inhabit the world behold the grandeur of Your MIGHT,
> Let every creature know that You fashioned it,
> Let every living thing recognize that You formed it,
> Let every creature declare that God is King,
> And His dominion extends over all creation.
> In Your great mercy, Lord,
> Bring us near to Your presence.
> Help us to break down the barriers
> Which keep us far from You:
> Falsehood and faithlessness,
> Callousness and selfishness,
> Injustice and hard-heartedness.
> Our hope is in You,
> For You respond in mercy
> When we sound the Shofar.'

I also recalled what Rabbi Hertzberg had said during the Jewish declaration on nature. 'In the imagery of many a rabbinic preacher we, men and women, are depicted as God's flock. He is our shepherd...It is written in the Scripture: "I will give grass in your fields for your cattle, and you shall eat and be satisfied". In this verse, Rabbi Hertzberg had noted, cattle are mentioned before men ... Judaism does know, of course, that there are wild and destructive forces within the heart of humankind. That is why God gave us His commandments, to teach us restraint ... And yet, the ultimate meaning of human life, in Jewish teaching, is not to restrain evil but to do good. God Himself, as He created the world, left some of it unfinished.' Here Rabbi Hertzberg raised the pitch of his voice: 'He did not make order of all the *tho va-vohu*, the primal chaos. He deeded onto us the task of being His partner in the act of creation ...'.

So many words about humility, patience, selflessness and respect for others and for nature. Everyone claimed to believe in them, to be duty bound to practice them. Surely the Rabbi was not alone in any sense, just an in-opportune example of the silence of communication we all indulge between the saying and the doing, the word and the deed, the intention and the reality. How many more from other creeds could the blowing of the shofar call to account?

'You do not know the other side of my character,' he thundered to a small gathering of Franciscan monks. 'I have been waiting for six hours now. If a car does not arrive immediately ...', he paused, tried to finish his sentence, but decided not to do so. One monk tried to persuade the Rabbi to take a taxi. The Rabbi agreed grudgingly. A taxi arrived and the Rabbi's luggage was loaded. The taxi driver emphasised he wanted $300. The Rabbi suggested the taxi driver should be paid now. The monks looked at each other in perplexed silence. Then one of them left to make a telephone call. He came back to advise that the Rabbi should pay the taxi and bill the World Wildlife Fund.

There was an explosion.

When the air cleared, the Rabbi's assistant had persuaded him to pay for the taxi.

A few moments after the Rabbi and his assistant had left, a car arrived. A monk indicated that I should get in the car. It was driven by a young Yorkshireman who was taking time off from teaching English Literature in a Japanese university to work as a volunteer in Assisi. He gave the impression of having emerged from nearby cover only on the appropriate signal. We made instant friends.

'Nice message, shame about the Rabbi,' he opened the conversation.

'We all know the message', I replied. 'It's the action bit we are truly ignorant about'.

He laughed. 'Still the ceremony was fun despite the organisational hiccups. A cacophony of hubbub with not much harmony', he said negotiating the meandering road out of Assisi. We laughed together; and spent the time on the journey discussing the notion of partnership in the Judeo-Christian intellectual heritage and Salman Rushdie's relationship with Günter Grass.

# ARTS AND LETTERS

ATHENS' CONCRETE DELUSIONS *by Iason Athanasiadis*
MEDITERRANEAN DEATH *by AbdelWahab Yousif*
ISTANBUL POEMS *selected and translated by Mevlut Ceylan*

# ATHENS' CONCRETE DELUSIONS

*Iason Athanasiadis*

Few ancient cities flaunt, obsess over but also degrade their antiquity like Athens. An Italian traveller sighting it in the seventeenth century, hailed the ancient city clustering around 'the most beautiful piece of antiquity remaining in the world', the Acropolis. But by the early 1800s, armies, Western aesthetes and looters fighting over its legend had already reduced its appearance so much that English Poet Lord Byron described it as 'the most injured, most celebrated of cities'.

Today, tonnes of concrete cover most of the city Byron witnessed, leaving contemporary arrivals four ways in which to approach it. Drivers must plough through several kilometres of seaside industrial facilities or haphazardly-constructed inland residential districts before encountering

Dense buildings surround the Parthenon. Buildings are subject to a law banning the construction of anything higher than the ancient monument, resulting in a mostly low-rise city.

anything reminiscent of an Instagram feed. Ferry passengers steam into a smoggy harbour replete with vintage dock machinery, crowded with apartment blocks, and dominated by the hulk of a skyscraper built, then abandoned, during the 1967–74 Colonels' dictatorship. Trains deliver their passengers straight to a downtown of dense, poor and multicultural neighbourhoods a world apart from the neoclassical villas scattered around the Acropolis' Arcadian foothills. Finally, air-travellers descend over the glittering waters and wind-turbine-studded islets of the 'Athens Riviera' (perhaps the only Riviera to have already been overbuilt and environmentally-degraded before being proclaimed as one) gliding over automobile and villa-sprawl into an airport constructed for the 2004 Olympics. An underground metro and a privately-operated highway winding through a forested mountain further shield new arrivals from the concrete organism splayed across the Attic Plain.

At first sight, visitors gasp at the informal urbanism and grasp for references. Some are struck by how dry, chaotic and Middle Eastern the city's energy appears. Others describe it as a Soviet-looking town of cement blocks transposed to a Mediterranean climate. Its strongly Modernist architectural traditions, developed along narrow, grid-patterned, motorcycle-strewn streets, reference districts of Damascus and Belgrade. But Athens' past is even more cemented-over, and its ancient buildings, streams and rivers subsumed under interminable rows of twentieth and early twenty-first century apartment buildings that scarcely evoke Europe. Even its glass-and-steel contemporary buildings look more like an approximation of the West encountered in Fujayrah than the City of London.

No two cities are the same and nothing we see today transpired accidentally. But contemporary Athens' layering, versatility and resonant absences manifest themselves through a procession of mostly misapplied ideologies: Athens' nineteenth-century Western liberators sought to conjure up a phoenix of Hellenic antiquity. But instead they unleashed a smorgasbord of currents that transformed the fragile antique city. The state they created was invested in promoting a homogenising Greek narrative that implicitly excluded Muslims, Jews, Armenians and any kind of healthy multiculturalism that was too reminiscent of the Ottoman Empire. The flight from the old condemned much of the older architectural traditions to the city because, unlike Romans or Parisians, Athenians were taught to crave the modern, leaving little space for respecting and preserving anything historical that wasn't ancient or Greek. Finally a singular lack of institutions insulated the city from political storms and instability, because the political culture remained clannish rather than national, consisting of groups that installed and replaced loyalists as they shifted in and out of power.

Athens' nineteenth century revival from parochial post-Ottoman backwater into European wannabe was driven by a pro-Westernism containing an incipient contempt for its Eastern identity and Ottoman past, and impelled forward by a speculative opportunism. The city of 'flat roofs intermingled with cypresses, ruins, isolated columns, the domes of the mosques crowned by huge storks' nests... each house with its garden planted with orange and fig trees' witnessed by Chateaubriand in 1805, was judged too backward to survive.

I was born in the late 1970s, long after Athens' expansion had brought it up against its encircling mountains, and spent my first fifteen years in a dusty under-construction suburb adjoining the brutalist new university campus, before we moved to a central neighbourhood famed for being a haunt of intellectuals in the 1960s. The following two decades were spent abroad in cities to Athens' West and East, an experience that gifted me some essential perspective on my frantic, lackadaisical and inscrutable birthplace. As I adjusted to life in London, Damascus, Cairo, Paris, Tehran, Istanbul, Kabul, Libya's Tripoli, Tunis and Boston, I was increasingly preoccupied by the perplexing differences and unexpected similarities encountered daily. What I'd been brought to believe was normal while growing-up proved elsewhere to have been at best an exception, at worse perverse. But I also discovered striking cultural similarities in the most frowned-upon places (usually to Athens' East). It all made me wonder how the waves of history sweeping across a weak and often bankrupt state's capital could end up moulding its habits, infrastructure, layout and traditions as much as (or more) than its own inhabitants.

Greece will mark the 200-year anniversary of its anti-Ottoman revolution in 2021, in a Balkan blur of pageantry and nationalism only moderately subdued by the necessities of austerity and its organisers' Europeanised aesthetics (the head of the committee is the same billionaire's wife who ran the Athens 2004 Olympics). As we approach that moment, it's worth pausing to reflect on the six ideologies whose misapplications most defined

Athens' complete transformation from low-rise and poor, post-antique Ottoman backwater into midrise and over-touristed investment destination.

Using a camera or drone I sought to best contextualise each location's significance within the city, identifying the buildings, districts and spaces that best tell the story of how it formed at each separate ideological stage, while providing visual evidence of how Athens evolved under the pressure of narratives just as much as circumstances.

### *Classicism: an antidote to the Ottomans*

In 1827, a joint English, French and Russian fleet regime-changed Ottoman rule in Greece, ending an inconclusive conflict fought for years among a shifting alignment of Greek and Albanian revolutionaries and

Athens developed through accretions and amputations. This solitary neoclassical building stands on the edge of a neighbourhood known as Vrysaki, demolished in the 1930s to uncover sections of the Agora of ancient Athens. The excavations ramped up during the Cold War, in a period when a United States wielding the Truman Doctrine and promoting a democracy-protecting narrative funded excavations as a source of historical legitimation. Vrysaki's demolition resulted in public outcry and was never repeated since. The Greek Ministry of Culture now continues uncovering the Agora through a slow and expensive policy of purchasing buildings to demolish them.

mercenaries, Ottoman and Egyptian militaries, and French and English philhellenes. When the smoke cleared, the Great Powers agreed that the best person to shepherd to maturity the fledgling country – a South Sudan or Kosovo of its era – was the King of Bavaria's underage son. A Bavarian

The recently renovated Fethiye Mosque (foreground), and the Hellenistic-era Tower of the Winds (background) which the Mevlevi order used as a tekke in Ottoman times.

The gateway of the *medresseh* of Athens is the only part of that building still remaining. Post-Independence, it functioned as a prison for decades before being demolished.

guard took over the Acropolis from the Ottomans in a ceremony marking the transfer of control over Greece from Ottomans to Great Power guarantors, and inaugurating a two-century attachment to the West that only started shifting back Eastwards over the past decade.

By 1830, Athens had shrunk to about 4,000 inhabitants and wasn't even the obvious first choice for capital. One popular idea among many Greeks was that – along with other cities – it could perhaps be a temporary, rotating capital, at least pending Istanbul's conquest, since many felt that only a reconquered Constantinople could be Hellenism's final capital. But *Augsburger Allgemeine Zeitung*, announced that 'the Capital of Greece must be Athens ... because of its mild climate, its fertile soil and excellent harbour as well as its magnificent monuments'.

The King of Bavaria was the father of Greece's appointed king and a great admirer of antiquity. He had already purchased the marble reliefs of Aegina's Temple of Aphaia and displayed them in his just-built and neoclassically-inspired Glyptothek museum in Munich. In Athens, he appointed a team of architects to design a neoclassical city of palazzos, squares and boulevards, bestowing on the city an architecture inspired from its past, but developed in Paris and Munich then exported 'back' to Athens in a reverse compliment loaded with significance.

*Cafés-chantants* no longer exist in twenty-first century Athens, but *rembetika* joints are still going strong.

The result was a city largely purified of Frankish, Byzantine and Ottoman accretions intended to express its past splendour in digestible, Europeanised form. Neoclassical Athens' construction marked a season of destruction not just for all previous periods of its history (Ottoman, Frankish, Byzantine, even classical), but for its Christian heritage too, as 120 Byzantine churches and chapels were demolished during the 1840s to make way for the rising city, seventy-two destroyed merely to provide building materials for the ambitious cathedral.

But angry landowners refused to sell up, real-estate prices rose, and a resulting lack of funds resulted in the city never quite looking as intended. This was not necessarily bad, given one German architect's intentions to emulate the practices of past conquerors by building the King's palace inside the Parthenon in neoclassical style. Ultimately, Otto's 'immense marble palace' was still criticised by French historian Jean Alexandre-Buchon for a grandiosity inappropriate to a town where 'two years ago scarcely a stone house existed, in a nation whose people had so recently been raised to being their own masters and where princes slept out of doors wrapped in their cloaks'.

The University of Athens, presented as part of a neoclassical triptych inaugurated in 1837 and housed in, is the most striking example of the grandiose neoclassicism envisaged by Athens' revivalists. Upon seeing it, one of the aged heroes of the simpler, less pretentious revolutionary period, Theodoros Kolokotronis, correctly predicted that 'this house will eat up that house', meaning that Western-style education would result in the monarchy's abolition.

## *Against the East*

Before evolving a state identity, Greek-speaking Christians inhabited each of the Mediterranean's three shores as polyglot trading minorities. Much like the Jews, the creation of a nation-state resulted in the shrivelling of their cosmopolitan communities, not just because they finally had a country to call their own, but because the transition from empires to nations resulted in their port-cities being integrated into countries, each with its own nationalistic founding myth that failed to include them.

As the imperial era transitioned to the nation-state, successive waves of Greeks 'repatriated' to a country they had never visited. Although the majority had lived in Arabic and Turkish-speaking countries, the social climate they encountered in Athens was contemptuous, ignorant and fearful of their nuanced and cosmopolitan backgrounds. One of the unspoken conditions of assimilation was to leave their acquired languages at the door, effectively amputating a cultural skill that could have aided Greece had it decided to situate itself less squarely in the West. The same was happening in neighbouring Turkey, where Kemalist efforts to fashion a nation-state out of a collapsed empire resulted in all minorities being urged to speak only Turkish, while Arabic and Persian words were cleansed out in favour of French derivatives.

While Athens was always measuring itself against Paris and Vienna, it was closer or inferior in functionality to Alexandria, Smyrna and Tunis, all modernising Mediterranean cities boasting large Greek minorities. In post-Independence Athens, luxuries were so scarce that an American missionary's home was renowned for its rocking-chair! By the 1880s, Athens may have lacked paved, lit streets and residents still queued at public fountains for water, but donkeys deposited bejewelled ladies and gentlemen decked out in evening dress before a brand new opera house, occasionally also interrupting performances with their braying. Even as late as the 1970s, Greeks living in Shah-era Tehran looked down on Athens as underdeveloped.

A bourgeois elite developed in Athens, much of it springing from strategic marriages between old Athenian and Phanariot families freshly-arrived from Istanbul, Wallachia or Odessa, where they had spent centuries serving international business and the Ottoman Sultan. The new urban aristocracy sidelined the mostly illiterate revolutionary heroes, dismissed bawdy, embarrassing customs derived from the countryside, and had a fear of the proletariat that expressed itself in efforts to reform them, both through efforts to eradicate illiteracy and through new forms of entertainment. Europeanised locals preferred the so-called *cafés-chantants*, featuring French songs and foreign dancers (marking a revolution in local sexual mores) to the *cafés-aman* where mostly-male musical groups played traditional melodies derived from common Turkish, Arabic and Persian musical cultures.

The cultural confrontations escalated when pro-fascist dictator Ioannis Metaxas banned *rembetika*, a type of music arising from the region's main ports – Thessaloniki, Istanbul and Smyrna – developed by refugees from Asia Minor settling in Athens' working-class districts. Already spatial social separations had been established as the bourgeois settled in freshly-built neoclassical villas and manors, while their builders, workers and servants clustered around the wealthy, planned districts, or occupied marginal areas next to quarries and factories. During the Civil War, these invisible divisions became bullet-riddled frontlines between Communists and Royalists. Even today, machinegun-armed riot police guard the separation point between the traditionally working-class and leftist Exarheia neighbourhood and aristocratic Kolonaki.

Athens' palm trees became another cultural battleground. Dozens were ripped up in intensely Westernising periods of the city's history, like the immediate post-Ottoman period, the developmental 1920s, and the 1967–74 Junta years. The cull was allegedly made to deny the city an Eastern look. In the 2000s, ahead of the 2004 Athens Olympics, hundreds were replanted to boost its exoticism in the eyes of visitors. Today, palm-trees exist in escapist parts of the city: the so-called Athens Riviera and the pedestrianised part of the centre earmarked for tourism, hotels and Golden Visa investors.

From the 1990s onwards, the Westernising tendency accelerated through the introduction of private television stations and lifestyle magazines instructing their readers how to dress, speak and act, which restaurants and clubs to eat and be seen in, islands to holidays in, and universities in the West to send their children too. The founder of one of these magazines once famously boasted that he was largely responsible for 'depeasantifiying' Greeks.

In Athens, the Westernising tendency manifested itself in American-style urban sprawl, as new and unregulated suburbs arose upon agricultural or recently-burned forest land. Life became heavily dependent on cars, public transport was chronically underinvested in, and the environment degraded by a patronage-based political system that placed industries too close to the city and intentionally failed to regulate them. The damage was completed by annual arson seasons intended to clear land for more construction, and wanton pollution of the sea through oil-spills and direct dumping of sewage.

As Athens expanded to cover most of Attica, social segregation grew. Greeks abandoned the city centre, and first-generation migrants seeking cheap rents and willing to work hard at jobs that Greeks now considered

Tzitzifies is a lowrise settlement of refugee housing built in the 1930s to accommodate some of the 1.2 million refugees from Greece's Asia Minor defeat against the Turkish army.

Local children ride their bicycles in the ancient Kerameikos (Ceramics) district of Athens in front of a building whose first floor still bears signs of the December 1944 British advance from the port of Piraeus into Communist-held areas of central Athens.

beneath them repopulated it. Once-bourgeois downtown districts first became marginalised in the nineties and noughties, then developed in the 2010s and 2020s as vibrant, multicultural hubs attracting artists engaged in popular and award-winning cultural production.

### *Megaloideatism: reviving Byzantium and the refugee backlash*

As time wore on and Greece won more Ottoman territory at the expense of other Balkan claimants, it sought to implement its irredentist Megali Idea (lit. the Great Idea): conquer all Byzantine territories that the Turks had claimed by the fifteenth century, and become a regional power astride two continents and five seas.

Egged on by the victorious but exhausted Allies in the immediate aftermath of World War One, Greece's charismatic Prime Minister Eleftherios Venizelos dispatched an army to invade an Ottoman Empire under occupation by three European armies and riven by internal political crises. The British, whose putative control over Mosul's oil reserves had been questioned by Turkey's dynamic military leader Kemal Ataturk, were particularly supportive of the Greek intervention. Three years of fighting later, the defeated Greek army withdrew, setting the stage for the burning of Smyrna and triggering the million-strong exodus of Greek-speaking Christians to Greece. A 1923 population exchange treaty between Greece and Turkey became Hellenism's tombstone in Asia Minor, ending a 3,000-year Greek presence there. Around 150,000 refugees were added to Athens' 300,000 population, resulting in the construction of several new neighbourhoods for them, many of which the descendants of the original families today rent out to more recent migrants and refugees from the Middle East.

In 1922, the geopolitical repercussions of the Great Idea project turned Piraeus, parts of the Agora, and even the entrance to the royal Palace into squalid refugee camps, full of disbelieving petitioners that the upstart new country which had so cavalierly represented their dreams, mishandled its military campaign to the point of squandering everything. The wartime rhetoric of unity evaporated as the locals expressed hostility towards refugee newcomers, who were also seen as a threat for generally being more skilled, multilingual and integrated into the global economy. Their arrival gave a distinctively Eastern feel to a city constructed as a Western

Located within eyeline of the Parthenon and a stone's throw from the US Embassy, the Hilton became Athens' most fashionable address but also a political hub.

The Hilton Hotel dominates the area around it with its bulk and design.

derivative, and further weaponised the twentieth century's domestic culture wars.

## *The Capitalist City*

With Communism banished, and British influence waning, Greece passed into US custody. It entered NATO in 1952, devalued its currency against the dollar to bring itself into line with Bretton Woods requirements, and initiated a construction boom whereby new highways, coastal entertainment zones and business districts extended the city along model capitalist grooves. The new consumer lifestyle was captured in the period's lavish movie production, much of it filmed inside new beach-clubs, office buildings, cabarets and luxury hotels.

Mass tourism commenced against a political backdrop of right-wing governments, internal repression of leftists, and a hefty troop and air force contribution to the US war against Communist China in Korea. Air-hostesses wearing haute-couture uniforms worked for the Onassis-owned Olympic Airways out of the starchitect-designed Ellinikon airport, apartment buildings built of cement churned out by the Hercules factory in Piraeus went up, and coal-miners descended into the shafts of the Kalogreza mines humming catchy tunes recorded at the sprawling Columbia Records recording-studio complex. Today, that high-living period of Athens' history is as dead as the half-demolished or vandalised facilities encapsulating Greece's industrial moment, and products that were once made in Greece are imported from China at a lower cost through Athens' Chinese-owned port.

Aside from being a model capitalist city, Athens also played a key military role in the Cold War: the US Sixth Fleet regularly visited Piraeus, half the international airport acted as a US military airbase, and an entire local economy developed around American sailors' entertainment needs. To symbolise Greece's binding to the West, a statue of US President Harry Truman was erected within eyesight of the Hilton, promptly becoming Greece's most vandalised public monument.

Athens' and Istanbul's geopolitical positions turned both these cities into Cold War stages for intelligence operations, assassinations and intrigue. From 1968 onwards, Athens airport figured in dozens of terrorist incidents and aeroplane hijackings, especially after Lebanon erupted into civil war.

No building captures that era better than the Hilton Hotel, opened to great fanfare in 1963 as a symbol of the purchasable American way of life. Its architect blasphemously declared that the marble-coated cement slab rising

The remnants of the Lipasmata factory in Piraeus, once the main producer of fertilisers and a great source of pollution.

The remains of the Columbia recording studio complex in a part of Athens inhabited by refugees from the Asia Minor campaign, then reinhabited today by North African migrants.

opposite the Parthenon had been modelled on the antique temple itself. The Hilton marked the first international hotel chain to open in Athens and became a favourite for frolicking starlets, businessmen and politicians.

In his novel *Lost Spring*, Greek novelist Stratis Tsirkas' character, an unrepentant leftist returning to Athens after twenty years of exile in Budapest, experiences shock when first catching sight of the huge building towering over the city: 'A monster, hubris, a gigantic chunk of cement provocatively erected between (Mount) Hymettus's eyebrow and the Acropolis' smile,' the character thinks to himself as he rides in the taxi from the port. 'When I first caught sight of it, I felt within me the shattering of that violet vision of an open-hearted, friendly Athens which I'd been carrying and nurturing over the exile years.'

### *The neoliberal dividend*

Greece was over touristed long before the term was invented. A traveller arriving in Athens in 1810, a decade before Greeks revolted against the Ottomans, found it full of foreign socialites and artists cheerfully vandalising the city's ancient monuments for mementoes or purchasing them ready-

Athens has completed its transformation from low-rise and poor Ottoman backwater into midrise and over touristed investment-destination.

severed from the locals, carving their names on ancient walls, and attending whirling dervishes spectacles in the Tower of the Winds. Accommodation was scarce: the well-connected, would stay as guests of their country's consuls, the rest lodged at the monastery run by the Capuchin monks.

Until Covid-19 stilled the world's airports, tourism was the city's only growth business, with buildings cleared of residents and rubble to reopen as hotels. A lucrative Golden Visa program saw non-EU residents, especially Chinese, Russians, Israelis and Turks, purchasing the right to live in Europe. Athens was transforming into a theme-park, with a newly-pedestrianised centre and design tweaks intended to evoke a halogen-lit, 1960s city-centre filled with cruising chrome-finned Chevrolets, humming high-rise emporiums, and an Omonoia Square dominated by a gushing, multicoloured fountain.

But change in the early twenty-first century also came from unexpected quarters. China appropriated a part of the port, intending to turn it into the 'head of the dragon' of its trans-Asian Belt and Road initiative. As Greece's population contracted, more and more refugees from Asia and Africa were granted asylum and settled in the seedier parts of the city centre's once-bourgeois neighbourhoods, from where Athens' social revival or demise would issue. Imperceptibly at first, but following time-honoured tradition, Greece was shifting direction towards where power lay, this time Eastwards.

So how did these ideologies impact Athens? Undoubtedly they helped a city that had declined as much as the empire it once belonged to, grow into the thrusting hub of business, industry and political corruption that it is today, reminding us that a country created on the basis of a narrative always runs the risk of remaining economically unviable and prey to the interests of others. Without a tradition in institutions and a conservation ethic, the repeated waves of development and destruction left behind little recognizable of the city of 1940, let alone 1820: 90% of the buildings constructed between 1850 and 1940 no longer exist, turning a neoclassical urban jewel into a vibrant, deformed, and polluted concrete jungle.

Athens forfeited other things that it failed to sufficiently defend: its Jewish community during the Nazi occupation, the accumulated experiences of Greeks moving to Athens from Arabic, Farsi, Georgian, Russian and Turkish-speaking communities of the greater Mediterranean and Middle East regions, and half a million of its youngest, most skilled and polyglot citizens, surrendered to an austerity-enhanced brain-drain. Despite being ideally placed to benefit from the talents of those arriving before, during and after the 2015 refugee crisis, Athens' universities and private sector didn't invest in attracting the best of the region for study and work, and so its squares and neighbourhoods, instead of nourishing a new generation of talented city-dwellers, became merely resting-places in the long corridor leading to Europe.

The small minority of asylum-seekers who stayed behind of their own will rather than because they were trapped by the EU's containment moat, knew full-well that the system would offer them no material goods. Mostly they tended to be poetic souls: there's the melancholy Iranian *saaz*-maker living in a basement off Victoria Square who carried his instrument with him across several Balkan borders, the Kurdish painter nourishing himself with *rembetika*, or the Iranian director of *Pari* (2020), whose long years in the city allowed him to produce possibly the moodiest and most mystical reading of the city committed to film. Perhaps the city's jaded and long-complaining residents cannot discern the city's insistent buzz; only those purified by years of trauma and a modern, trans-Continental pilgrimage undertaken across inhospitable geographies can perceive Athens' centuries-deep energetic accumulations. Perhaps that energy – impervious to all ideologies – is what elevates this mongrel of a city into still being one of humanity's profoundest.

# MEDITERRANEAN DEATH

*Abdel Wahab Yousif*

During August 2020, a rubber boat packed with forty-five African migrants sank into the Mediterranean Sea shortly after setting off from Libya on its way to Europe. On board, was a young Sudanese poet, Abdel Wahab Yousif, twenty-nine years of age, known affectionately amongst the young generation of African poetry fans as Latinos. Born to a poor family in Manwashi, Southern Darfur, Latinos managed against the odds to study for a bachelor's degree in the Faculty of Economics at the University of Khartoum. However, despite his qualifications, he was unable to get a job. Desperate to secure his future, and as a last resort, Latinos, like scores of Darfurian youth, made his way to Libya, a gateway through which successive waves of Africans continue to brave all perils in the hope of getting safely to European shores. On his departure from Sudan, he wrote:

I'll run away from a homeland scourging my back with lashes day and night;
From a woman who doesn't know how to feed my soul from her body's nectar.
I'll run from everything,
nonchalantly embrace demise.

His tragic departure sent shock waves among his friends and poetry fans in Sudan. Adding to the tragedy was the realisation that the way he died was a perfect demonstration of a scenario that was depicted in his recent verse:

You'll die at sea.
Your head rocked by the roaring waves,
your body swaying in the water,
like a perforated boat.
In the prime of youth you'll go,
shy of your 30th birthday.
Departing early is not a bad idea;
but it surely is if you die alone
with no woman calling you to her embrace:

'Let me hold you to my breast,
I have plenty of room.
Let me wash the dirt of misery off your soul.'

The poet hit the zenith of despair in the last poem he published shortly before his death:

You are destined to go;
Today, tomorrow,
or the day after.
No one can halt the heavy wheel of destruction
running over life's body.
It's all in vain
no last-minute saviour will come
and rescue the world's body.
It's all in vain
no flash of light,
to scare away the darkness.
Everything is dying:
Time. Language.
Screams. Dreams.
Songs. Love. Music.
All in vain.
Everything is gone,
except a violent vacuum
dead bodies wrapped in melancholic silence
and a heavy downpour of destruction.

Translated by Adil Babikir

# ISTANBUL POEMS

## *Selected, Translated and Edited by Mevlut Ceylan*

Layer upon layer of civilisations. Religious and cultural heritage stretching back thousands of years. Rich complex history at every street corner. Its name evokes beautiful memories, allows imagination to run riot. Istanbul is the Eternal City, a perpetual destination. Not surprisingly, it has inspired countless poets. Just as in Sufism the mystical experience is described using the language of profane love, yet always contrasted with divine love, the poets address Istanbul hyperbolically as mistress, as girlfriend, as wife, with all the ambiguities such relationships involve. She is an undying and ever young lover. Torment and angst are her middle name. She's always youthful, beautiful and alluring. Istanbul is a demanding mistress whose favours are courted by many:

> I fell in love with you when I saw you,
> I can't forget you till the end of my life

After a long period when her beauties were obscured, mosques, colleges and mausolea, neglected and allowed to decay, and the Golden Horn turned into an industrial sewer, Istanbul has returned to its former glories. During the last decades, mosques have been refurbished, *caravanserais* converted to new usage such as craft workshops or hotels, the 'golden' Horn cleansed. In places like Khodja Mustafa Pasha and the Booksellers Bazaar, never invaded by modernity, it is still possible to recapture something of the past of the peerless city recorded by the English architect and artist, Thomas Allom (1804–72), in his engravings in the early nineteenth century. This was prior to the Tanzimat reforms and the degradation of the Islamic environment due to an uncritical adulation of everything Western. That so much of this beauty was allowed to vanish accounts for the poet's nostalgia. The consummation of the poet's love affair comes when he sees the city in everything: 'Istanbul, I touch you with a hundred thousand hands'.

These poems, covering a span of over hundred years, take us to the physical and emotional heart of the city and reveals some of the mystique of the city. Some of the great poets ofTurkish literature take us to a journey along the city's promenades, pleasure places and cafeterias: Kagithane Square, Sadabad, Camlica, Hisar, and Kucukcekmece, the site of caves at Yarimburgaz where Paleolithic culture flourished. Sometimes the poet address Istanbul directly; other times they describe her charm. But there is always an invitation: come and embrace the undying lure of Istanbul.

**Dreams of Istanbul**

Mehmet Akif Ersoy (1873–1936)

The boat was rolling over in an ocean…
The dream threw me on the shores of Marmara!
I saw from only a couple of miles away
Your blackened Istanbul clear as crystal,
Its forehead shining like a crescent:
She's laughing; coquettish, charming and attractive.

What base destitution now, alas!
What arrogance, what ostentation!
Many schools are opened, men and women study;
Factories are in full steam, textile industries progress.
Printing houses work day and night.
New companies emerge for the benefit of the people,
New parties arise to enlighten the people,
Economy prospers
And ships unload wealth from length to length of her shores.

**End of September**

Yahya Kemal Beyatli (1884–1958)

The days are brief, old folks of Kanlica
Remember all the autumns of the past.

Life is too short to love this district only...
I wish summers to last and days to be longer...

That rare drink quenched our thirst for years...
Ah! Life is too short for such a joy.

Death is our end, we're not afraid of it,
But it's hard to be away from the motherland.

Not to return from death's night to this shore,
Is worse than death, this is the heart's desire.

**Kodja Mujstafa Pasha**
Yahya Kemal Beyatli (1884–1958)

Kodja Mustafa Pasha! Poor and distant Istanbul!
Since the conquest you're a devout believer, and needy,

Here live those who deem sorrow is pleasure.
I was with them all day in this lovely dream.

Our motherland and nation are inseparable twins.
Thus we alone have been seen, and have been heard.

The moral frame radiant for five centuries;
Death is near, so close.

Sun followed an April rain.
On such a day reality mingled with dreams.

Doomsday is on the scene, very near,
So near there's no dividing wall between,

One is a step away from the other,
Seeing the beloved beyond is certain.

## The Derelict Temple of the Mihrimah Sultan Mosque

Riza Tevfik (1869–1949)

I came and wore down your threshold.
You're encircled by thorns and thistles.
I saw writings on your High Pulpit,
Were they remnants of happy moments, perhaps?
A glance from the setting sun faded,
Left your Qiblah in the dark,
The destiny of the unlucky Ummah
Casts shadows upon your ruined domes.
In a happy time of Islam
Its fountain had the elixir of life.
Now in its ruined baldaquin
The singing birds are rare.
There are sacred words of wisdom on your inscription,
There's something to be learned from your speech.
The cries of Tekbeer were suffocated
In your heavenly ruins.
Hey Riza, prostrate yourself before Him, and cry,
Your sufferings will make the stones talk.
I'll tell you fables, weep, and listen;
That glorious past was only a fairy tale.

Galata tower, photo credit: Mevlut Ceylan

**Domes**

Arif Nihat Asya (1904–1975)

Yesterday, mobilization started, hands are ready;Lead was melted and marble blocks cut down.
It wasn't money that built these domes,
These minarets, but love.
In such a ship, Noah defeated water
And the soul set sail with these wings.
...........
O traveller, if you could find a place,
A golden moon on everyone's brow,
Watch the mosques of Istanbul,
Count the minarets and domes!
..........
Here the sky opens quite blue,
It stands on silver pillars...
Shadows of some on the ground
And water reflecting others,
The roads to the Lord are here.

**My Dear Istanbul**

Necip Fazil Kisakurek (1905–1983)

They have melted my soul and frozen it in a mould;
They have named it Istanbul, and put it on earth.
There's something smoking inside me; air, colour, grace, and climate;
That's my beloved who came from beyond time and place.
Its flowers are golden stars, its water is sweet;
The moon and the sun have always been Istanbulian.
The sea and the earth have reached their union in her
And the dreams have turned to reality in her.
Istanbul is my life;
my motherland...
Istanbul,
Istanbul...

History has eyes, the riddles on ancient walls;
Cypresses, cypresses are of fine stature, they're the curtains
of two worlds…
A steed rears up on the clouds;
Diamond domes, perhaps there are billions of steeds…
The minarets are index fingers pointing to the sky.
In every embroidery a meaning: we must die.

Death is more alive than life, mercy is greater than sin;
When Beyoğlu is drowning in worldly pleasures,
Karacaahmet weeps…
Seek the meaning, find it!
Find it in Istanbul!
Istanbul,
Istanbul…

The Bosphorus, the silver brazier of the Bosphorus, boils the coolness;
The depths of heaven on earth are in Çamlica.
Playful waters are the guests in the basement of the sea-side house;
A photo of the sad face of a former diplomat hangs on the wall.
Every evening flames on the windows in Üsküdar,
A haunted house, big as the city…
A song from the Ud or the Tanbour?
It sings "Katibim" behind the bay-windows…
Its women are like sharp knives,
Warm like fresh blood,
Istanbul,
Istanbul…

Time on the seven hills embroiders
Seven colours, seven voices, endless manifestation…!
Eyüp is an orphan, Kadiköy is dressed up, Moda is haughty,
Wind in the Island plays tricks with the girls.
Each dawn, the arrows fly from their bows.
Cries come from Topkapi Palace still.
The mothers are the best of sweethearts, Istanbul is the best of places;

Never mind the cheerful crowd, those who cry are happier.
Its night smells hyacinth, Its Turkish the nightingale's voice.
Istanbul,
Istanbul...

**My Country**

Asaf Halet Çhelebi (1907–1958)

the tree grew out of
Osman Ghazi's heart,
streams,
meadows,
herds.
the land I live in
my Murad, my Yildirim, my Fatih,
my janissary,
my Evliya Çhelebi,
my Bursa, my Istanbul,
especially my Istanbul;
my history, my fine arts,
my mother, my father,
my neighbours,
Nerkis the black maid,
Nevres my Circassian nurse;
sea lights reflect on my house in Jihangir.
I've not fallen from heaven on this place;
this place is my Istanbul,
these people are mine,
these skies are mine;
Omer the sweet child is mine,
my forefathers my country and my
everything is hers.
In the dream Osman Ghazi saw
Omer and I are there.

**The Language of My Istanbul**
Asaf Halet Çhelebi (1907–1958)

my mother's tongue,
my father's tongue,
my Istanbul's tongue,
my Istanbul's tongue.

my Istanbul's Effendi
  and its Lady
guardian of my streets,
seller of yogurt, fishmongers,
you're my life,
interpreter of my soul.

this tongue sang my lullaby,
this tongue told my tales.
I listen to my folk songs from this tongue.
I've recited my poems with this tongue,
"oh, oppressor, stop prodding me to speak
  my innermost self".

**Istanbul**
Cahit Irgat (1916–1971)

Don't ask what's in Istanbul,
What's in Istanbul?
There's Istanbul in Istanbul.

**Gift**
Ilhan Berk (1916–2008)

I wrote this poem in nineteen forty nine,
I had more trouble than I could handle.

I was looking at Istanbul,
            my hands in my pockets.
Many horses passed before me,
            pouring sweat
I remembered your strength, I felt relaxed
my thoroughbred,
my beautiful steed,
all day long, the horses before me,
I wandered in Istanbul.

**Istanbul**

A. Kadir (1917–1985)

There are seas
there,
limpid and full of light,
that make you reflect.
Here are ships at anchor;
who knows
the weight of their chains.
Sarayburnu,
    Kizkulesi,
        Haydarpasha…
Look, here's the Bridge,
all day trampled underfoot,
and creaking, screeching roads;
and there, you see
Sultanahmet Square.
At last, the seafront,
where the fish smell good.
And then the Islands
    and all their pinewood.
Moonlight was sweet as heaven,
they say,
you lived in a dream world there.

Such is your vision of Istanbul, I think,
if you stand before a postcard
and look with hungry longing.

**Longing for the Sea**
Ilhan Geçer (1917–2004)

Your soft coolness is in my hand,
the time is in bluish memories.
Your wind is all over blue
and blows through my evenings.

In open sea the sail is homesick,
foaming sea-gulls are on my horizon.
My looks desire salt
and greet bright seasons.

I wish I was in a sea city,
I wish my feet to touch sea-weed,
I wish my song to be sung
by rough waters.

I wish the fishes to swim by my shores,
tiny and handsome fishes.
I wish they'd wave good-bye,
My dear Istanbul.

**Emirgan**
Salah Birsel (1919–1999)

All of you will run to Emirgan
In September or October
And sit before samovars
Drinking your tea and tea again.

Work and things will be forgotten
Under the plane tree till evening,
You'll be stretched out as if
You're in your own home,
You'll eat corn and corn again.
Gentlemen, there's no way out,
All of you will laugh and shout,
Sit down and get up
and smoke hubble-bubble, hubble-bubble.

Hubble-bubble, Photo Credit: Zaid Sardar

**The Bosphorus**
Necdet Evliyagil (1920–1992)

Istanbul,
Every season
appears
with her
beauty.

Autumn,
each side of the strait
envelops itself in the wind's blueness.
Sea is blue,

sky is blue,
the old plane tree is blue
The fisherman's eyes are blue
who waits his kismet by the sea.

**Istanbul**
Mucap Ofluoğlu (1923–2012)

Istanbul was cloudy today.
It's still six o'clock in the morning;
it's the nineteenth
of June
in Kadiköy Harbour
and the day is Monday.

It's still six o'clock in the morning;
it's been some time
since I've seen Istanbul
at this time of day.
It's drizzling, I'm looking at Istanbul the giant city
from hundreds of years ago.

This city turned over
to Mehmed the Conqueror
in fourteen hundred and fifty-three,
on a night in May.
Pulled overland on rollers
the galleys lay in the harbour side by side
against Byzantium's line of defence.
Amid laughter
The Conqueror's vessels walked on land.
Scimitars were brandished on the towers
and javelins hurled at the walls,
When Islam spread
and Constantinople became Istanbul.

**Yakacik**

Mehmet Çinarli (1925–1999)

I fell in love with you when I saw you,
I can't forget you till the end of my life, Yakacik.
As the moon lights us as its pleases,
O Yakacik! What a sweet evening we had.

As you'd expect to be in such a place
You showed us all your gifts.
We gave all our grievances to the wild winds,
O Yakacik! What a sweet evening we had.

We sat facing Marmara
And added new tunes to the songs,
As if we climbed to the seven heavens.
O Yakacik! What a sweet evening we had.

All the drinks took their taste from your water.
The beloved drank it and became ever sweeter.
We had the time of our life until late night,
I cannot forget you till the end of my life, Yakacik!

**The Cloud of Istanbul**

Arif Damar (1925–2010)

Heaps of clouds are coming,
They're white in the island, and in Moda,
They're black over the Golden Horn
And they disappear in Topkapi.

**Istanbul**

Umit Yasar Oguzcan (1926–1984)

A room in the house, in the room Istanbul
A mirror in the room, in the mirror Istanbul.

A man lit his cigarette; Istanbul smoke,
A woman opened her bag, Istanbul in the bag.

I saw the child cast his fishing line in the sea,
He started to pull it up, Istanbul on the hook.

What sort of water is this, what kind of city?
Istanbul's in the bottle, Istanbul's on the table.

When we walk she walks, when we stop she stops; we were confused,
She's on one side, I'm on the other, Istanbul in the middle.

Once you love, you're in trouble.
Wherever you go, Istanbul is there.

**Lost Days**

Metin Eloğlu (1927–1985)

Bring me some Istanbul,
fill the bowl with the sea;
let them sift my days in a bag.
Whatever was left of Üsküdar from
 that summer with Elif,
stuff them in your pockets;
if they don't have them, the neighbours might,
they knew me and will be pleased.
Tell them Metin sent you.

**Istanbul**

Mustafa Necati Karaer (1929-1995)

Perhaps the water of the Bosphorus has changed;
I've found you on this Istanbul morning.
I don't know how to say it -
When I come to Istanbul, I become Istanbul.
Your hands are in Bebek, your face is in Küçüksu,
You're wearing a sea-blue blouse;
Like a poplar tree long and slender,
I've found you on this Istanbul morning.

A good-morning fell on the windows
Near the houses, streets will awaken soon.
Yesterday, today, and tomorrow are in one line.
I've found you on this Istanbul morning.

Clouds take me to Eyüp,
Perhaps they know something.
Beyoglu is my wine, my bread is Üsküdar,
When I came to Istanbul, I became Istanbul.
I'm wet, I've come from far away,
My business is to love, not to write poetry;
Please don't disturb my dreams,
I've found you on this Istanbul morning
When I came to Istanbul, I became Istanbul.

**I Love Istanbul**

Ayhan Inal (1931– )

Her lover for years,
I love Istanbul.
Beylerbeyi, Küçükyali,
I love Istanbul.

I love Istanbul
With her sweet accent,

Her poverty, her sufferings,
Her Kumburgaz and her Sile.

Sultanahmet, Dolmabahçe,
From inside
To outside,
Are like lace work on canvas.

Visitors wear out the threshold
Of mosques where the Qur'an is recited.
Its corners are sacred.
I love Istanbul.

Our best ornament.
We're grateful to Him,
Our heaven on earth,
I love Istanbul.

The Bosphorus has no equal, the Golden Horn is blue,
Let's walk in the moonlight in Küçüksu.
How can we tire of this city?
I love Istanbul...

Sweet shop in the grand bazaar. Photo credit: Zaid Sardar

**Before the Sunrise in Sehzadebasi**
Sezai Karakoç (1933– )

In the courtyard of the mosque
he looks for a place to sit
on a cold stone
before the sun rises in Sehzadebasi,

Holding tight his head between two hands,
and picking up birds' feathers
from the attic of nights,
before the sun rises in Sehzadebasi.

Covered with dust the camels
charmed by poetry;
roses scatter from the saddlebags
before the sun rises in Sehzadebasi.

Few children on the road,
light holds the dome,
fresh sounds in the grave
before the sun rises in Sehzadebasi.

Fountains made of tulips,
fountains of violets,
tombs like waterfalls,
before the sun rises in Sehzadebasi.

Yunus Emre,
Aksemseddin,
Mimar Sinan,
they are all in Sehzadebasi__
before the sun rises.

only a humble tree
bears the sky on its branches,

its roots embrace the earth
before the sun rises in Sehzadebasi.

Higher that the Qaf Mountain,
longer than the Great Wall of China,
the ebb and flow within us,
before the sun rises in Sehzadebasi.

Princes before daybreak
carrying torches,
wander around in Sehzadebasi,
before the sun rises in Sehzadebasi.

Convoys from the country of djinns
pass riding mules,
playing a long song on the violin,
before the sun rises in Sehzadebasi.

Greetings to the crimson horizon
from Süleymaniye and Beyazit.
Of course I want to be there
before the sun rises in Sehzadebasi.

The sun is risen, the day is born,
the dawn will break, this is certain.
The day will conceive many days
before the sun rises in Sehzadebasi.

**The Golden Horn**
Kemal Özer (1936–2009)

Istanbul has been awake for some time,
the domes and minarets
have pierced the twilight and come out
like working hands, the eyes, and feet

have been awake
without sipping enough of their tea;
they're on their way to work;
the factories are hungry.

Istanbul has been hungry for a long time,
the sky scrapers are gluttons,
they're impatient and ready
for their meals,
the big hotels are ready for their visitors,
and casinos, and amusement centres;
merchants have untied their appetite's collar
to devour the golden horn.

**Your Eyes Suddenly Became Istanbul**
Yavuz Bülent Bakiler (1936– )

A fine rain starts with you,
The beauty of a poem fills my heart.
The sea gulls perch on my shoulder,
Your eyes suddenly become Istanbul.

I'm away from you, from nights and evenings
My poems are winds blowing in far away mountains...
Like still waters I'll diminish
One day if you don't suddenly appear.

You'll come with songs; sensitive, thoughtful;
'Just look into my eyes', you'll say.
Slowly when my hands touch your hands
You will disappear.

My one hand will draw you on all the windows,
The other will caress you;
My heart a rainbow a thousand times a day
Will become alive.

What joy to find your face in every face.
And lose you almost everywhere.
What joy to miss the ferry,
And be quite alone on the quay;
A fine rain starts with you.

The beauty of a poem fills my heart,
The sea gulls perch on my shoulders,
Your eyes become suddenly Istanbul.

**The Pigeons**
Erdem Bayazit (1939–2008)

The tree was swallowing a tombstone in Çarsikapi
"Istanbul is moving within us".
A child was selling the waterless state of temples
In a water jar whose voice we could not remember,
the sun stood over us
like our sins.

Why do these pigeons exist?
To bring a memory to life?
Or to carry an immortal voice beyond,
In the palms of the mosques?

********
Chait Zarifoglu (1940–1987)

he ripped off a face from the text in his hand,
a face that was starting a speech.
"gentlemen", it said,
"fatih sultan mehemet han
when he entered istanbul
there was a pretty girl,
and such a beauty,

she was so pretty.
if the padishah loves the land

she was the land.
She ran and ran
and kissed the floor in front of his horse".

"Dear fellows, I wish you
    knew the turmoil
        within me.
I wish you knew youth, and youthfulness,
I wish you knew the sultan
    who was loved by his foes".

(When the governor visited her village
an old woman said: "Long live my Padishah!")

**Ghazal**
Akif Inan (1940–2000)

Before your eyes touched my heart,
O Istanbul, where were those birds?

Sea is my tongue's lexicon;
Songs, my brother, where were they?

Lasting rain clouds are within me;
Forest, rivers and roses, where were they?

Your fingers are reflections of light,
Where were my mother's and daughter's hands?

Before your eyes touched my heart,
Sorrows, laughter and dreams, where were they?

Entrance to the Grand Bazaar. Photo credit: Zaid Sardar

**Istanbul**

Ataol Behramoğlu (1942–

I'm drawing an Istanbul on my chest
With my thumb, in the shape of a butterfly;
In front of the mirror like a child
I'm stroking my face and my hair.

Any bit of sea from Kadiköy,
A half-empty tram from Sisli
From Samatya, perhaps from Sultanahmet,
I remember fig trees.

I'm drawing an Istanbul on my chest
With my thumb, in the shape of a butterfly,

I haven't much hope, I'm a bit tired,
I like my eyes best.

**Cheerful Loneliness**
Mehmet Ragip Karci (1945–2020)

A deer is passing in your eyes
And you're carrying the hoarse voice of Istanbul
in your hair.
Then on the wettest April day
on the pavements
you seek your childhood.
You're running, running
and so much happiness on your face;
you're unrecognisable.

The doves land gently next you,
you start singing a love song.

Your cavalry rides full gallop.
in your cheerful loneliness
Are you laughing?
Or the stars assembling
in your dovelike looks?

**Cafeteria**
Kamil Esfak Berki (1948– )

In Istanbul in Beyoglu
Today I noticed a code of practice:
in this cafeteria of the future
There's not much food
and not much talk.

**The Bitter End**
Cumali Ünaldi (1949– )

Shattered life! O spear that hits the heart!
Georgios Francis leans back on an old Byzantine
fountain and tells the story of Paleologolos
the defeated King - our valiant foe -
He talks of the King's lost water, the sea,
his last moments, the loneliness, and the King
who confronted death proudly;
his longing was a rose beautified by the Conqueror.

**The Architect**
Mehmet Atilla Maras (1949– )

Oh Sinan
you're the holy architect of eternity
you're the minaret
elegant, deep and faithful
you're the fountain of ablutions
you're the dove
you're the limpid river
you're the coolness of stones
you're the architect

**Rumeli Kavaği**
Mustafa Özer (1949– )

By the old plane trees of Kanlica
Winds from the South West rest.
All the colours indulge in an orgy,
all the friends embrace each other
Time, History, and I.

Rumeli Kavaği melts with the breeze,
pomegranate trees hang,
    hair of the Bosphorus.
Pomegranate trees, beautiful girls,
and the candle melts and drops fine drops.
Time, History and I.

**An Ode**

Besir Ayvazoğlu (1953– )

When the shadow of the Padishah wanders
In old Istanbul through the seven seasons

Suddenly a silky silence grows
Mahmud the Second goes to his summer house

The phoenix wand opens in a thousand and one hearts
And brings Leyla from the heart breaking tales

Said Effendi who is from the Thousand and One Nights
Tells countless funny jokes

O beloved who embroiders love on my eyes
Now I'm with you in longing

From the thin lips of silence
Play the songs with one long kiss

Like the sun's free spirit scattered on the earth
Let the waters shine on your beauty

Let the crescent rest on the players' fingers
Let them breathe their music to the sky

**Looking for Istanbul**
Arif Ay (1953– )

This is Istanbul in the sun.
When you look at her
She is standing on guard
And resists your attacks.

These are the minarets
That convey news
From heaven to earth
And from earth to heaven.

When a generous heart
Looks with love,
Doors open to the sea
And streets mirror the morning.
Only with love does she come to you,
When you turn your eyes,
This is Istanbul.

**War of Roses**
Ahmet Kot (1953– )

The guns you loaded
With water they say
Fired roses
Into the breast of Byzantium

**The Fires**
Ibrahim Demirci (1955– )

One day we shall find the way
to explain silence

To transmute voices into words
and those wise designs
into telling calligraphy

**Fragments of Memory**
Necip Evlice (1956– )

we're in Istanbul
the giant city,
three of us in the early morning
On a sea-gull sea;
we're terrific passengers.

we're watching an island
through the angry looks of the crew,
which ship,
which island,
which sea?

**Stop My Friend**
Ali Göçer (1956– )

I'm looking at the world
looking at oceans of hatred
flowing past
from the Bosphorus,
or the middle-east,
or from the world's jugular vein.
Stop my friend,
Stop and wait for me.

**History**
Mevlut Ceylan (1958– )

I am in front of demolished walls
shaking the nights, gathering
the eyes of history

I am the one singled out
to cultivate the well-toiled field
of exile

I am asked to feed
the magnetic north to empty words
we must know where we stand

**Istanbul**
Rahmi Kaya (1960– )

Water is heavy with grief in the Golden Horn.
The roads of wet Istanbul are sick with panic.
Buildings and laws descend on my heart
like frontier walls.
O Istanbul, only your chaos and echoes remain.
Water is heavy with grief in the Golden Horn.

**The Monumental Kiss**
Necat Çavuş (1959– )

Mimar Sinan seized the loveliest parts of Constantinople
and kissed her over and over and created Istanbul.
Perhaps in Sehzadebasi or Süleymaniye
one kiss became a popular tree in the wind,
one, alchemy against the ages,
one, music's blossoming rose,

one, a sound in the sea
In Üsküdar or Samipasa.
Dear God! What a kiss it was. I don't
think anyone ever gave Istanbul such a kiss!

Istanbul at night, photo credit: Mevlut Ceylan

# REVIEWS

# CONSIDER OTHERS

*Katharina Schmoll*

When I close my eyes, I can still hear the sounds of the rattling dishes and trays. It was early morning, and we had gently been woken up first by the *azan*, and then, after sweet moments between sleep and wakening, by our hosts preparing the breakfast. When arriving the night before, the family had generously offered us their salon for our night's stay. The salon was the only big room they seemed to own, a building in itself, surrounded by vast swathes of lush green grass and a kitchenette tucked away in a rickety stone shed with a tin roof. This was my first stay in Morocco, together with a small group of French and Moroccan university friends, and through someone's contacts we had ended up in rural Morocco close to the city of Al Jadida. By European, and also Moroccan standards, our host family was not well off. And yet, I fondly remember the most delicious and generous Moroccan breakfast I have ever had, even after more than ten years of travelling back and forth between Morocco and Europe. Trays and bowls kept being brought to the salon where we had assembled around the table, laden with fragrant fruits, homemade jams and cheese, boiled eggs, olives, honey, freshly baked bread and *meloui* pancakes, mint tea, and *harira*, the traditional Moroccan Ramadan soup sometimes also served for breakfast in the countryside. Before dipping into the delicacies, I sneaked out of the salon, over to the kitchenette, where an elderly, majestically wrinkled lady prepared pancakes on a stove. I shyly asked whether I could take a picture of her. In this moment of writing, I am holding her picture in my hands. She looks straight into my eyes, smiling, graceful, full of force and wisdom. For years to follow I was at a loss for words that would describe the look in her eyes and the kindness of our hosts who seemed to give so good-heartedly and demand nothing in return. After what seemed like an endless search and longing for elucidation, I have finally found what I was looking for without knowing it existed, the Islamic concept of *ihsan*, meaning perfection, goodness and righteous deeds, the highest form of worship.

Fast forward to my early years in East London, and to a very different impression of Islam and Muslims. It was the time when the British Muslim teenage girl Shamima Begum made international headlines when she and two girlfriends were captured at Gatwick Airport on their way to join the 'Islamic State of Iraq and Syria' (ISIS) in February 2015. The narratives and debates about Islam I then found among British Muslims, in British newspapers, universities, libraries, online media and wider society alike commonly centred upon headscarves, Muslim women's supposed oppression, terrorism and ISIS, halal food and cosmetics, the government's 'Prevent' strategy, and narrow legalistic Shariah debates about halal and haram, often backed up by selective *ayats* of the Qur'an and (at times questionable) *ahadith*. What a distance!

These memories of such contrasting experiences arose after I happened to find solace in two books that offer compassion, nuanced explorations of where and how we turned, and gleams of hope on the horizon: Azadeh Moaveni's *Guest House for Young Widows: Among the Women of ISIS* and Muqtedar Khan's *Islam and Good Governance: A Political Philosophy of Ihsan*. The books' topics, ISIS and *ihsan*, could not be further apart, and yet there is much to be gained from a joint analysis; an analysis that will also build on Omar Saif Ghobash's beautiful book *Letters to a Young Muslim*.

In her powerful account *Guest House for Young Widows*, the acclaimed American journalist and writer Azadeh Moaveni sets out to understand why young Muslim women around the globe are joining ISIS. No small task. So many reports, analyses and studies have been written about ISIS and its female members in the last years that one is tempted to ask whether another attempt to grasp women's appeal to ISIS and its rigid Sunni-Salafi jihadist doctrine is necessary. But Moaveni's account differs. Rather than re-hashing security concerns, pathological psyches, Islamist ideologies or ISIS's sophisticated propaganda, she immerses herself in these women's lives through extended in-person interviews, taking us with her on a journey from (pre-)revolutionary Tunisia and Syria, stopping off in Germany and the UK, to the Islamic State in Syria and Iraq. And she does so masterfully. Her voice dissolves in the women's life stories, carrying those narratives to the reader without ever adding her own baggage. It is non-fictional storytelling at its best.

Azadeh Moaveni, *Guest House for Young Widows: Among the Women of ISIS*, Scribe, London, 2019
Muqtedar Khan, *Islam and Good Governance: A Political Philosophy of Ihsan*, Palgrave Macmillan, London, 2019
Omar Saif Ghobash, *Letters to a Young Muslim*, Picador, London, 2018

*Guest House for Young Widows* is loosely organised in five parts. Moaveni begins by recounting the pre-ISIS lives of her chosen protagonists Nour, Rahma and Ghoufran in Tunisia, Asma in Syria, Lina, Emma/Dunya in Germany and Sabira in England (later to be completed by the story of Shamima and her friends, the girls from Bethnal Green who made international headlines in 2015). This first part reads like a powerful summary of all potential fractures and failures that indicate trouble long before they were stirred together and exploited by ISIS. Broken family structures and their momentums during periods of liminality such as puberty or divorce; migration, modernity and grappling with belonging and identity issues in postcolonial times; strangled aspirations and powerlessness in Arab authoritarian systems.

Parts Two to Four then gradually shift the focus from micro-level perspectives to macro-level considerations, carefully weaving together the women's individual experiences with information about the 'War on Terror' and Islamophobia in the West, the unfolding revolutions in Tunisia and Syria that had been fuelled by socio-political failures and discontent in the postcolonial Arab world, and the increasing power grab in Syria and Iraq by ISIS from 2014. It is this mixture of individual and socio-political fractures and failures that eventually culminate in the protagonists' decisions to join ISIS in Syria and Iraq. Without ever overwhelming the lay reader, Moaveni manages to gently and subtly fold in the necessary political analysis, always careful not to undermine the women's voices. She expertly and nuancedly depicts the Arab world's encounters with modernity, postcolonial power and identity struggles, the Western 'War on Terror' in Muslim lands as well as the global rise and appeal of Islamism, both violent and moderate strands. It is her expertise shimmering through the pages which allow for compassion to these women's struggles and attraction to ISIS beyond the compelling individual life stories.

The last part finally reveals the logic of the title. It portrays the hardships of life under ISIS, such as the death of martyr husbands, mourning, and widows' dreadful lives in so-called guest houses where women temporarily stay before being married off to the next husband. It also allows a glimpse into how un-Islamic and grotesque ISIS really is beyond the obvious brutality of the regime: pressing martyr widows to remarry before the end of the four-month Islamic mourning period, flogging women for wearing light make up under the compulsory niqab, commanding couples to use contraception since young fathers would be less willing to fight and die.

What makes *Guest House for Young Widows* so outstanding are its complexity and its compassion. Moaveni resists a dogmatic and simplistic conclusion of why women join ISIS. Each individual female life story that Moaveni portrays reveals a slightly different picture of why Islamism, including radical Islamism, is appealing to some Muslims. Most notably though, she points again and again to how the women's societies and families have failed them: a British teenager who, sickened by Islamophobia and groomed by a dodgy British Salafist, almost reluctantly decides to follow her beloved brother who initially left to fight the Assad regime in Syria; two Tunisian sisters whose hopes for a more prosperous and economically stable life in post-revolutionary Tunisia are betrayed and who find respect, meaning and even a moderate income through a local Salafi organisation; a pious Lebanese-German woman who manages to file for a divorce following years of neglect and abuse from her husband and in-laws after finding support online by conservative Muslims; a Western-oriented Syrian marketing student whose hopes are crushed after ISIS invades her home town Raqqa and who starts working for ISIS for the lack of alternatives; a German convert for whom promises of Islam are mixed up with dreams of a loving home similar to the ones of her German-Turkish friends; four London-based teenage friends whose limited options for a halal yet fun lifestyle lure them into murky promises of romance, adventure and justice under ISIS through social media. As Moaveni mentions herself in the epilogue, it is only after the decline of ISIS and many years of research and travels that she finally finds the ISIS woman she 'has been waiting for': a strongly ideology-driven jihadist, someone who 'believes it all' – rather than a lost soul. In a way, after all the pages where Moaveni mostly steered clear of any judgement and interpretation, this can be read as taking a more explicit stance, namely, that many, often young ISIS women are in fact not evil perpetrators but victims of their fates, groomed by Salafists, estranged by Islamophobia, pushed to the fringes of society for being the Other, neglected by their families, left behind and squeezed out by oppressive Arab tyrannies.

It is this compassion towards the women of ISIS, the socio-political contextualisation and the nuanced storytelling, that help in grasping where we went wrong and how, perhaps more so than all the other humanly detached reports, studies and analyses on ISIS. Moaveni witnesses and listens where others analyse, and usually fail. She sees life through the women's eyes. Through these intimate perspectives and insights *Guest House for Young Widows* then indirectly shows how in the West, we could work towards diminishing the appeal of radical Islamism by fostering belonging and civic participation, economic opportunity and greater equality, and rethinking our domestic and foreign policies.

But Moaveni's strength to recount the female protagonists' lives with compassion and in all their complexities is also continually at some risk of turning into a weakness. In times of increasing polarisation in Western societies and rising right-wing extremism trumpeting simplistic narratives about Muslims and Islam as dangerous and incompatible with Western values, Moaveni deserves praise for giving the wider non-Muslim Western public access to female Muslim voices and for shedding light on the socio-political underpinnings of their struggles. But at the same time, it is clear that female members of ISIS have been heavily involved in both ideological and physical extreme violence. They are not just victims of their circumstances, they have agency.

For decades, female Muslim women academics and activists in the West have fought against the Orientalist image of Muslim women as passive and oppressed. Here, it seems, that struggle is abandoned to counter the new image of Muslim women as aggressors and threats to Western societies. Similarly, Moaveni is in risk of abiding by the liberal left-wing trend to demand everything from the state and nothing from the individual. What started as a postmodernist discourse in academia is now gradually filtering through wider society. It is a narrative which criticises Western institutions and wider society for marginalising and discriminating against minorities. No doubt, there lies truth in these accusations. In her book, for example, Moaveni illustrates very well the failures of the British counterterrorist 'Prevent' strategy and how British tabloids have fuelled Islamophobia. I can only pray that these pages will be carefully studied by those concerned. But Moaveni's understandable preference for female voice leaves the accusations made against Western states and societies without a fair argumentative balance. At times Moaveni simply seems too harsh with the failures of Western states that can by no means be equated to the failures of Arab tyrannies. As the American political scientist Muqtedar Khan recently pondered in a talk on his YouTube channel, what *is* the Muslim state that people would like to live in? How come so many people including Muslims wish to emigrate to the West?

Likewise, in Moaveni's book there is no enquiry into ultra-conservative and rigid interpretations of Islam that are increasingly common in European Muslim communities, and no debate about contemporary Muslim identity politics which have championed banal aspects of Muslimness that diminish rather than foster social cohesion, tolerance and wisdom in Western societies.

In his bravely and exquisitely narrated book, *Letters to a Young Muslim*, written with his own son in mind, the Emirati diplomat Omar Saif Ghobash insists on a different narrative which is all too rare these days: that we always have a choice, and that 'there is always more than one way of dealing with obstacles'. A 'choice to give priority to certain principles and certain values'. A choice whether to embrace humility and humanity, cooperation, doubt and enquiry – or dogmatism and zealotry, narrow hate and anger, 'militant devotion' and 'theatrical piety'. While we should continue demanding states and institutions to do better, as Moaveni seems to suggest, we should also demand more from ourselves. Too much energy and time have been lost on scapegoating the West and nurturing a narrative of Muslim victimhood that we could spend so much more productively and creatively on taking destiny into our own hands. Energy and time that we could spend to pursue *ihsan*.

Muqtedar Khan is among those Muslims to have recently joined Ghobash's narrative of choice, agency and cooperation. In his new book *Islam and Good Governance*, he calls for bringing the long-neglected virtue and practice of *ihsan* – one of Islam's three central tenets *islam*, *iman* and *ihsan* – back centre stage in discussions on what role Islam can and should play in Western and Muslim-majority societies in the twenty-first century. Notably, his book envisions an Islamic-inspired politics 'based on a concern for the interests of others rather than just self-interest', 'away from the now failed vision of Islamic states'. While *ihsan*, in simplified terms meaning goodness, self-purification and righteous deeds, has found ample recognition and interest among scholars and adherents to the mystical tradition of Sufism, or *tasawwuf*, Khan aims to move *ihsan* from the realm of mysticism to mundane politics and civil society. The reason for advancing his political philosophy of *ihsan* is grounded in Khan's worry that, simply put, Islam and Muslims might have gone astray from the straight path. He criticises existing Islamic orthodoxy with its focus on identity politics and its binary logic of Muslims vs the West, worldly-oriented political ideologies and narrow legalistic and unforgiving interpretations of Shariah which have fuelled global hostility towards Islam. Khan believes that 'the disproportionate attention Muslims pay to identity formation and symbolism detracts from a focus on substantive issues such as the revival of Islamic spirituality, Islamic ethics and values, and the goodness that Islamic sources teach'. Identity, he continues arguing, has too often been a 'form of narcissism', with Muslims 'performing' Islam for others rather than living it genuinely and for the greater good of wider society. He instead aims to foster a more compassionate, spiritual and virtuous version of Islam that will 'make Islam a force for the good in the global society' through character building, worship, service and *sadaqah*, purification of the soul, and defending social justice for all of humanity.

While Khan often remains vague about the more practical aspects of implementing *ihsan*, his inclusive narrative on Islam about spiritual purification, character building and good deeds is hopefully just the prelude to a wider debate among Muslims about the role of Islam in twenty-first century politics and society. I hope that in this century, we will finally overcome the constant urge to defend Muslim identity, a discourse and practice inherited from the scars of colonialism and modernity. It is clear that many Muslims find great meaning, purpose and pride in their religion. A new inclusive Islamic maxim that asks what we can give rather than take, that seeks to understand rather than to be understood is a promising alternative to identity politics. It has the potential to transform the narratives of Muslim victimhood and dangerous Muslims hostile to the West into a narrative about Islam as a religion of love, compassion and contribution, which can revive a sense of pride among Muslims about their religion. It is a maxim that shows us a way out of the societal and political gridlock and foster social cohesion in Western societies. By embracing Khan's vision of Islam away from outward-oriented identity politics to inward-oriented character building, and from taking to giving, we might eventually also overcome global hostility towards Islam and the appeal of radical Islamism.

I am taking the picture with the elderly Moroccan lady back into my hands. She still looks at me, gently smiling, graceful, full of force and wisdom. I am smiling back at her. In the hope that one day, God willing, we will be able to raise a next generation of Muslims full of compassion, mercy and *ihsan* just like her. A generation that judges less and instead asks what it can contribute, a generation that gives lovingly and proudly, to all of humanity.

# BAGHDAD (MIS)REPRESENTED

*Zainab Rahim*

Of the many who have died from unnatural causes in modern-day Iraq, I often think of two of my own uncles who were killed approximately two decades apart. In 1981, at the age of 31 and with a baby on the way, my maternal uncle was targeted and arrested as a political dissident under Saddam Hussein's regime. My family never heard from him again. His body, like countless others, was never recovered. In 2004, my paternal uncle who had been a vocal advocate of an Iraq free from dictatorship had his life cut short by the liberators. Driving across a bridge in Baghdad with my cousin sat next to him, he was accidentally caught in crossfire between Americans and Al-Mahdi Army on either side. He was shot in the kidney and died in hospital hours later, his family receiving nothing more than an apology. Shit happens in war, right? These are just two stories which present a stark visualisation of some of the dramatic directions the country has been pulled in. Over a year ago I wrote an article for The Platform describing how Iraq has fallen victim to the loss of its own memory, each wave of conflict veiling the last, each tale lying namelessly in a mass grave. That's why for an Iraqi diaspora exhausted by reductive explanations and statistics, the telling of those tales is a welcome change – but they have certainly been few and far between. Who tells those stories is equally important.

It was with this at the forefront of my mind that I learned of the series *Baghdad Central*, a six-episode crime thriller set in the immediate aftermath of the Iraq War of 2003 in the transition to a 'New Iraq'. The Brits and Americans are very much still in town in this television drama, which

*Baghdad Central* (English/Arabic). Based on the novel by Elliot Colla, written by Stephen Butchard, directed by Alice Troughton. Euston Films, 2020. Broadcast on Channel 4 in February 2020.

follows the story of Muhsin al-Khafaji (Waleed Zuaiter), a former Baathist police officer approached by coalition forces to join them as a detective. Desperate to support his daughter Mrouj, who relies on dialysis, and quietly looking for his rebel daughter Sawsan, Muhsin accepts the job. The series has been compared to *Homeland* – in which Zuaiter himself plays a terrorist – offering just enough suspense to keep viewers going, assisted by a talented cast from various non-Iraqi Arab backgrounds, as well as a familiar backdrop, no doubt influenced by Iraqi producer Arij al-Soltan.

The opening of *Baghdad Central* reminded me of my first visit to Baghdad, which was around the same period in which this story is set. Defaced murals of Saddam, the famous literary Al-Mutanabbi Street bustling anew, checkpoints everywhere, and the sandy roads punctuated by concrete blocks, are all well reflected in the cityscape of Morocco's Rabat where the series was filmed. Inside the homes, too, the mise-en-scene aptly encapsulates daily life in Iraq. A steaming *istikaan* of *chai* is regularly in view, the kitchens are minimal with very few perishable items left out in Iraq's heat, old-model electric fans blow in the background, and electricity frequently goes out without anyone thinking to make much of a fuss about it. The lanterns, of course, are always ready. That's not to say that the show's creators have paid attention to every detail. Iraqi critics have pointed out that the police uniforms used in the show do not match the post-Saddam time period and I cannot recall seeing Baghdad apartment complexes like those in the show. The script features some brilliant unmistakable Iraqisms in the Arabic dialect, however, and the actors have done a decent job of maintaining the Iraqi accent, aside from a few occasional Palestinian slips. Yet the creators have gone for a 'dual-language' production with the majority of the dialogue in a heavily accented English, which may sound jarring to some listeners and unnecessary to those who prefer subtitles.

Although *Baghdad Central* has been much-lauded for offering an Iraqi perspective, I would argue that it fails in its task of representing the complexity of an Iraq torn apart by dictatorship and invasion, and in fact, centres the architects of the Iraq War in a way that can be quite misleading. By choosing not to root the characters and stories in real contexts, the writers leave holes in the plot and generalisations in their wake. Sawsan (who is given terrible disguises throughout) is a confused and unconvincing rebel who initially welcomes change in Iraq, but then turns her focus on a single revenge plot pertaining to a rape case and a former British policeman Frank Temple (Bertie Carvel), who becomes the focus of her anger. Fellow rebel Zahra and Professor Zubeida Rashid of Baghdad University are some of the strongest characters of the series, but neither of their motives appear to have a valid basis within the reality of transition faced by Iraqis at the time, where many of those from the professional and academic classes would have taken up roles in the new Iraqi government with enthusiasm.

The writers seem at least to be aware that, for American and British personnel, war can be a vessel for a lucrative career path steeped in orientalism. After a tense scene, Frank Temple reflects on his purpose: 'I came here to help ... Gonna reclaim my money. Resign and get out of this shithole once and for all. Write a fucking book. *Iraq: After the Bombs Stopped Falling* by Francis Paul Temple.' His saviour intentions are framed as a sincere will to help this forlorn place, tainted only by an arrogant wish to write a bestseller. Despite this overt admission, I cannot help but feel that the makers of the show are coming from the orientalist position of Frank Temple. After all, the book which this series is based on is written by an American scholar of the Middle East. In this show, Iraq *is* a shithole with no past or future, governed by youth gangs and a marked lack of cultural practice. By forcing an ambiguity on the religious and cultural identities of the Iraqi characters – in what is historically a richly diverse nation – the characters become unrelatable and roll into a seeming Iraqi tendency towards hostility and violence. Rather than this ambiguity being a potent strength, as previously seen in Mohamed Al-Daradji's film *The Journey* (2017), the non-specificity of the insurgency we see in Sawsan's and Zubeida's circles, is stripped of any socio-political context – the non-specificity itself is orientalising – and viewers can only conclude that such insurgency stems from being Iraqi.

This spills into gendered representations too: the lead female characters with their presentable hairstyles and lack of veiling, although not uncommon among Iraqi women, serve here to erase Iraq's religious and cultural tapestry in favour of a blank secular character. In reality, post-Saddam Iraq featured a sudden public display of Shia identity, previously subdued, with street commemorations of calendar events and scholars competing for social and political space in the 'New Iraq'. The annual pilgrimage to Karbala began to attract millions of visitors every year on the occasion of *Ashura* and the *Arbaeen*. This is the grassroots sentiment that would have been bubbling underneath the surface but is so glaringly absent from the show. The Iraqi characters hoping for change envision not only a democratic Iraq, but one that is secular and superior in nature.

What is particularly striking in *Baghdad Central* is how the chaos caused by Western intervention is contained, manageable and almost amateur. The three-letter word that made British Petroleum (BP) lobby the British government to go to war in Iraq barely gets a mention. Apart from a familiar sequence of the first bombs dropped on Baghdad in 2003 and a short clip of torture in the opening, we do not see the horrors of Abu Ghraib, nor are they referenced in any great detail. In fact, the gruesome torture we do see is towards various American characters. The coalition raids on civilian homes appear quite justified and are conducted politely during the day, with extra respect paid towards those who've been rattled – a far cry from the boots-on-the-ground tactics in Iraq explained, for instance, in the soldiers' own testimonies in a recent documentary, *War School* (2020). Both British Frank Temple and US Captain John Parodi seem like fairly reasonable people, with Parodi emerging as the voice of reason. That Temple becomes centred as the only potentially guilty party responsible for a criminal operation, is immensely reductive and erases the multiple challenges that would have been faced by Iraqis at the time.

The severe bombardment of Iraq by US and British forces following a ruthless thirty-year dictatorship would have presented a plethora of immediate concerns at the time – a tangle of humanitarian, economic and environmental problems. People would have been preoccupied with the counting of losses, a distribution of resources and the rebuilding of Baghdad. We know that 10,870 cluster bombs were dropped by coalition forces in the first phase of the Iraq War in 2003, with 100,000 bomblets that failed to explode on impact. Like this potentially explosive munition, historic hazards have been building up and shattering every facet of Iraqi life at intervals. We cannot quantify the damage wrought, but we can certainly depict it from a perspective that does not naively present the invaders as noble.

In addition, the protagonist Inspector Khafaji could have been a symbol of the tumultuous transition if he had been placed firmly in the context of the mismanaged 'debaathification' process which saw an axing of people who had worked for Saddam's regime. Instead his character seems to indicate that crimes recorded during Baathist rule are bogus and questionable, an unhelpful and dangerous assertion in a show which explains nothing else of that era. Yet the truest reflection of the complexity of Iraq's history is in Khafaji's simple reply to explain how his wife died: 'cancer and sanctions'. Though this is given no further context, Iraqis will remember the infamous line by Madeleine Albright, then US Ambassador to the United Nations, that the death of half a million kids due to sanctions following the 1991 Gulf War was 'a price worth paying'.

One of Khafaji's final messages – 'we are all guilty' – which I can only assume was intended to invite introspection for both the characters and viewers, ends up providing a smokescreen to the compounding layers of historical events that were out of the control of ordinary Iraqis, the same circumstances which killed both my uncles. I'm afraid we are not all guilty.

The decentring of authentic Iraqi experiences is the reason I'm inclined to avoid English-language television shows set in Iraq – and I wasn't proven wrong with *Baghdad Central.* The bottom line is there were no Iraqi decisionmakers or lead Iraqi actors in this particular series. A recent BBC documentary series, *Once Upon a Time In Iraq*, tells the post-2003 story through a personal archive of civilian and soldier interviews. This could be the start we need to encourage better programme-making. If we are to create successful shows based on stories which resonate with audiences, television commissioners and creators must embed Iraqi experiences into the writing and directing processes, support in unpicking the stories we were never able to tell – and sit and reflect in the discomfort of their own orientalism.

# DO VISIT (SOME OF) OUR MOSQUES

*Abdullah Geelah*

Mill Road in Cambridge, England, is an unassuming yet bustling thoroughfare of independent shops, restaurants, cafes, pubs and student flats. The mundanity of this urban scenery was broken by an exciting addition in spring 2019. The new £23 million Cambridge Central Mosque is perhaps the most audacious and successful attempt at innovative mosque design in the UK. Absent are the garish pastiche of Indo-Saracenic design features, common amongst many British mosques. Praise be to Allah: there are no dreadful minarets, tacky calligraphy or bearded *unclejis* to inform you that you're destined for hell on account of your fresh trim. And whilst the average worshipper may fail to notice it from street level, a beady-eyed six-foot person like me is able to discern a golden dome atop the magnificent building. Alas, a small and sad capitulation to orthodoxy. More interestingly, visitors are welcomed by a meticulously-manicured *chahar bagh* – a quadrilateral Indo-Persian garden evocative of the Muslim paradise – with English oak benches and crabapple trees adjoining an octagonal stone fountain. The calming murmur of falling water distracts the ear from the surrounding cacophony of pagan and holy tongues.

The garden leads to a portico with an adjacent cafe, and thereafter an atrium, both columned by the mosque's crowning glory: octagonal, intertwined and latticed timber colonnades. 'Say: God is One' – the expression of Islamic monotheism – covers the walls of the mosque in geometric Kufic script, albeit not rendered in cheap gold paint or Shiite black, but assembled skilfully in Cambridgeshire Gault brickwork. The interlaced arboreal theme, conceptually reminiscent of English Gothic vaulting, extends to the prayer hall: its walls bleached in austere white, its floor carpeted in delicate morning blue and the large space illuminated by skylights. Though open to both genders (a rarity), the prayer hall is disappointingly segregated – an ornately latticed timber screen marking the sexual divide. My female companion, a practising twenty-something English Anglican (another rarity), engaged in conversation with me across the barrier. We chatted, rather astonishingly, without the scolding of exasperated worshippers shocked by the wanton flouting of Islam's strict gender norms. If that came as a surprise, the ablution facilities were a revelation. Overcome by foreboding on approach to the area, I anticipated the inevitable effluvia of feet, rusty pipes and structural damp. Instead, the ritually unclean are greeted by resplendent turquoise walls – with argentine slate and exquisite plants, modern plumbing and tilework, glistening in a naturally sunlit space. Rainwater from the heavens, a key feature in the mosque's sustainable design, flushes away, spiritually and physically, their impurities.

Shahed Saleem, *The British Mosque: An architectural and social history*, Historic England, 2018

The mosque is the work of Marks Barfield Architects, alongside geometer Keith Critchlow, garden designer Emma Clark, and artists Amber Khokhar and Ayesha Gamiet. They have weaved horticulture, sustainability, Islamic geometry and English craftsmanship together to create something unique. The mosque's architects and trustees wanted an English mosque. Yet the cultural reference seems misplaced at times as the minimalist arboreal design, subtle colours and simple furnishing could suggest Scandinavian. Indeed, if Allah likes IKEA, this is the House for Him. At any rate, the mosque generally is a triumph of Anglo-Islamic architecture.

In *The British Mosque*, Shahid Saleem suggests that the Cambridge Central Mosque 'marks a step change in the narrative of British mosque design' as 'it is not a building conceived and commissioned by immigrant Muslims' but one which caters to a multi-ethnic and non-sectarian British Muslim polity. It shouldn't come as a surprise that it has taken British Muslims 130 years to articulate an indigenous approach to mosque design in the UK. For British Muslims, 'the visuality of the mosque has been one of the fundamental strategies through which Muslim communities have made their presence in Britain known.' As such, 'the mosque needs to symbolise its identity quickly and easily to as many of its users as possible, in essence, replicating known and popular images from around the world.'

It's important to underscore that the double-minareted, onion-domed caricatures we see in major British cities aren't triumphalist manifestations of Islam's presence. These were an aesthetic attempt to signal to a nascent immigrant community a continuing link to (and nostalgia for) 'home' in this 'foreign' land. However, this narrative sits uneasily with younger diverse generations of Muslims, like myself, who find the current mosque landscape incongruent with our more rooted identity. Saleem's argument is historically accurate in describing the relationship of mosque aesthetics and identity in twentieth-century Britain, yet there seems to be no reason why these now long established communities should continue to adhere to the neo-traditionalist canon. Oskar Verkaaik, in *Designing the 'anti-mosque': identity, religion and affect in contemporary European mosque design* (2012) observes that 'it is not uncommon' to view these mosques as 'unreflexive and inauthentic imitations' which could be symptomatic of a failure to integrate in European society owing to these mosques' architectural expressions of loyalty to the so-called homeland: be it some obscure village in the Kashmir valley, the hills of Sylhet or a backwater in the Middle East. Indeed, Christian Welzbacher in *Euro Islam architecture: new mosques in the West* (2008) sees it as indicative of a stagnant mentality.

There is some merit in these arguments. The narrative of neo-traditionalist mosque architecture, as reflecting a wistful 'home' or parochialism, is applicable to an older, unsettled immigrant population. But this doesn't square with the realities of young British Muslims whose identities and experiences are more grounded and multifaceted. Indeed, young British Muslims have a plethora of multiple identities: from religious to secular, traditional to modern, national to ethnic, cosmopolitan to international, and parochial was well. Young British Muslims want mosque spaces that reflect this multi-dimensional lived experience: a modern environment which communicates their temporal and spiritual feelings. So why aren't we seeing these?

In the twentieth century, there was a need for the 'preservation and transference of religious tradition [when] communities faced discrimination and exclusion in all spheres of their lives in Britain'. The mosque has always been a sanctuary – a *haram* – for the faithful and it's understandable that focusing on aesthetic sensibilities during a time of heightened racism was inappropriate. Hence, many early British mosques were converted terraced houses, disused pubs and unused churches: cheap buildings readily available to house the spiritual and secular needs of the community. The increase in purpose-built mosques (including the existing buildings consecrated as Islamic) designed in the neo-traditionalist way, not only showed an attachment to an ancestral 'homeland', but also cultural independence and financial security during a time in which British society became somewhat more accomodationist and tolerant. That said, the current discourse on mosque design seems stuck in the rigidity of a bygone era due to the 'community leaders' who still run the various mosque committees in the country. They are an *ancien regime* of corpulent, bearded men who still call the shots in informing mosque design (amongst many other things). Saleem interviews Scottish convert and a historian of Islamic architecture, Yaqub Zaki, who points out that British mosques are:

> commissioned by [the] mosque committee, and the mosque committee consists of the cash and carry walla, the take-away tycoon, who don't know the first thing about mosques. So what they do is they take out the Yellow Pages, they pick out [an architect] quite arbitrarily, the man comes for a meeting with the mosque committee and the mosque committee are all contradicting each other, so he [the architect] goes to the library, takes out one or two books on Islamic architecture, picks a feature from here and feature from there and combines, and the result is an inconsistent mish-mash.

It's sad that these men have, in their senior days stymied the creativity and opportunity which could have inspired Muslims to commission beautiful and meaningful mosques. And for a group that never fails to invoke the pathos of the glorious Islamic past, they seem to overlook the visionary patronage of their antecedents in commissioning great buildings: Al-Walid I (the Great Mosque of Damascus and the Dome of the Rock); Abd al-Rahman I (the Cordoba Mosque); Muhammad I of Granada (the Alhambra); and Shah Abbas I (the Shah Mosque). Such myopia extends to other European Muslim communities. Take, for instance, the competition to design the Strasbourg Mosque in France. The late British Iraqi architect,

Zaha Hadid, submitted an innovative futuristic proposal: a mosque and community centre complex draped in rippling forms based on the visualisation of the mournful cadences of the *Azan* – the call to prayer. This was too much for the committee and instead a safe domed structure was selected (by the modernist Italian architect Paolo Portoghesi who also designed the Rome mosque).

This conservatism contrasts with advances in mosque design in Muslim-majority countries where one might expect the local minareted-and-domed model to reign sultan. One noteworthy example of this trend is the award-winning Sancaklar Mosque in Istanbul. Taking inspiration from the cave in which Prophet Muhammad received his first revelation, it is highly disruptive of the pervasive Ottoman mosque typology. The mosque is set partially underground in the Turkish countryside and it is surrounded by terraced landscaping with light-grey stonework, foliage and reinforced concrete. Another is the Education City Mosque in Doha whose conceptual reference is the cursive Arabic calligraphy; its structure is almost spaceship-like.

Jonathan Glancey, in a 2002 piece for *The Guardian* on British mosques, juxtaposes the work behind the construction of Britain's first purpose-built mosque in Woking (a cute Grade I listed nineteenth-century Indo-Persian style pavilion), as a 'meeting of high minds, with great learning and a degree of wealth and culture' with recent mosque design driven by 'zealous religion that all but eschewed luxury, sensuality and ornamentation... underpinned by poverty'. Glancey's comparison is somewhat lazy and simplistic, and fails to account for the construction of million-pound grandiose yet kitsch mosques the architectural failings of which can hardly be blamed on Muslim penury – even if the likes of the Woking Mosque were financed by wealthy royal patrons. However, he is not entirely wrong to point out that a puritanical fervour underlies the refusal to create extravagant buildings. This instinct has its roots in tradition: Muhammad built the first major mosque in Medina from beaten clay and palm leaves. As Saleem highlights, the austerity of the mosques of revivalist Muslim movements, such as the Deobandis (and to an extent, the Salafis), has been informed by their doctrinal puritanism in promoting the functional aspect of the mosque, rather than its decorative or aesthetic appeal.

In a focus group of young British Muslims I conducted last year, participants highlighted three reasons as to their disengagement from mosques: design, *diniyat* (the Islamic education taught in these places), and diversity. On the last point, it's no wonder some Muslim women in 2015 founded Britain's first all-women mosque in Bradford. Similarly, the establishment of the Inclusive Mosque Initiative in London in 2012, which is dedicated to creating an accessible, inclusive and diverse place of worship for marginalised groups, highlights the exclusionary nature of current conventional mosques. For those few (but growing) mosques which have female spaces, the facilities are derisory. Whereas the men parade exultantly through the main doors of the hallowed house, the womenfolk scuttle in through a back entrance like rats – lest the sight of their uncovered ankles or the sound of their honeyed voices cause the men to fall into ritual impurity. Another one of these progressive 'third spaces', though set firmly within the confines of theological orthodoxy, is Rumi's Cave in Kilburn, London, which was established to cater to the diverse north-west London Muslim community's spiritual, social and cultural needs. It's an arts and community hub, rather than a simple place to perform the prosaism of prayer. Children run riot, boys and girls chat, giggle and flirt while the oldies chill. The community is currently fighting a proposal by the local council to demolish the centre and nearby buildings in order to build luxury flats. This led one friend to proclaim, 'I'd rather see all the mosques closed down than to see Rumi's Cave demolished.' These spaces aren't mosques in the traditional sense nor are they housed in architecturally interesting edifices. They are interesting, however, in that they are an example of new generations reinterpreting the mosque to fit with their own complex modern identities. Although a discussion of these 'third spaces' would have fallen outside the overall theme of Saleem's book, their omission, as examples of social phenomena within the British mosque landscape, is rather disappointing.

That said, Saleem's classification of mosque design in the UK is to be welcomed. His periodisation helps us more precisely to delineate the history of British mosque design. It aims to find, amidst the chaotic styles, an identity to define the different phases of British mosque development. Much as English ecclesiastical architecture may be identified as Gothic Revival or Baroque, English mosques can now be distinguished as neo-historicist (e.g. Leicester's Mamluk-inspired Jame Mosque) or modernist (e.g. Sir Frederick Gibberd's Regent's Park Mosque). Across the border, the Edinburgh Central Mosque is an example of an Islamic Scots Baronial style.

The Prophet declared that 'the whole world is a mosque'; a simple, clean area can act as a prayer space for Muslims to perform their religious duties. This absence of religious stricture in Islamic architecture allowed it to adopt and synthesise the styles of conquered polities or local realities: from Byzantine domes to West African mudbrick, Hindu chhatris to Chinese pagodas, Roman temples to Sassanian arches. It may be a while before we see a Stirling Prize-winning British mosque, but attitudes are changing given the open-mindedness and activism of young British Muslims to inspire renewed thinking around religion and identity. This chimes with the efforts of the Muslim Council of Britain, the closest thing British Islam has to a synod, to provide training to mosque trustees on best practice in design, diversity and good governance. Saleem is wise to conclude with the Cambridge Central Mosque in his detailed survey of British mosques – it is a source of optimism for the future of mosque design in the UK.

# ET CETERA

LAST WORD

# ON PATRIARCHY

*Shehnaz Haqqani*

In my graduate school religion class, I brought up patriarchy constantly. So one day my professor asked: 'why are you still a Muslim if there's so much patriarchy in your community?' (I hope he said 'community' and not 'religion'. I don't remember his question verbatim. Only the point.) And it suddenly dawned on me that he, like many others, didn't get it. Not only do too many people not get it, but it turns out, I need to be more cautious about who I have such intimate conversations about my faith with.

I had never thought about the question before. I had never asked myself why I am *still* a Muslim *despite* the patriarchy that appears to be so ingrained in the tradition and faith that I am committed to. This question makes so many problematic assumptions, all of which I am going to raise in the form of questions. Is patriarchy only the enterprise of Islam, Muslims, and the Islamic tradition? Would we ask a feminist non-Muslim, perhaps a Christian, the same question – why they are still Christian when there's so much misogyny in the faith and community they are devoted to? Is patriarchy a problem only in religious contexts? Is it even possible for me to leave Islam and suddenly begin to be a citizen of a world without patriarchy – in other words, does a world without patriarchy currently even exist? And, most disturbing, can only misogynists lay a claim to Islam as their faith, leaving all non-misogynists no other choice than to walk out of it?

Since that graduate class, this question has come up a lot more – though explicitly and vocally only in Muslim spaces, in spaces where I feel safe enough to answer it. I have sensed it arising in non-Muslim spaces, where I suspect an observer is desperate to express their pity on me for being a Muslim woman or otherwise express some desire to enlighten me about my status as an oppressed Muslim woman. Their looks of commiseration speak plenty. But besides this pity committee, as Mohja Kahf calls them, many of my Muslim friends, male, female, and non-binary, who are committed to an egalitarian practice of Islam have asked if their fight against sexist bigotry is even worth it.

My answer is an unequivocal, unapologetic yes, our fight will always be worth the struggles. Not least because 'Islam' as we know it is a process, and its teachings – besides the most essential, monotheism and belief in Muhammad as a prophet – a matter not so much of truth but of power. That is, what a specific belief in Islam means is not a matter of some objective Truth but of who has enough political, social power and influence to make it appear 'true', to endorse it so that it becomes mainstream. For instance, even as all Muslims agree that there is only One God, they disagree on what that actually means, how a Muslim is to actually implement this knowledge in their everyday life. Muslim scholars have always attempted to explain the meaning of the oneness of God, but their answers need to be acknowledged as simply attempts. We do not all agree on what constitutes *shirk*, besides the idea that belief in the divinity of other Beings is certainly *shirk*. I, like many other Muslim feminists, for example, believe that patriarchy is *shirk*. This argument was first put forth by amina wadud as part of her *tawhidic* paradigm, which rests on the foundational Islamic doctrine of *tawhid*, the absolute, unconditional oneness and incompatibility of God, and has three components to it: sexism is a form of *shirk* because it relies on a hierarchy in which men are granted a God-like status over women; equating interpretations of the Qur'an with the Qur'an itself (God's words) is a form of *shirk* since, among other issues, it assumes that the words and claims of humans, historically only men, are the same as God's; and claiming to have the correct interpretation of the Qur'an is a form of *shirk* because it is an assumption of God's role and knowledge.

In my experiences as a blogger of Islam and gender-related topics, I have received many emails from Muslim women in which they share their struggles with the Islam that they grew up with and that their communities continue to force on them. A couple of the ones I am still in touch with have left Islam altogether, and most were relieved to know that they could embark on a journey that would offer alternative ways to practise their faith. My intended audience for my blogging and vlogging activities are Muslims who have experienced the harm of traditional and traditionalist, mainstream interpretations and practices of Islam, which privilege cis-heterosexual men and marginalise the rest of us. Non-cis-heterosexual men are privileged, to varying extents, in all patriarchies everywhere. Since non-Muslims of faith, such as Christians, have a similar trajectory in their tradition, one thing we can glean from this is that this is not a religious issue. It is, as I said earlier, an issue of power. Those who control the dominant versions of Islam, as of any other religion, are those with power, privilege, influence. The support they receive, the social capital and influence, allows them to mainstream their religious claims and ultimately sell it as the religion they claim to follow.

For instance, a few years ago, I gave a talk at a university, where I spoke on religion and feminism. I had situated the Islamic feminist movement as part of a broader, larger, transnational religious feminist movement around the world where women/feminists/non-cis-heterosexual males, people who have not historically been recognised as legitimate interpreters of scriptures, are engaging scriptures in creative, constructive, and compassionate ways that prioritise the impact of interpretation. A Christian feminist student came to me afterwards with tears in her eyes, sharing that it was the first time she was hearing validation of her feminist and Christian values. She had been struggling with Christianity, a version of Christianity that was founded on patriarchy, and she explained that even her supposedly progressive church community was not receptive to her feminist values. In my teaching experiences since then, I have had other female students share that they have recently completely left their religion because they were being forced to choose between their feminism and their Christianity; others struggle, searching for resources that will assuage their anxieties around gender and religion, allowing them to believe that they do not have to compromise their feminist convictions in order to accept patriarchal interpretations of the faith they believe in. Similarly, Jewish feminists have been fighting almost identical battles with their communities that Muslim feminists are fighting today, such as equal access to sacred spaces and ritual and other religious authority. The same can be said of Hindu, Zoroastrian, and other faith communities where patriarchy has contributed in harmful ways to the ways the religions are practiced. The key word, the common denominator, in all these is patriarchy.

I recently realised that Muslims who tout their favourite statement – 'that's not Islam! That's culture!' – to lay claim to a supposedly culture-free Islam actually mean to say, 'That's not Islam; that's patriarchy!' Culture in this context simply means patriarchy, and there is a lot to be said about the tragedy of reducing 'culture' to the violence that are part and parcel of it. When we reflect on the specific contexts in which this statement is invoked, and the specific examples that are used to 'prove' it, they are all tied to gender. For example, 'It's not Islam that allows forced marriages; it's culture!' Or 'It's not Islam that allows people to commit honour killings; it's culture!' And so on. I believe that identifying the correct problem here (patriarchy) might allow us to contribute solutions more effectively and faster.

My struggle with patriarchal Islam was ultimately exactly what led to my pursuit of feminist Islam. Through blogging, I accidentally came across other Muslim women's articulation of the problems with traditional, mainstream Islam, and it drove me away from patriarchal Islam, the harmful, destructive forms of Islam that lead to so many of us questioning what I have learned is something so beautiful and profound and safe (Islam) - for me, as a human, as a woman, as a Muslim. And that is a kind of Islam that is guided by compassion, rooted in the conviction that compassion overshadows everything else.

There are two significant facts about God that I have found to be profoundly liberating and that have affected my views on my Creator: the actual meaning of *Rabb* and the connection between the word *raḥm* and God's names *Raḥman* and *Raḥim*. In an Arabic class in Morocco in 2013, when learning the Arabic for 'I was raised in …' (*rubbibtu*), I asked my teacher if this word was connected to Rabb, the word for God that is often mistranslated as 'Lord'. She looked stunned and responded that she was not sure but perhaps so. I began to look into the word, relying on various Arabic dictionaries, and I discovered that the root of the two words is indeed the same. This new knowledge affected me greatly. Why had no one who knew ever taught me this? I have always had issues with the translation 'Lord' – which masculinises God and presents God as some sort of a Being obsessed with power and control. How can this be when, in most supplications, we recite *Ya Rabb* or *Ya Allah* when invoking God's mercy, God's love, God's forgiveness, God's bounty? I have seen the word *Rabb* for

God translated as 'Sustainer' in Sufi texts and have begun to use either the original Arabic *Rabb* or, if translation is necessary, then 'Sustainer'. 'Sustainer' or its equivalents – a colleague's friend recently proposed 'Caretaker' – reflect more correctly what *Rabb* means, as *Rabb* is One who nurtures us, provides for us, sustains us by bestowing on us blessings that allow us to live and exist in the universe.

As for *raḥm*, the term literally means the womb, the uterus. While this is not likely to imply that God, *al-Rahman* and *al-Rahim*, has a womb, the relationship between these names and the term again point to some nurturing taking place. In a patriarchy, which is founded also on the false dichotomy of male and female, or the masculine and the feminine, this might also simply be pointing to God's attribute of compassion, which the patriarchy associates with the feminine.

Wondering why these two facts were not known to me until recently, I realised that they are both related to patriarchy. Not only is it a patriarchal act to withhold empowering and liberating knowledge from people, especially those who are harmed by the lack of such knowledge, but also, the association of nurturing and the womb with God contradicts every vision of God that the patriarchy survives on. In monotheistic religions, God has been depicted as a man, and the pronoun 'He' is imagined to make sense, even by those who otherwise claim that God has no gender. If God has no gender, why are these same people then so shocked when they hear or see 'She' as another possible pronoun for God? In monotheistic patriarchy, God cannot be imagined as anything but male because it is as though patriarchal monotheists' belief in God is conditional, founded exclusively on the imaginary belief that God is male and masculine, and so if She is feminine or non-masculine, then God does not exist.

How has patriarchy become so ingrained in mainstream Islam? Leila Ahmed excellently maps patriarchy's journey into Islam, beginning with the Middle East and neighbouring regions centuries before Islam. As she shows, over the course of several thousand years, the Middle East went through many different kinds of civilisations and conquests, including the Babylonians, the Assyrians, the Persians, the Romans, the Greeks, the Christians. Each group of people who conquered the Middle East imposed their own will, their cultures, their religions, their attitudes on the conquered peoples. Over time, the indigenous cultures and practices became so submerged in the conquerors' that we can seldom identify the origins of a belief or practice. Institutionalised Islam picked and chose from all these empires, communities, and cultures that had become a seemingly innate part of Middle Eastern life by the time Islam was being established. One of the most striking findings of Ahmed's is that in all this cultural exchange that took place with the spread of Islam and other religions before it, the good ideas and attitudes towards women were not consistently being adopted, but the misogyny was. Over time, the misogyny that had become a part of the cultures at the time that Islam was spreading began to be normalised and universalised, embedded into Islam through texts, through the interpretations of the Qur'an.

amina wadud argues, in her ground-breaking *Qur'an and Woman*, that one's perceptions of women influence their interpretations of the Qur'an, and the reader's intentions, biases, opinions, experiences are reflected in their interpretation. Put another way, our interpretations of the Qur'an are shaped and affected by our contexts, our background, our experiences, who we are, and what we want and expect from the Qur'an. Some of the examples she gives in the book have now become mainstream enough for some readers to dismiss them as irrelevant. But because wadud is engaging the historical interpretations of the Qur'an, such a dismissal only proves her point that how we interpret the Qur'an is a matter of who we are and what we want from it rather than some objective divine meaning of the Text. A careful reading of all the examples she gives shows excellently how male perceptions, men's biases against women made it into the application of the Qur'an. Two examples here will suffice.

The first is of the creation story in the Qur'an. Even though we now know that the Qur'an never blames Eve for causing the downfall of humanity by deceiving Adam to eat the fruit, the entire male exegetical tradition of the past (at least before the twentieth century) blames Eve for everything. Since the Qur'anic account of the creation is not very detailed, past exegetes relied heavily on the Bible to fill in any gaps, since the Bible is more detailed. These scholars – or 'scholars' – relied almost entirely on the Biblical tradition, that too on the patriarchal version of it—because there are non-patriarchal versions of it, too, thanks to Jewish and Christian feminists – and decided that God created Adam first and then Eve from his ribs and then expelled both of them from heaven because Eve ate the fruit first and deceived Adam into doing so as well. This is, objectively speaking, not true because the Qur'an never blames Eve exclusively; it blames either Adam alone, Iblis alone, or Eve and Adam together. This is related to wadud's argument because it illustrates precisely what it means that human readers of the Qur'an read into it what we want – the 'scholars' read the creation story this way because it seems to have been the dominant version of the creation story, because it seems to have made sense to them, even though it contradicted the Qur'an.

Another example is the word *zawj* in the Qur'an. Too many translations and interpretations of the Qur'an imagine the word *zawj* to mean 'wife', even though this word is either masculine or gender-neutral and can therefore either mean 'husband' or 'spouse'. However, since the people who have had monopoly over interpretations of the Qur'an historically were all men, they imagined themselves and other men to be the audience of the Qur'an, therefore reading themselves into the text, and concluded that the Qur'an is speaking to them when it speaks of *zawj/azwaj* in heaven. Finally, the last example I want to give here is that of the word *nushuz* in Q. 4:34 and 4:128.

In 4:34, which is a very complicated and difficult verse with various interpretations, the word *nushuz* is used to refer to a certain kind of women (as spouses); in 4:128, the same word is used for a certain kind of men (as spouses). But the two are not translated the same way in most translations of the Qur'an. In 4:34, for women, the translations typically tell us that when a woman commits *nushuz*, she is being 'rebellious' or 'disobedient' (to her husband); yet, for 4:128, the translations tell us that when a man commits *nushuz*, he's being 'contemptuous' or 'not treating his wife well', 'abandons his wife', or 'is oppressive towards his wife'! The irony seems to be lost on these interpreters that they just read another part of 4:34 to mean that a husband can hit his wife in order to discipline her, but then also read 4:128 to warn men who 'are oppressive' towards or who mistreat their wives.

To me, all of these examples point to the same thing – the patriarchy that has been read into the Qur'an has been mainstreamed so powerfully and deeply that it often feels as though, for many Muslims, there is no distinction between patriarchy and Islam. Such Muslims reject an idea, a practice, an alternative way of practicing Islam solely because it is not patriarchal. They seem to be asking, Wait, is it even Islamic if it's not patriarchal? The tragedy of such an approach to Islam cannot be understated. This is the dilemma the Muslim feminists face – where to even begin explaining that, in fact, it's possible to believe that if it is patriarchal, then it is not Islamic because patriarchy is inherently unethical and, we must insist, if it's unethical, then it's not Islamic. An Islam that supports and promotes gender egalitarian interpretations is too commonly dismissed because for so many centuries, the mainstream version of Islam has deprived us of alternatives; it has thrived on the erasure of alternative forms of Islam that are not oppressive to any group of Muslims or people. It has denied us the opportunities to interpret the Qur'an creatively and fairly.

One thing that I've learned from my decade of research and study of Islam, as well as my study of gender and religion generally, that I cherish myself now and that I'm trying to share with as many other Muslims who struggle with Islam as possible is this: the patriarchal Islam we all grew up with, the harmful kind that hurts us all in so many terrible ways, is not the only possible way to be Muslim. There are alternative destinations – some are not at all patriarchal, some are less patriarchal. This is nothing new in Islam. The Islamic tradition is filled with a plurality of ways for people to be Muslim, and none of what we know now is a matter of objective facts, reality and truth – they are the fruition of politics, and conclusions of debates that (all-male) scholars had with each other for generations, and they passed those conclusions down to us. So a feminist Islam is as valid - subjective, sure, but as valid – as the patriarchal Islam that too many of us are familiar with. We are allowed, in fact encouraged, to walk away from what hurts us; I am of the opinion that is our obligation.

In fact, while many people of faith ridicule the idea of 'picking and choosing'; in a given religion, the Islamic tradition is replete with instances of scholars and lay Muslims doing exactly that – yet, picking and choosing the best possible interpretation available, or that they could come up with, in order to practice Islam. There's even a word for it in the tradition – *takhayyur*, literally picking and choosing the best possible option. Male scholars have relied on this strategy too, for instance, when arguing for certain kinds of reforms to be made to historical interpretations of Islam. Religious people have always cherry-picked from their traditions because it is through such a practice that religion, all religions, survive and remain meaningful to their practitioners. In order to make sense of Islam in their specific context and positionality, Muslims have always negotiated and re-negotiated with the Islamic tradition to extract the best possible meanings out of scripture and its interpretations. The difference, however, is that today, unlike the past, women and feminists are an active part of the discourse, engaged in the re-negotiation and cherry-picking processes, showing that Islam is not just the realm of men or an elite scholarly male body but also for others to contribute to. The reason, then, that picking and choosing is viewed as unacceptable today is not that there is anything un-Islamic about it or that it is unprecedented; it is deemed unacceptable solely because Muslim feminists rely on the tool of *takhayyur* and others similar to it to support their interpretations of Islam.

The flexibility that is allowed to Muslims according to the historical Islamic tradition can be illustrated through other terms as well, besides *takhayyur*. *Tarjīḥ*, *talfīq*, and *maṣlaḥa*, among others. *Tarjīḥ*, often translated as preponderance refers to the idea that the opinion with the strongest evidence is the most correct opinion; *talfīq* means combing multiple existing opinions, even if contradictory, in order to form one; and *maṣlaḥa* is the idea of public interest, which means that if an existing practice or interpretation has a harmful impact, then for the common or public good, a new interpretation is necessary so that the damage can be prevented further. Whether the scholars who developed these concepts meant for them to be used in this way or not, all of these concepts are evidence that alternatives are always possible. What is crucial here is also that producing these alternatives was not and is not the realm of the scholarly elite alone; ordinary, lay Muslims can engage Islam and make decisions for themselves as well. That is also proven by the fact that the concept of fatwa exists to create ease in our lives: if we do not agree with or do not like a certain fatwa from an individual mufti that we sought an opinion from, we can go to someone else and obtain another one. Read collectively, all of these terms demonstrate that a principle that was clearly integral to medieval Muslim jurists was a multiplicity of viewpoints from which both scholars and the laity could choose. The purpose was to create ease and accommodate an individual's convenience, or offer a practical approach to Islam. There is no valid reason why we cannot continue to interrogate the unkind Islam that we grew up with for a kinder one, for a better one, for a harmless one.

I have never been able to articulate in any language the betrayal I felt upon discovering the plethora of options available to me in my knowledge and practice of Islam. I have thus committed my life and my future to working to uproot the patriarchy from Islam to any and all extents necessary. My blogging and vlogging activities are founded on the fact that we have choices within Islam, not a singular dogmatic destination, and it is our moral and ethical responsibility as Muslims to adopt those that make us better humans, better Muslims.

So why am I 'still' a Muslim when there's so much misogyny? Because, as it turns out, religions are only to a small extent a matter of truth – the rest of it is all about power, a matter of who had enough political support and social capital to win and make it a history. If misogyny could be read into the Qur'an, into Prophet Muhammad's practices, then so can non-misogyny – so can feminism. Just because feminist Islam is not mainstream does not mean it is not a valid or correct way to practice Islam. A non-patriarchal Islam exists, and I consider it my religious and moral obligation to contribute towards mainstreaming it.

# TOP TEN SYNTHETIC WONDERS

Creativity and innovative thought have been essential tools for the flourishing of human culture and civilisation. But originality, imagination and pioneering cultural products require serious effort and hard work. So why not simply copy others or just buy the signs of sophistication. Have you noticed, when you travel East to West and North to South, that several elements appear to have an unsettling amount of similarity. Perhaps this is simply a coincidence. Or maybe it is an unimaginative copy. Or (deep) fake, or even a virtual representation. We'll let you be the judge.

*1. Mock Islands*

Before China had co-opted the art of island-making to subdue international sea treaties and resolve neighbourly territory disputes, Dubai had created the Palm Islands. Beginning in 2001, the three islands – Palm Jumeirah, Deira Island, and Palm Jebel Ali – were constructed for much more lucrative and peace-time purposes. Financed largely by access oil revenues, the Palm Islands give the small nation a unique (bordering on absurd) aesthetic and a new luxury territory for private hotels and residences, a bit distanced from the painfully normal Arabian Peninsula. But the islands have been faced with numerous unintended consequences. These creations face great risks from increase wave height, storm frequency, soil weakness due to sea level rising, and coincide with an increase in water pollution. Erosion will be the biggest challenge for these fake islands but beneath their coastal waters looms threats to marine ecology and natural sediment distribution along Dubai's coast.

*2. Big Ben Duplicate*

The most sacred city in Islam is not exempt from a horrid example of architecture copying. The Makkah Royal Clock Tower looms high, casting a shadow over the *Haram*, the Sacred Mosque in Mecca. The Clock Tower is the centre piece of the *Abraj Al-Bait* (Towers of the House) consisting of a seven-skyscraper complex of hotels. It has been reported to resemble a similarly famous clock in London. But the clock face on the Makkah Royal Clock Tower is the largest clock face in the world and its tower is the third-tallest building in the world and the fifth-tallest free-standing structure in the world. The Abraj Al-Bait complex is part of the King Abdulaziz Endowment Project, centred on modernising the city in service to its pilgrims. One complaint from a hotel patron noted that it provides a perfect, birds-eye view of the Kabba but he wished he stayed a few floors lower as the Kabba looked miniscule from the forty-second floor. The Abraj Al-Bait project cost approximately £12 billion. The whole project earned considerable controversy, especially from the Turks who were irked by the demolition of a eighteenth century Ottoman fortress to make way for the complex. But in the rapid artificialisation of our world one can't be too sentimental about such things.

*3. Borrowed Culture*

No one in the Muslim world seems to do artificial like the United Arab Emirates. While the French will, without hesitation, claim the responsibility for inventing art, culture, cuisine, civilisation, and nearly everything else, nobody mentioned that it couldn't be sold or bought. The term priceless is not so easily tagged to works of art, at least not since $525 million bought Abu Dhabi the name 'Louvre' for their art museum in 2007. An additional $747 million price tag would be placed on top of the name for art loans, special exhibitions, and management advice. The 'selling' of French art was vehemently opposed by the various artist circles of France, but in 2017, its doors were officially opened. Designed by a French architect, Jean Nouvel, the museum is said to be inspired by the way sunlight hits a palm tree in a mythical oasis. While the project is designed to be an artistic collaboration between East and West, such high price exhibitions, like Leonardo da Vinci's *Salvator Mundi* reveal a bias in what drives ticket sales. Controversy surrounded the condition of workers who built the museum: reports of forced labour and massive human rights violations could not be suppressed despite earnest efforts. Jean Nouvel defended the practice by declaring that the working conditions were no worse than those found in Europe! So now we can all feel better, right?

*4. The Simulated City*

Imaginative skyscrapers and terraforming are the tip of the iceberg for the developers behind Neom, the 'mega-city' of the future. Saudi Arabia has pledged at least $500 billion to develop the project which, Covid-19 and global economic crisis aside, is planned to be fully functioning by 2025. As the first city to span multiple Middle Eastern State borders, Neom will spread into Jordan and Egypt (which shows high ambition as Egypt and Saudi Arabia do not share any land borders). Inspired by the wonderfully esoteric Garden by the Bay of Singapore, Neom will cover 26,500 square kilometres, thirty-three times the size of New York City. A state-of-the-art smart airport will accompany flying cars, robot maids, holographic teachers, artificial rain, animatronic dinosaurs, and a giant artificial moon. This will be truly remarkable as developers have pointed out that the technology for such wonders has not yet been created. Following the 2018 assassination of Jamal Khashoggi, even Saudi Crown Prince Mohammad bin Salman has admitted finding investors for the city has been problematic. Numerous advisors and architects have distanced themselves from what appears to be a troublesome climate in Saudi Arabia. But fear not! An estimated 20,000 Saudi citizens will be forcefully relocated to the dream city. Isn't the future so bright and shiny.

*5. Manufactured Dark Ages*

By Western reckoning, the period from the fifth to fifteenth century (or from the Fall of the Roman Empire to the Renaissance) is referred to in Europe as the Medieval Period. This period was characterised by loss of centralised dominance, mass migrations, constant war and invasion, pestilence and disease, deurbanisation, population decline, abandonment of reason, and overall depressing times. So it was dubbed the Dark Ages. But the Dark Ages were not limited to Europe – Western history universalised it and the history of the entire world for this period came to be seen as the Dark Ages! Somehow the Muslim world really mucked up this neat consignment of the rest of the world to the dustbin of history. While it was doom and gloom for Europe, the Islamic world was thriving and revolutionising thought and culture, science and learning, industry and society. Religion motivated thought in both Medieval Europe and the classical Muslim world, but while Christian thought sought to snuff out any non-Christian thought as well as rationalist, Islamic thought championed reason and embraced thought and learning of other cultures. Despite extensive recent historical research, the Dark Ages moniker still persists.

### 6. *Mock Human Rights*

After she was revealed to the world at the 2016 South by Southwest Festival, Sophia, the AI robot, jumped to the world stage in 2017 by being granted citizenship by the Kingdom of Saudi Arabia. Sophia also became the first robot to have a nationality. The great irony of course is that most women in Saudi Arabia do not have the same level of citizenship, especially if they were not born within the Kingdom. The laws of the time held women under the guardianship of their husbands, a legal identity equivalent to a minor in other countries. Restrictions on women included workplace limits, segregation from men, restrictions on public appearance and numerous other limits to freedom. While Sophia was modelled after the Egyptian Pharaoh Nefertiti, technically robots do not have a sex. In fact, at the time of her gaining citizenship she was little more than a torso, head and arm without discernible genitalia. Developer David Hanson, of the Hong Kong based Hanson Robotics, hoped Sophia would use her citizenship and nationality to fight for women's rights in the Kingdom. How she might do this has not been suggested – yet!

### 7. *Replica Capitalism*

Islamic banking and finance have a distinguished, if somewhat controversial, history. The concept of sharia-compliant banking and finance picked up particular steam following the 1970 Conference of Finance Ministers of Muslim Countries held in Karachi. Since then banks and financial institutions have levied principles and regulations that provide for an economic system believed to be more beholden to the standards of the

Qur'an. From the beginning, Islamic economics fell under the more dominant field of economics, which has itself been dominated, during the last fifty years, by neoliberal capitalism. Therefore, the project of Islamic economics has largely become the project of rediscovering capitalism through the Sharia. Greed, a history of exploitation, and the profit above all else – the main principles of Western capitalism – leaves much to be desired. We can legitimately ask: is that it, the end product of fifty years of research and development, setting up of numerous Islamic banks, university courses and academic journals? Can't Islamic economics give us something better than neoliberal economics?

### *8. Counterfeit Alcohol*

One Sharia complaint thing that has more success than Islamic economics is alcohol. The proclamation of alcohol as haram need not dissuade the pious from indulging in the delectable beverages that symbolise high class and leisure. Wine and beer can be made to follow the Sharia like anything else in the world. Numerous methods exist for making alcohol-free beer and wines, but generally the process remains the same, except a final step is added to remove the alcohol by-product. This can be done by heating the solution, but the process can alter the taste. So a vacuum filtration method has been adopted to preserve the taste while removing the intoxicating elements. Consumers of the 'real' thing have noted that Sharia-compliant wine or beer tastes like wine or beer, but without the alcohol!

### *9. Reclaimed Copies*

Our apologies to the French. You did not invent civilisation; rather, you copied it from the Muslim civilisation. Both the twelfth and eighteenth century 'European Renaissance' emerged on the back of Muslim achievements in science, philosophy and art and ethics. Europe only discovered its 'Greek heritage' thanks to the Muslims, who not only translated the Greek philosophy and learning but also took it to new heights. Muslim philosophers made sure that Plato, Aristotle, Euclid and the rest made it out of ancient Greece. Numbering systems, algebra, and geometry too were copied by Europe. And, yes, this includes the Scientific

Method, evolution, and key medical advancements and understandings that remained common practice through the nineteenth century. Mind you, hospitals and universities were novel concepts that also came from the Muslim world. Oh, and don't forget freedom of religion and speech headlined the many achievements in the development of ethics and law. Notions of constitution and international law often taken for granted date back to the life of the Prophet. Poetry, arts, and crafts combine with advancements in engineering, plumbing, and public sanitation standards developed a style of society that were gladly copied by ungrateful Europe. Heck, we say to the French, you even copied how to sit and eat properly on a dinner table!

*10. Spurious Ends*

And finally prepare for your DOOM! Thanks to the evil Covid-19, for the first time in centuries, hajj has been cancelled. This is a clear indication of *Qayamat*, the End of Times, the arrival of the Day of Judgement! Of course, Mecca has seen a few epidemics in its history; for example, the cholera epidemics of 1821 and 1865, and more recent outbreaks of MERS and SARS. But Covid-19 is in a class of its own. For one thing, it is, as quite a few traditional scholars have pointed out, mentioned in the Qur'an. Yes, indeed: the time of the virus's appearance, its global spread, and the reason why it has appeared are all mentioned in the Qur'an (allegedly in 74:8-13) – a bit like electricity, relativity and quantum mechanics which are also all clearly mentioned in the Qur'an. According to a hadith in Sahih Bukhari, we are told, the day of judgement won't take place until the hajj is abandoned. QED: given that hajj 2020 had been cancelled (or, rather, limited to locals), thanks to a virus that is mentioned in the Qur'an, we should all prepare for the imminent arrival of the Day of Judgement – which, by the way, can be witnessed on YouTube.

# CITATIONS

## Introduction: To Hell and Back by Samia Rahman

Zora Neale Hurston's novel, *Their Eyes Were Watching God* was published by Virago Press, London, in 1937. Other citations include Christian Lange, Paradise and Hell in Islamic Traditions (Cambridge University Press, 2015) and Al Ghazali, *The Revival of the Religious Sciences*, various parts of which can be downloaded from: https://sufipathoflove.com/the-revival-of-the-religious-sciences-by-al-ghazali/

See also, Annemarie Schimmel, *Gabriel's Wing: A Study Into the Religious Ideas of Sir Muhammad Iqbal* (Iqbal Academy, Lahore, 1989).

## New Territories by Ebrahim Moosa

The quotes from Toni Morrison's *Song of Solomon* (Plume, New York, 1987) are from page 222; and Manto quotes are from 'Sareh tyn ane' which appears in *Sa'ādat Ḥasan Manto, Jahān-I Manṭo: Sa'ādat Ḥasan ManṭO Ke 151 Shāhkār Afsāne,* edited by *Fārūq Argalī* (Farid Book Depot, New Delhi, 2012), pages 578-85. The quote from Deleuze is from Gilles Deleuze and Félix Guattari, What is Philosophy (Columbia University Press, New York, 1994), p27.

On Reinhart Koselleck's ideas, see his *Futures Past: On the Semantic of Historical Time* (Colombia University Press, 2004) and *The Practice of Conceptual History* (Stanford University Press, 2002).

See also: Gilles Deleuze and Feliz Guattari, *A Thousand Plateaus : Capitalism and Schizophrenia* (Univeristy of Minnesota Press, Minneapolis, 1987); Michel Foucault and Jay Miskowiec, Of Other Spaces' *Diacritics* 16, no. 1 (1986): 22-27; and Jordan Kisner, *Thin Places: Essays from in Between*. Vol. 116 (Farrar, Straus and Giroux, New York, 2020).

## A Stroll Through KL by C Scott Jordan

For more on the development and history of Kuala Lumpur see Ziauddin Sardar's *The Consumption of Kuala Lumpur*, (Reaktion Books, London, 2000), Barabara Watson Andaya and Leonard Y. Andaya's *A History of Malaysia*, (Macmillan Education, London, 2017), British Pathé's 'Views of Kuala Lumpur' (1920-1929) on Youtube, https://www.youtube.com/watch?v=9IY6z4OmkGw, and Andrew Ng Yew Han's 2015 documentary *Kuala Lumpur Sdn. Bhd.*

On the background to UMNO and the development of contemporary Malaysia post Merdeka, see Philip Mathew's (editor) *Chronicle of Malaysia: Fifty Years of Headline News* (1963-2013), (Editions Didier Millet, Kuala Lumpur, 2013), Sultan Nazrin Shah's *Striving for Inclusive Development from Pangkor to a Modern Malaysian State*, (Oxford University Press, New York, 2019), For more on the May 13th Tragedy, see The National Operation Council's *The May 13 Tragedy: A Report, 9 October, 1969*, (Silverfish Books, Kuala Lumpur, 2019), Kua Kia Soong's *May 13: Declassified Documents on Malaysian Riots* (SUARAM, Petaling Jaya, 2007). For more on Saloma see Adil Johan's *Cosmopolitan Intimacies: Maaly Film Music of the Independent Era*, (Nus Press, Singapore, 2018), and Saidah Rastam's *Rosalie and other love songs,* (SIRD, Petaling Jaya, 2014).

For more on the 1MDB Scandal, see Tom Wright and Bradley Hope's *Billion Dollar Whale: The Man Who Fooled Wall Street, Hollywood, and the World* (Hachette Books, New York, 2019), the reporting of the team at the Sarawak Report, www.sarawakreport.org, and the episode of Netflix's series *Dirty Money* titled 'The Man at the Top,' season 2, episode 2, posted in 2019. For the background of Pudu Prison and development in KL, see Clara Chooi's 'No heritage site for Pudu jail, development will commence' *Malaysian Insider*, 21 June 2010, https://web.archive.org/web/20140813071649/http://www.themalaysianinsider.com/malaysia/article/no-heritage-site-for-pudu-jail-development-will-commence, and Malayasiakini's KiniTV report 'Pudu prison demolition' 20 October 2009, found on Youtube, https://www.youtube.com/watch?v=x679XpPGrLc.

## Wanderer by Hafeez Burhan Khan

To find out more about psychogeography read *London Orbital* by Iain Sinclair, (Penguin 2003). Works by Medieval Muslim scholars/travellers include *The Travels of Ibn Battuta*, ed. Tim Mackintosh-Smith (Picador, 2003), and *Ibn Fadlan and the Land of Darkness: Arab Travellers in the Far North*, translated by Paul Lunde and Caroline E M Stone (Penguin Classics, 1 Dec. 2011).

## My Qur'anic Voyage by Shanon Shah

This article only skims the surface of contemporary Qur'anic and Biblical scholarship. The five recent texts discussed in the article are: Garry Willis, *What the Qur'an Meant and Why It Matters* (Viking, New York, 2017), Muhammad Abdel Haleem, *Exploring the Qur'an: Context and Impact* (IB Tauris, London, 2017), Musharraf Hussain, *The Majestic Quran: A Plain English Translation* (Invitation Publishing, Nottingham, 2018), Bruce B. Lawrence, *The* Koran *in English* (Princeton University Press, Princeton, 2017) and Karl-Josef Kuschel, *Christmas and the Qur'an* (Gingko Library: London, 2017). In *Sacred Misinterpretation: Reaching Across the Christian-Muslim Divide* (William B. Eerdmans Publishing, Grand Rapids, 2019), the Lebanese Christian scholar Martin Accad critically analyses how Muslims and Christians have engaged in hostile readings of each other's scriptures (and apologetic readings of their own sacred texts). For an overview of the evolution of tahrif in Muslim intellectual history, a good place to start is Abdullah Saeed's 2002 journal article, 'The Charge of Distortion of Jewish and Christian Scriptures', in *The Muslim World* 92(Fall): pp. 419–36.

On contemporary scholarship that looks at the intertextuality between the Qur'an and Jewish and Christian scriptures – including much apocryphal material – I referred to two additional examples for this essay. Geneviève Gobillot focuses on Muslim-Jewish intertextuality in her 2013 chapter, 'Qur'an and Torah: The Foundations of Intertextuality' (pp. 611–27) in *A History of Jewish-Muslim Relations: From the Origins to Present Day*, edited by Abdelwahab Meddeb and Benjamin Stora. Princeton: Princeton University Press. On historical Muslim thinking on Christology, see Tarif Khalidi's

*The Muslim Jesus* (Cambridge, Massachusetts, Harvard University Press, 2001). Ziauddin Sardar's account of his wedding needs to be appreciated in full, and can be found in the chapter 'Bhawalnagar Wedding' in his sumptuous *Balti Britain: A Provocative Journey Through Asian Britain* (London, Granta, 2009).

I have relied on memory and my previous writings to revisit the infamous Second International Muslim Leaders Consultation on HIV/AIDS in Kuala Lumpur and the vitriol directed at amina wadud, especially 'Muslim 2 Muslim' (pp. 95-107) in *Body 2 Body: A Malaysian Queer Anthology*, edited by Jerome Kugan and Pang Khee Teik (Petaling Jaya, Matahari Books, 2009). 'Introduction to Poetry' by Billy Collins is accessible online at: https://www.poetryfoundation.org/poems/46712/introduction-to-poetry

## Berlin Exiles by Amro Ali

This is an edited and abridged version of the essay that originally appeared in the German magazine *dis:orient*. The full version can be see at: amroali.com

Writers quoted and mentioned include: Hannah Arendt, *Between Past and Future: Eight Exercises in Political Thought* (Penguin, 1977) p14 and *On Revolution* (Penguin, 1973); Stuart Braun, *City of Exiles: Berlin from the Outside In* (Noctua Press, 2015) p13; Byung-Chul Han, *The Agony of Eros* (MIT Press, 2017) p1, *The Burnout Society* (Stanford University Press, 2015) p49, *In the Swarm: Digital Prospects* (MIT Press, 2017) p13, p52-53, p45, and *The Transparency Society* (Stanford University Press, 2015P p.30-3; Václav Havel, and Paul R. Wilson. *Open Letters: Selected Writings, 1965-1990* (Vintage Books, New York,1992) p177; Peter Schneider, *Berlin Now: The City after the Wall* (Macmillan, London, 2014) p7, p8; and Edward W. Said, *Reflections on Exile and Other Essays* (Harvard University Press, Cambridge: 2000) p173

See also: Sofian Philip Naceur, "Q&a with German Mp Stefan Liebich: Revealing German Arms Exports to Egypt." Mada Masr (16 November

2017). https://madamasr.com/en/2017/11/16/feature/politics/qa-with-german-mp-stefan-liebich-revealing-german-arms-exports-to-egypt/.

Mohamed Naeem, "Mother of the World, against the World and Outside of It." Mada Masr (9 June 2016). https://madamasr.com/en/2016/06/09/opinion/u/mother-of-the-world-against-the-world-and-outside-of-it/.

"Two Thirds of Germans Think the Country Has a Major Loneliness Problem." The Local Germany (23 March 2018). https://www.thelocal.de/20180323two-thirds-of-germans-think-the-country-has-a-major-loneliness-problem.

Jeremy Peter Varon, *Bringing the War Home: The Weather Underground, the Red Army Faction, and Revolutionary Violence in the Sixties and Seventies* (University of California Press, Berkeley, 2004) p306.

Dina Wahba, "Diaspora Stories: Crippling Fear and Dreams of a Better Home." Mada Masr (16 August 2018). https://madamasr.com/en/2018/08/16/opinion/u/diaspora-stories -crippling-fear-and-dreams -of-a-better-home/.

## Strangers in a Strange Land by Robert Irwin

The authors quoted in the essay: Francesco Suriano, *Treatise on the Holy Land*, ed. and tr. Theophilus Bellorini and Eugene Hoade (Jerusalem, 1940); *The Pilgrimage of Arnold von Harff*, ed. and tr. Malcolm Letts (London, 1946); Niccolò da Poggibonsi, *A voyage beyond the sea, 1346-1350*, ed. and tr. Bellorini and Hoade (Jerusalem, 1945); *Travellers in Disguise: Narratives of Eastern Travel by Poggio Bracciolini and Ludovico de Varthema*, tr. John Winter Jones (Harvard, Mass., 1963); *The Wanderings of Felix Fabri*, tr. Aubrey Stewart, *London Palestine Pilgrim Text Society*, 4 vols. (London, 1896-7); *Le Voyage en Egypte de Félix Fabri, 1483*, tr. Jacques Masson, 3 vols. (Cairo, 1975); Ulrich Haarmann, 'The Mamluk System of Rule in the Eyes of Western Travellers', *Mamluk Studies Review*, vol. 5 (2001) pp.1-24; *Relation du pèlerinage à Jérusalem de Nicolas de Martoni, notaire italien (1394-1395)*, tr. Léon Le Grand (Paris, 1895); *Visit to the holy places of Egypt, Sinai, Palestine and Syria in 1384*, (Leonardo, Frescobaldi, Giorgio Gucci, Simone Sigoli), tr. Bellorini (Jerusalem, 1948); Meshullam of Volterra in *Jewish Travellers*, ed. Elkan Nathan Adler (London, 1930); *Itinerarium Symonis Semeonis Ab Hybernia Ad Terram Sanctam*, ed. and tr. Mario Esposito (Dublin, 1960); *The Bondage and Travels of Johann Schiltberger*, tr. J. Buchan Telfer (London, 1879); *Croisades et Pèlerinages: récits,chroniques et voyages en Terre Sainte XIIe-XVII siècle*, ed. Danielle Régnier-Bohler (Paris, 1997) includes extracts from Wilhelm von Boldensele; Louis de Rochechouart, Simeon Semeonis, Nompar de Caumont and Emannuel Piloti; Mignanelli has been translated in Walter J. Fischel, '"Ascensus Baroch". A Latin Biography of the Mamluk Sultan Barquq of Egypt', *Arabica* vol. 6 pp.57-74, 152, 172; *Oeuvres de Ghillebert de Lannoy, Voyageur, Diplomare et Moraliste* ed. C. Potvin, (Louvain, 1878); Bertrandon de la Broquère, *Le Voyage d'Orient: espion en Turquie*, tr. Hélène Basso (Toulouse, 2010); Pietro Casola, *Pilgrimage to Jerusalem in the Year 1494*, tr. Margaret Newett (Manchester, 1907); *Itinéraire d'Anselme Adorno en Terre Sainte (1470-1471)*, ed. and tr. Jacques Heers and Georgette de Groer (Paris, 1978); *The Book of Margery Kempe*, ed. and tr. Anthony Bale (Oxford, 2015).

## Invisible Thessaloniki by Boyd Tonkin

Mark Mazower's *Salonica, City of Ghosts: Christians, Muslims and Jews 1430-1912* (HarperCollins, 2004) is the indispensable English-language resource for anyone who seeks to understand the city and its past, and I have gratefully drawn on it. Bruce Clark's *Twice a Stranger: How expulsions forged modern Greece and Turkey* (Granta, 2006) narrates and explains the ethnic cleansing that resulted in the radically simplified nations of today. Leon Sciaky's *Farewell to Salonica* (Haus Publishing, 2007) is a poignant and passionate memoir of a lost world of connected communities. Bea Lewkowicz's *The Jewish Community of Salonica: history, memory, identity* (Vallentine Mitchell, 2006) employs interview sources to tell many similar stories, and to put them in context. Victoria Hislop's novel *The Thread* (Headline Review, 2011) revisits the city and its varied peoples before and after the 1917 fire in the form of well-researched, and historically astute, popular fiction. Nikos Gabriel Pentzekis's *Mother Thessaloniki* was translated by Leon Marshall (Kedros Publishers, 1998), and *Poems of Nazim Hikmet* by Randy Blasing and Mutlu Konuk Blasing (WW Norton, 2002). Jason Goodwin's *Lords of the Horizons* (Chatto & Windus, 1998) spans the broad arc of Ottoman imperial history, while Eugene Rogan's *The Fall of the Ottomans* (Allen Lane, 2015) follows the empire's breakdown before and during the First World War. Roderick Beaton's *Greece: Biography of a Modern Nation* (Allen Lane, 2019) traces the country's protracted formation as a cultural as much as political entity, and Andrew Mango's biography *Atatürk* (John Murray, 2003) shows how one Salonican helped imagine and realise another new nation. On the latest wave of incomers to Thessaloniki, the Refugees in Towns report *To Integrate or Move On?*, by Mohamad Kasra, Osman Mohammad, Rabih Saad and Ioanna Terzi, with Anjali Khatri, can be found at fic.tufts.edu. The 2019 investigation by Refugee Support Aegean, *Reception Crisis in Northern Greece: Three years of emergency solutions*, is at rsaegean.org. For recent reportage and analysis of the migration emergency, see Aris Roussinos, 'What the hell is happening with migrants in Greece?', vice.com, 3 April 2020; and Patrick Strickland, 'After the EU Turned Greece into a Refugee Warehouse, a Backlash', nybooks.com, 4 March 2020. To hear the mingled music of old Salonica, listen to Savina Yannatou's album *Primavera en Salonico: Songs of Thessaloniki* (ECM, 2015). Roy Sher's evocative documentary film *My Sweet Canary: a journey through the life and music of Roza Eskenazi* was released on DVD in 2012 but – like so much of the culture it celebrates – is now hard to track down. Her songs appear in CD anthologies such as the *Rough Guide to Rebetika*, while the singer Mor Karbasi explores the Sephardic legacy in her album *The Beauty and the Sea* (Mintaka Records, 2008).

## Strands of Kazak Cultures by Natalya Seitakhmetova Zhanara Turganbayeva and Marhabbat Nurov

This article was prepared in the framework of a joint research project 'Islamic Studies as a Dialogical Project of the Humanities: Discourse and Praxis of Kazakhstan and France' with Abai Kazakh National Pedagogical University.

On the sacred texts of Zoroastrianism, see William Malandra, *An Introduction to Ancient Iranian Religion: Readings from the Avesta and the Achaemenid*, University of Minnesota Press, 1983. See also: I.M. Oransky *Introduction to Iranian Philology*, Eastern Literature Press, Moscow, 1960. On recent archaeological discoveries, see K.A. Akishev, *Issyk Barrow*, Art Press, Moscow, and 1978; D.D. Vasiliev, *The Collection of the Turkic Runic Monuments of the Yenisey Basin*, Science Press, Laningard,1983. For languages and cultural history of the region, see E.E. Bertels, *Selected Works. The history of Persian-Tajik literature*, Eastern Literature Press, Moscow, 1960 and *Languages of the Peoples of the USSR*. Volume 2. Turkic language, Science Press, Moscow, 1966.

See also: 'Where does the history of the Turks begin?' at: // http://e-history.kz/ru/publications/view/1294; and www.e-history.kz

## Inner Journeys by Saimma Dyer

The quotes in this essay are from Kabir Helminski, *Living Presence* (Tarcher, New York 2017), introduction p ix-x; *Rumi: Jewels of Remembrance*, translated by Camille & Kabir Helminski (Shambhala, Boston 1996), p130; *Mevlevi Wird*, translated by Camille Helminski (Soquel, London, 2000), p7; Abd al-Khaliq Ghudjuvani, *The Laws of the Khwajagan* as quoted on p139 in *Rumi's Sun: The Teachings of Shams of Tabriz*, translated by Camille Helminski & Refik Algan (Louisville 2017); and *Rumi: Jewels of Remembrance*, translated by Camille & Kabir Helminski (Threshold Books, Boston 2012), p270; and Charles Upton, *Rabiah: Doorkeeper of the Heart* (Pir Press, Vermont 1998) p48.

## Fieldwork by Chandrika Parmar

On qualitative research and open interviewing, see David Silverman, *Doing Qualitative Research* (Sage, London, 2017), fifth edition; James Holstein and Jaber Gubrium, 'Active Interviewing', in David Silverman, editor, *Qualitative Research: Theory, Method and* Practice (Sage, London, 1997); A Fontana, A. and J H Frey, J.H. (2005), ;The Interview: From Neutral Stance to Political Involvement' in N.K. Denzin and Y.S.

Lincoln, editors, *The Sage Handbook of Qualitative Research* (Sage, London, 2005), third edition; and N K Denzin, *Interpretive biography* (Vol. 17). (Sage, London, 1989). On Raimondo Panikkar's ideas on pilgrimage, see his *The rhythm of being: The Gifford lectures* (Orbis Books, London, 2010).

See also: 'From I and Thou' in A D Biemann, editor, *The Martin Buber Reader* (Palgrave Macmillan, New York, 2002); and Gilles Deleuze, *Fold: Leibniz and* Baroque (University of Minnesota Press, 1992).

Reports of BAPS Earthquake Relief Work and the Ramakrishna Mission are available on their websites.

## Assisi by Ziauddin Sardar

The Assisi Declarations, from five faiths, can be read at the Alliance of Religion and Conservation website: http://www.arcworld.org/downloads/THE%20ASSISI%20DECLARATIONS.pdf
A detailed analysis of the outcome of the Assissi meeting, and other religion and nature conferences and declarations held and made during the 1980s and 1980s, see Martin Palmer and Victoria Finlay, *Faiths in Conversation: New Approaches to Religion and the Environment*, World Bank, Washington D.C., 2003.

## Athens' Concrete Delusions by Iason Athanasiadis

For more on the history and development of Athens see: Homer Thompson & R E Wycherley, *The Agora of Athens, The History, Shape and Uses of an Ancient City Center*, American School of Classical Studies at Athens, 1972; William Miller, 'The Centenary of Athens as Capital', *The Journal of the Historical Association*, Volume 19, Issue 75, 1934; Ahmed M Ameen, *The Kucuk Camii of Athens*, Turcica, Volume 47, pp 73-95, 2016; and Molly Mackenzie, *Turkish Athens, The Forgotten Centuries, 1456-1832*, Ithaca Press, New York, 1999
See also: Ilay Romain Ors, *Diaspora of the City: Stories of Cosmopolitanism from Istanbul and Athens*, Palgrave Macmillan, London, 2017; William St Clair, *That Greece Might Still Be Free: The Philhellenes in the War of*

*Independence*, Oxford University Press, 1972; and Maria Kaika, *City of Flows, Modernity, Nature and the City*, Routledge, London, 2005.

## Last Word: On Patriarchy by Shehnaz Haqqani

amina wadud explains her argument in detail in *Inside the Gender Jihad: Women's Reform in Islam* (Oneworld, 2006), specifically chapter 1. Also see *Qur'an and Woman: Re-reading the Sacred Text from a Woman's Perspective* (Oxford UP, 1992). While I am convinced by Leila Ahmed's argument in her book *Women and Gender in Islam: Historical Roots of a Modern Debate* (Yale University Press; New Ed edition, 1993), because she shows that women's contributions to Islam were not considered legitimate enough to be sewn into the fabric of institutionalized Islam, a critique of her argument can be found in Pernilla Myrne, *Female Sexuality in the Early Medieval Islamic World: Gender and Sex in Arabic Literatur*e (London: I. B. Taurus, London, 2020), specifically the Conclusion.

For more on the terms Tarjīḥ, talfīq, and maṣlaḥa and their relevance to gender and Islam, see Shehnaz Haqqani, "Islamic Tradition, Change, and Feminism: The Gendered Non-negotiable" PhD Diss (University of Texas at Austin, 2018).

See also: Mohja Kahf, "The Pity Committee and the careful reader: How not to buy stereotypes about Muslim women" in Eds. Rabab Abdulhadi, et al. *Arab & Arab American Feminisms: Gender, Violence, & Belonging* (Syracuse UP, 2010), 111-123.

# CONTRIBUTORS

**Amro Ali** is lecturer in political sociology and Andrew W. Mellon postdoctoral fellow at the American University in Cairo ● **Iason Athanasiadis**, an award winning multimedia journalist writing about Mediterranean urban cosmopolitanism from Athens, Istanbul and Tunis, is the current holder of a Balkan Investigative Reporting Network fellowship for Journalistic Excellence ● **Mevlut Ceylan**, poet and translator, is Associate Professor of Cultural Studies at Çanakkale Onsekiz Mart University, Çanakkale, Turkey ● **Saimma Dyer** is the co-creator of RAY of God, a non-profit organisation that promotes feminine spiritual wisdom ● **Abdullah Geelah**, a lawyer and Fellow of Winston Churchill Memorial Trust, is writing a report on British mosques ● **Shehnaz Haqqani**, Assistant Professor of Religion at Mercer University, runs a YouTube channel called What the Patriarch and blogs at: http://orbala.net ● **Robert Irwin's** latest book is *Ibn Khaldun: An Intellectual Biography* ● **Scott Jordan** is Executive Assistant Director of Centre for Postnormal Policy and Futures Studies ● **Hafeez Burhan Khan** was an adventurer before (reluctantly) becoming a teacher ● **Ebrahim Moosa** is Mirza Family Professor in Islamic Thought & Muslim Societies and Co-director, Contending Modernities at the Keough School of Global Affairs, University of Notre Dame ● **Chandrika Parmar** is faculty member at S P Jain Institute of Management and Research (SPJIMR), Mumbai ● **Zainab Rahim** is the editor of the website The Platform and the non-fiction editor of the Khidr Collective Zine ● **Tamanna Rahman** is a broadcast journalist and documentary maker ● **Katharina Schmoll** is Lecturer in Media and Communication, Centre for Global Media and Communication, School of African and Oriental Studies, University of London ● **Shanon Shah** is a Visiting Research Fellow at King's College London and teaches religious studies at the University of London Worldwide ● **Boyd Tonkin** is a writer and literary critic ● **Zhanara Turganbayeva** has just received a doctorate in Islamic Studies from Al-Farabi Kazak National University, Almaty ● **Eric Walberg** is a Toronto based journalist and writer ● **Abdel Wahab Yousif** was a young Sudanese poet who tragically died crossing the Mediterranean Sea.